Little League, BIG DREAMS

The Hope, the Hype and the Glory of the Greatest World Series Ever Played

CHARLES EUCHNER

PHOTOGRAPHY BY ISABEL CHENOWETH

SOURCEBOOKS, INC.®
NAPERVILLE, ILLINOIS

Published by Sourcebooks, Inc.
P.O. Box 4410, Naperville, Illinois 60567–4410
(630) 961–3900
Fax: (630) 961–2168
www.sourcebooks.com

Library of Congress Cataloging-in-Publication Data

Euchner, Charles C.
  Little League, big dreams : the hope, the hype and the glory of the greatest
World Series ever played / Charles Euchner.
    p. cm.
  ISBN-13: 978-1-4022-0661-0
  ISBN-10: 1-4022-0661-5
  1. Little League World Series (Baseball) (2005) 2. Little League World Series
(Baseball) I. Title.

GV880.5.E83 2006
796.357'62—dc22

                                                          2006012970

        Printed and bound in the United States of America.
            BVG 10 9 8 7 6 5 4 3 2

To a few who taught me along the way

WAYNE COFFEY
JIM LEESON
ALEX HEARD

Contents

For millions of American children,
spring begins with tryouts
for Little League.

PREGAME

---•◆•---

"Put Me In, Coach"

*I*N THE SIXTY-EIGHT YEARS SINCE A CLERK at a local oil-supply company in a small Pennsylvania town created Little League, upwards of forty million kids have played in all fifty states and more than one hundred countries around the world. Most of us have not been very good. When people talk about "Little League plays," they're talking about comical stuff, Larry-Moe-and-Curley routines—fielders dodging grounders and overthrowing balls, baserunners arriving at the same base at the same time, long sequences of wild pitches and passed balls, innings long on walks and short on action.

At the same time, Little Leaguers and their parents and coaches often take the experience very seriously. From the very day that he decided to create a boys baseball league—Title IX and the National Organization for Women forced Little League to admit girls in 1974—Carl Stotz wanted players to act like miniature versions of big leaguers. He wanted teams to wear spiffy uniforms, play on well-manicured fields, hire umpires to call balls and strikes, and assign scorekeepers to keep track of standings and statistics.

It's natural for kids to imitate adults. Girls put on their mothers' dresses and heels and apply rouge and lipstick, and boys dress up in cowboy gear and Daniel Boone hats and baseball uniforms. *New Yorker* cartoons poke fun at the make-believe mannerisms of Little Leaguers. In one 1999 cartoon, a coach tells two parents: "Would you explain to your son that there's no free agency in T-ball?" A 1970 cartoon shows Little Leaguers celebrating a championship by pouring cans of soda over each other.

But in Little League, kids don't only imitate adults, but participate in a worldwide multimillion-dollar organization that *organizes* that dressing up and imitation for them. One long-running lament about Little League is that the parents take it much too seriously. Fathers devote not only whole summers to running the teams, but spend off-seasons plotting out their course. They scout players whose age is in the single digits. They make complicated strategy for player drafts. They contemplate trades (seriously). They work with designers on uniforms. They often care more about Little League than their jobs or family life.

Kids line up for their chance to try out for the Original Little League in Williamsport, Pennsylvania.

Little League has a strange un-*Peanuts* quality that has become the norm in America today. In the classic comic strip by Charles Shultz, the children lead lives free of adults. Charlie Brown, Linus, Lucy, Peppermint Patty, and the whole Peanuts gang create their own world of fantasy and play. Adults are neither seen nor heard, except for the occasional squawking sounds of teachers in the background. But in Little League—and other programs for sports, music, camps, and other activities—the adults have come to set the rules and manage every aspect of children's play.

The adults script the action in Little League and its ultimate event, the Little League World Series, down to the last detail. The kids, in turn, mimic the adults' words and actions. No matter what the issue—pitch counts, curveballs, other teams and coaches, umpires, swimming in the pool—the kids say whatever the adults said, in fewer but similar words. When they're together, you see the child constantly looking to the adult for approval and permission. The easiest way to get parents' approval is to mimic their words and mannerisms. To an eerie degree, that's the story of the Little League World Series.

And that's why so many of the adults enjoy the experience so much. Coach after coach told me that he liked working with twelve-year-olds because they didn't talk back and argue. You say something, and they let it soak in and try to make it their own. The word "sponge" came up again and again—as in, "these kids are sponges; they'll absorb everything you say without a whole lot of resistance." After Little League, parents, teachers, and coaches say they encounter more resistance when they try to teach kids. The kids start to think for themselves and push back more aggressively.

———————◆•———————

Like millions of people, I know something about the pros and cons of Little League from personal experience.

I started playing Little League in the summer of 1970 when I was nine years old. My parents just moved our family to a small town on the Mississippi River called Muscatine, Iowa. We didn't know anyone in town, and my parents thought Little League would be a good way for me to get out and meet other boys. My parents were casual baseball fans—they rooted for the New York Mets, the city's replacement for their former favorite team, the Brooklyn Dodgers. No one in my family was especially athletic, but my parents liked the idea of their kid playing Little League.

I hated the idea.

My parents had to force me to go. I tried to avoid it. I hid once or twice and I grumbled about why do I have to play that *stupid* game in that *stupid* league. It didn't help that my team, the White Sox, was terrible. Or that *I* was terrible. I couldn't hit, or field, or throw. I was posted in right field, where my chances to mess up were minimal.

But sometime during that first season—as I stood out among the dandelions, watching those endless innings—I started to like baseball. The game's rhythm and episodic action pleased me. I peppered my father with questions about the infield fly rule and scorekeeping. I liked chasing and, occasionally, catching the ball. I never could hit, but I drew a fair number of walks and considered myself quite the baserunner. Before long, I followed my parents' lead and became a Mets fan. I started imitating my favorite players—Tom Seaver, Tommie Agee, and Cleon Jones—when I

With some pitches reaching the plate at a major-league equivalent of 100 miles an hour, it's a wonder anyone manages to make contact with the ball.

put on my uniform. That uniform was just a black T-shirt with the team name and Little League insignia silkscreened in white. But it was enough.

We played fourteen games—winning just two of them—and when school let out I wanted to play more. In the neighborhood where we lived, kids from all over would gather near my house, on a cul-de-sac, to play in the street. Even though (or because) we didn't have uniforms or keep score, it was a lot more fun than Little League.

We played with kids ranging in age from seven to about fourteen or fifteen. We usually played half-field, because the street wasn't wide enough for a full diamond. We often played without teams. Different kids would play the positions and move around the diamond—right to left in the outfield, then third to first base in the infield, and finally pitcher to catcher—until they got a shot at bat. If you caught a fly, you'd trade places with the hitter, which created the perverse incentive of not hitting fly balls beyond the infield.

We wore out dozens of baseballs—not because we hit them hard, but because most of them were inexpensive and poorly made. For the cheapies, we paid 69 cents. Sometimes a kid would bring a more expensive ball, but not often. We'd hit the cover off the ball and then tape it up, again and again. Sometimes we let the cover stay off and we hit the ball until the string trailed along the ball as it wobbled across the street.

All these years later, I give Little League the credit for introducing me to baseball. I have not always been a dedicated fan—I have other interests too—but I have always come back to baseball. A number of years ago, when I was studying urban affairs, I wrote a book about the politics of sports in major-league cities. For years, when I lived in Boston, the

Red Sox were part of the everyday rhythms of my life. Walking on the street, I'd call out to perfect strangers, "What happened?" and they'd tell me the Red Sox score. They knew what I was asking about.

Baseball is a great game both because of the tension of a low-scoring game (which I prefer) and the dizziness of a slugfest (which can be fun occasionally). I like to see a power pitcher like Pedro Martinez overwhelm the opposition and a finesse artist like Greg Maddux flummox the other side. I like to see Manny Ramirez smash the ball out to the Mass Pike. And I like to see singles hitters like Ichiro Suzuki hit the ball exactly where the fielders *ain't.*

But I don't just like baseball at its best. Like a lot of people, I have seen a few Little League World Series games on TV over the years. More often than not, the quality of play was strong enough to keep me tuned in.

The best Little League players are very good. They pitch hard, locate their pitches not only *near* the strike zone but in the *right part* of the strike zone. They hit the ball hard—amazing, when you think about it, because balls whistle in to the plate at a major-league equivalent of ninety, ninety-five, even 100 miles an hour. (Those equivalents are determined by how much time a batter has to hit the ball; because the Little League field is smaller, a seventy-two-m.p.h. pitch allows as much time to swing as a ninety-four-m.p.h. pitch on a standard field.) The best Little Leaguers field well, keep their eyes on the ball, and know where to throw when they get the ball. They know how to hit the cutoff man and get a baserunner caught in a pickle.

The very idea of televising kids' games has always seemed strange to me, but then again, the mass media always look for oddball stories. For years, the championship game was aired on *Wide World of Sports,* ABC's sports anthology. *Wide World* showed any event that could be turned into a contest, so the annual Little League game didn't strike me as too strange.

In the last generation, the Little League World Series has lost its status as the elite showcase of kids' baseball in America. Tens of thousands of travel teams have come into being. Those teams play in hundreds of tournaments across the U.S., all year long. Even though Little League's national tournament gets ungodly exposure on TV, the best baseball gets played elsewhere. The best 100 or 200 travel teams are probably better than the teams in the Little League World Series.

Little League might not even have the best talent in community leagues anymore. Cal Ripken Baseball, the PONY League, and even Dixie Baseball now attract players as good or better.

But TV keeps shining the spotlight on the Little League World Series. In 1984, a new cable TV network called ESPN—hungry for programming of any kind—started broadcasting more and more games from the Little League World Series. Every year, the Little League World Series TV schedule expanded. By 2005, thirty-seven games were broadcast on either ABC or ESPN.

It's like Little League has done the impossible and invented a perpetual motion machine. Little League got TV to broadcast the games as a novelty; as the years have gone by, more and more games have gotten on the air, which draws a bigger and bigger national audience, which draws some ringers from travel teams, which makes for a good show...and that convinces the suits at ABC and ESPN to keep broadcasting the games.

———————— • ◆ • ————————

To supporters, Little League offers a priceless opportunity for kids— and their parents and neighbors—to get together and play the game at the community level. Because they're volunteers, coaches do it for the love of the game, and that spirit infuses everything the teams' families do together. Even though most coaches have not played at a high level, they are usually lifelong enthusiasts of the game and have plenty to teach kids about hitting and pitching, fielding and teamwork.

Over the course of a season, teams often come together in ways that amaze everyone involved. Little League becomes a primary way for neighbors to get to know each other, and the spirit of teamwork continues off the field. After the fathers and mothers have dragged equipment to the field, prepared potluck meals, and traveled together to tournaments, they become a big extended family.

Along the way, the children learn not only the great game of baseball, but also something about how communities work together. If baseball is part of America's civic religion, then Little League provides the village churches that animate that spirit.

To detractors, Little League and its annual World Series represent the worst aspects of modern childhood. Rather than simply letting kids run free in the summertime, to play games and swim and build forts, modern parents insist on organizing and professionalizing childhood. Kids get signed up for Little League, swim teams, computer camps, basketball tournaments, music lessons, church retreats and don't have a chance to make their own worlds.

Parents and coaches are so determined to win that they put their kids through grinding summers of practices and tournaments with travel teams. Before their arms have fully developed, kids are throwing curveballs that could ruin their arms forever. The kids are told to commit fully or get off the team. When they travel to tournaments, they aren't allowed to swim in hotel or dorm pools for fear that they'll stub a toe or overtax their developing muscles. When they lose, they get chastised. When they win, they're told they didn't win by enough.

When an umpire blows a call, the coaches and parents complain bitterly. They stomp around and scream (as I heard countless times following Little League tournaments), "You suck, ump!"

Behind the scenes, some families quarrel with each other. With TV time on the line, some parents snipe about playing time. *Why does her kid get to pitch? My kid's better!* When a manager makes a questionable decision on the field, parents are quick to complain. After games, cell phones ring with grievances about field strategy and treatment of kids.

Experts on youth sports have a term to express the problems that swirl around major events like the Little League World Series—Achievement by Proxy Disorder, or ABPD. When parents and coaches depend on their children to succeed for the sake of the adults, competition becomes corrupted. Kids should play for enjoyment, to develop their bodies, and learn teamwork and fair play. But the adults often turn the game into their own field of dreams.

Sometimes, you wish the adults would just leave the field and let the kids run their own games, like the *Peanuts* characters.

"It felt like the players were the pawns on the chessboard for those coaches and adults," Mike Ludwikowski, Little League's trainer, told me after one bitter contest between teams from California and Florida.

———————•◆•———————

In reality, both assessments of Little League are right. The poet Keats talked about "negative capability," the ability to hold contradictory thoughts in your mind at the same time without pushing too hard for some resolution—in his words, "capable of being in uncertainties, mysteries, doubts." To understand Little League, you need that approach. Little League is both good and bad, richly rewarding and exploitive, a special little cocoon and a harsh microscope, fun for fun's sake and a corporate hustle, a place of new friendships and a time of wrenching homesickness, an opportunity to learn a great game and a place where coaches often teach the wrong lessons.

Somehow, coaches and parents need to find a way for kids to experience the exhilaration of competition while also acknowledging that the kids are just kids. Some children thrive on the pressure and others wilt. Competition can be great. I wouldn't want to shield children from any kind of competition or test. But it's also important for adults to keep the game a kid's game, to know when enough is enough—and give the kids an easy way to say when they've had enough.

During the New England regional tournament, a player from Westbrook, Maine, named Sean Murphy got so stressed he had trouble breathing. After pitching three strong innings, he went to his manager, Richard Knight. "Hey, Rich, you got to start warming up Joey," he said.

Knight was confused. "Why?" he asked. "You're doing great."

"Well," Murphy said, "I'm really, *really* nervous. I'm hyperventilating."

Knight worked out a signal. If Murphy returned to the mound but decided he was still too nervous, he would tap the top of his cap. That meant he wanted to come out of the game. He went out for the fourth inning but left after one batter.

You can quibble with Knight's approach—maybe he should have taken Murphy out then and there—but I think he struck a good balance. The key was that Murphy felt he could tell his manager he was nervous. All too often, eager-to-please players don't feel they can approach their coach and speak honestly about their physical or emotional limits. All too often, the coach does not respond well when a player *does* speak up.

Finding the right balance might be the hardest task of a parent or coach. How the adults and kids seek this balance at the Little League World Series—or ignore the need to do so—could tell an intriguing story about the nature of sports and growing up in twenty-first century America.

———— • ◆ • ————

To understand the challenges of Little League—and all youth sports today—I watched Little League games all summer and traveled to Williamsport for the Little League World Series.

The book is organized thematically. The first three chapters provide general background. Chapter 1 places Little League and its premier event into a larger context of youth sports. Chapter 2 describes the excitement of teams arriving in Williamsport. Chapter 3 tells the story of Little League from its founding to the present day.

Chapters 4 and 5 describe the teams from Hawaii and Curaçao, which played each other in the championship game of the 2005 World Series.

The next two chapters get into the nitty-gritty of baseball. Chapter 6 describes the training strategies of several teams. Chapter 7 explores the pitching injuries that result from overusing pitchers in the Little League tournaments—and what might be done to prevent such a rash of injuries in the future.

The next three chapters get into the culture of the Little League World Series. Chapter 8 looks at the culture of "hustling" in the series—whether it's corporate marketers promoting their products or Little League enthusiasts trading pins. Chapter 9 delves into the growing importance of religious faith in sports. And Chapter 10 explores how different teams responded to winning and losing in the series.

The following chapters step back and look at youth baseball from a broader perspective. Chapter 11 explores Little League's growing challenge from travel ball and other youth leagues. Chapter 12 explores the different styles of play that teams from different parts of the world bring to the game of baseball.

Chapters 13 and 14 conclude the story, with an account of the dramatic series finale—in which Hawaii beat Curaçao in extra innings—and a visit with the winners after they returned home to parades and new educational opportunities.

The book closes with a "Postgame" essay that considers how Little League might reform itself to put children back at the center of the game.

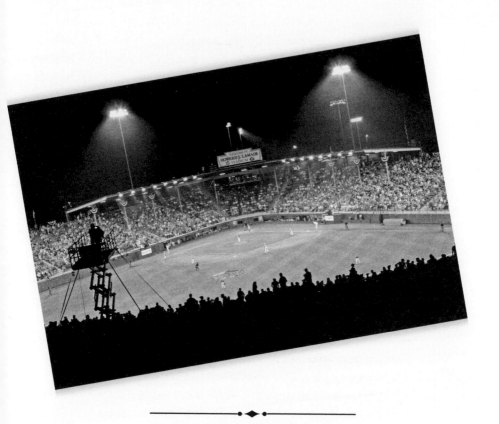

Howard Lamade Stadium
is the promised land for millions
of Little Leaguers.

CHAPTER 1

"The Greatest Sporting Event on the Planet"

*I*T WAS 10:30 AT NIGHT AND THE CRICKETS were making a racket and all of the sixteen teams in the 2005 Little League World Series had already padded up the long hills to their dorms at the Olympic-style village called International Grove.

The all-stars from Maitland, Florida, finished batting practice almost an hour before. Since then, I talked with two of their coaches and fathers. Dante Bichette and Mike Stanley were not typical Little League coaches. They were former major league stars.

Bichette and Stanley did not know each other well before they became coaches for the Maitland team. They're an odd couple. Bichette is Oliver Hardy, soft and voluble, full of childlike enthusiasm. Stanley is Stan Laurel, more angular and circumspect, always deflecting attention off himself. In the first days in Williamsport, reporters repeatedly asked Stanley how the Little League World Series ranked among his baseball accomplishments. "It's not my accomplishment," he said. "It's my son Tanner's accomplishment."

Between them, Bichette and Stanley played nineteen seasons in the big leagues, collected 3,044 hits and 461 home runs, and earned almost $59 million. Combined, those numbers would add up to one Hall of Fame career. But Bichette and Stanley never made it to a World Series. The manager of the Maitland team, a bank executive named Sid Cash, joked that it took their kids to get them anywhere *near* a World Series. Cash had been coaching Little League for almost three decades, and he had never been anywhere near a World Series either. Maitland's team, an underdog all summer, kept winning and winning. Bichette planned to spend the summer playing in an independent league, but cancelled those plans when Maitland won the district, sectional, state, and regional tournaments—all of them tough, since kids play baseball in the Sunbelt twelve months a year.

Long after the players climbed back to their dorms in the sparkling Little League complex, Bichette and Stanley explained how you teach baseball to a bunch of eleven- and twelve-year-old boys. The key, they agreed, is constant repetition. Keep trying even the most difficult physical feats, and you keep getting better and better.

Take hitting, which Ted Williams famously called the single most difficult act in all of sports.

What makes hitting so hard in Little League is the miniature fields. Carl Stotz, Little League's founder, decided back in 1939 to use a field with dimensions two-thirds the size of a standard field. But kids get bigger and stronger every generation. The mean weight of a twelve-year-old increased from 94 to 111 pounds between 1970 and 2002. Most teams have a few kids who weigh 150 pounds or more. Those monsters can overwhelm opponents. A twelve-year-old kid throwing seventy miles an hour was once uncommon, but now it's not. All the top pitchers now throw in the seventies, some in the mid-seventies. And some in the eighties. The smaller field makes the pitches seem even faster. A hitter facing a seventy-m.p.h. pitch on a Little League field has as much time to react as player on a standard field facing a ninety-one-m.p.h. pitch. A hitter facing an eighty-m.p.h. pitch has as much time to react—read the pitch and swing—as a major leaguer facing a 104-m.p.h. pitch.

Little League speed (m.p.h.)	Standard field equivalent
70	91
71	92
72	94
73	95
74	96
75	98
76	99
77	100
78	101
79	103
80	104

Think about that for a moment. The kind of major leaguers who throw that fast—*occasionally*—are intimidators like Randy Johnson, Billy Wagner, and Roger Clemens. To hit against pitchers like that, hitters have less than two-tenths of a second to swing their bat.

Every time I think of kids hitting pitches coming in that fast, I think of the skinny arms with knobby elbows that poke out of short-sleeved jerseys. And then I think of the thick, muscled arms of big leaguers like Barry Bonds or Gary Sheffield. The kids have to get their bats across the plate as quickly as major leaguers, with fractions of the bodily mass and power. How fair is that? I'm amazed Little Leaguers *ever* hit that stuff, much less hit it hard.

But Dante Bichette says you can teach any decent little athlete to hit that impossible heat.

"The learning curve is just unbelievable," Bichette said. "A lot of kids think they can't hit a seventy- or seventy-two-mile-an-hour fastball. So you go to a pitching machine and put in balls at seventy and at first they're five feet behind. So they adjust, and then after a while they're three feet behind. So they adjust again and eventually they get around on it. They can get an image in their mind about when to swing."

Despite the excitement, the World Series also had its slower moments, as Canada's Mitchell Burns can attest.

Hitting becomes a matter of deciding when to put the bat over the plate. You make a decision as the ball tumbles out of the pitcher's hand. *Whatever you do, don't keep your eye on the ball.*

This is not your father's Little League.

After talking about baseball and kids, passionately, for almost an hour, Bichette and Stanley started to walk up the hill.

Bichette needled Stanley. At first, Stanley didn't believe that you could teach kids so much about hitting and fielding. All Stanley wanted was for his son Tanner to have some fun and win some games. But Bichette showed that you could teach these kids almost anything. As Bichette spoke about proving Stanley wrong, Stanley smiled and nodded.

As they trudged up the long incline toward the dorms at International Grove, the path wrapped around two stadiums bathed in the major-league lights. No one was playing any baseball at this hour. No one would play any baseball for another three days. But the men who run Little League could not resist creating this vivid scene of stadiums glowing in the quiet of the night.

Dante Bichette, for one, was moved.

As we walked up toward International Grove, Bichette paused. He announced, with a potent pause between every word: "The—Little—League—World—Series—is—the—greatest—sporting—event—on—the—*planet*."

And then he continued his climb up the hill.

———————— • ◆ • ————————

The Little League World Series is a lot of things—among them, certainly and strangely, the most famous and visible of all youth sporting events in the United States.

People all over the globe work for years and years to reach this small old town on the Susquehanna River. All of them have watched the Little World Series on TV and some of them have made a pilgrimage to the series. Something about the event—the beauty of the stadiums or the tension of the ten-day tournament or the vividness of the characters—captured their imagination and made them want to perform on the stage themselves.

Jace and Brenn Conrad, players for the Little Leaguers from Lafayette, Louisiana, watched the event on TV since they were in diapers. Dante Bichette Jr., the star player for the Maitland, Florida, Little Leaguers, dreamed of pitching in the World Series when he came to Williamsport as a spectator with his famous dad three years before. Blaise Lezynski, a star with the Council Rock Little League in Newtown, Pennsylvania, can tell you about every great feat in Little League World Series history.

The adults also fantasize of reaching Little League's peak, maybe more than the kids. Rich Knight, the manager of the team from Westbrook, Maine, has brought kids from his local Big Brothers program to Williamsport for years and dreamed of returning as a manager. Hirofumi Oda has been working to bring a team from Chiba City, a suburb of Tokyo best known as the home to Japan's Disney World, for twenty years. After watching the World Series on TV, he carried vivid images of the event in his head. When he got a tour of the stadiums from his translator, whose family was one of the original sponsors of Little League in 1939, he started to cry. "Now, I am here," he said.

Advancing to the Little League World Series is a quest, every bit as much as *Raiders of the Lost Ark* or anything else Hollywood has to offer. Between the 8,000 or so teams and the ultimate prize lie all kinds of obstacles to overcome—trickery and cheating, homesickness and cabin fever, illnesses and injuries, internal strife, jealousy, cynicism, distractions, economic hardship, boredom, and dumb luck, to name just a few.

———————— • ◆ • ————————

Having won sporting's greatest game of "Survivor," they settle into this old town for two weeks of constant baseball.

The environment is a big part of the experience. Williamsport has all the charms of a small town because it never grew out of its old form. In the late 1800s, Williamsport was the lumber capital of the world. Cutters took down white pine, Eastern hemlock, and hardwoods in the Allegheny Mountains and sent them down the Susquehanna River to Williamsport's mills. The wealth from those operations produced the nation's largest collection of millionaires per capita. Those moguls built an elegant downtown, with a city hall, public library, churches, parks, law and insurance offices, a grand hotel, bookstores, cafes, clothiers, and restaurants. Just off the downtown core is a row of Victorian houses called Millionaires' Row.

When a pair of Biblical floods wiped out the city in 1889 and 1894, the timber industry was already in decline, and city leaders eventually decided not to try to revive the industry. When the federal government built Interstate 80 twenty miles south of Williamsport, the city missed the development that vast transportation networks foster. The city has struggled to attract industry. A city planning document calls Williamsport's history "a story of unceasing struggle for survival." In the 1990s, Williamsport became a magnet for "influx people" when public-health officials decided that Williamsport's small-town serenity was attractive for drug and alcohol addicts trying to resist temptation and settle into healthy routines. At one point, influx people comprised 10 percent of the city's population.

The town still looks great. Partly because of its economic stagnation, downtown looks like a quaint set for a 1940s movie like *Shadow of a Doubt.* Chain retailers like Staples, Starbucks, McDonald's, and the Gap haven't taken over downtown because they can't find enough customers to survive there. So downtown has an old-timey feel, with its small-scale men's clothing store, candy shop, cafe, bookstore, microbrewery, and Greek restaurant. The downtown is great for TV visuals.

The World Series itself takes place across the river in South Williamsport. Games are played in two stadiums—Howard J. Lamade Stadium (named after the publisher of a local newspaper called *Grit*) and Volunteer Stadium. In Lamade Stadium, the place where the big games are held, two grassy ledges create semicircles beyond the outfield fence. That's The Hill. Fans come and lay down blankets like they're at a G-rated Woodstock—no booze, no rebellious music, no nudity—and watch the games morning, day, and night.

The Hill is not just a grassy bleacher. It's also a playground. Kids throw baseballs and Frisbees and footballs. They find pieces of cardboard and climb to the peak, up by the Little League administration building, and slide down The Hill over and over. During the course of the World Series, so many people slide over the grass that the edges of hills turn from bright green to a heavy brown.

Total attendance for the ten-day World Series usually surpasses 300,000. Some *major league teams*, like the 1979 Oakland A's, have drawn fewer fans over the course of a whole season.

———————•◆•———————

Whatever else you say about the Little League World Series, remember this: it's probably the hardest tournament anywhere to win. At the beginning of the summer, more than 7,000 Little League organizations across the United States select players for all-star teams. They play as many as twenty games in qualifying tournaments, starting in early July and concluding in the middle of August. Only eight of those teams survive and win a berth in the Little League World Series.

Hundreds of teams from outside the United States compete for a berth in the series. They all play their own regional tournaments to qualify for Williamsport—four in the Americas (Canada, Mexico, the

Caribbean, and Latin America), one in Asia, one in the Pacific, one in an amalgam region called EMEA (Europe, the Middle East, and Africa), and one in a grab-bag region called Trans-Atlantic, which consists of American and other ex-pats living overseas at military bases and corporate outposts. The foreign teams usually have a lighter load; some play only six or seven games to get to Williamsport.

It's hard to handicap the Little League World Series at any stage.

The Sunbelt teams are usually the best, but teams from Connecticut and New Jersey have pulled some famous upsets. Teams from Southern California have historically done the best in their very difficult West division, but teams in places like Nevada and the rest of California are strong every year too. Sometimes, it's the weakest teams that reach Williamsport. In 2005, teams from Owensboro, Kentucky, and Davenport, Iowa, made repeat appearances in Williamsport. But that's just because the competition was weaker in their regions—the Great Lakes and Midwest regions—and not because they developed nationally competitive programs. Sure enough, both teams went 0–3 in the World Series for the second straight year.

Internationally, the Asia, Pacific, Caribbean, and Latin America divisions are strongest. Japan emerged as the top team in Asia in 2005, winning the tournament despite having the same records as Hong Kong and Chinese Taipei. (Little League's tie-breaker rule, which gives the victory to the team that yielded the fewest runs, gave Japan the title.) Guam won the Pacific title for the second time in three years. Curaçao, the defending champions, prevailed for the fifth straight time in the Caribbean tournament. And a team from Venezuela won the Latin America tournament.

The World Series begins with pool play. The tournament's sixteen teams are divided into four pools of four teams each. Each team plays three games against other teams in the pool, with the top two teams in each pool moving to the next round. Then the teams play one, two, or three single-elimination games.

———————•◆•———————

Any time you create an event that provides TV glory and riches to the winners, some contestants are going to bend and break the rules to win.

Ever since the Danny Almonte scandal of 2001, Little League has struggled mightily to police teams playing in the qualifying tournaments for the World Series. But making regulations often just emboldens people to look for ways to get around those rules.

In 2001, Almonte played for a Bronx Little League team that went to Williamsport. Almonte pitched a perfect game and became a national celebrity. President George W. Bush praised him and Mayor Rudolph Giuliani gave him the keys to the city. But *Sports Illustrated* discovered that Almonte was fourteen years old—two years older than he said—and it turned out that he didn't live in the Bronx, go to school there, or even play on a regular Little League team. After the series was over, Little League stripped the Bronx team of its honors and banned its president and coach. Almonte's fraud became a morality tale, a story of how people who want something *too much* ruin it for everyone.

The PR fallout from Almonte's fraud was so great that Little League started to require three kinds of proof of age and residency, including birth certificates. Parents are told to keep records handy, in case a dispute arises. The mother of Kalen Pimentel, the star pitcher for the Rancho Buena Vista all-stars from California, had to run home for his birth certificate during one tournament when the other team challenged his age.

But enforcing even the simplest rules can be hard. Teams that want to win will always find ways to cheat. And some of them will slip through Little League's dragnet. In the qualifying tournaments in the Latin America region, another age scandal challenged Little League's ability to keep its competition fair and honest.

Because Venezuela hosted the Latin America tournament, the country got two entries, and they met in the championship game. Altagracia beat Valencia for the title. But before the tournament even started, Altagracia's participation was the subject of a formal protest and investigation. The San Francisco Little League, another Venezuelan team that had lost to Altagracia in the national tournament, filed the protest.

It wasn't the first complaint against Altagracia. In 2003, the Sierra Maestra Little League complained about Altagracia after it won the Venezuela title. In 2004, the Coquivacoa Little League issued a formal protest because of Altagracia's use of the same player who was under suspicion in 2005.

"We were defeated by Altagracia in the national finals there in Los Puertos and since we saw the boy with some physical characteristics unusual for a twelve-year-old boy, we asked the board of directors for an investigation," Luis Flores, president of the Coquivacoa Little League, told *Diario Panorana de Maracaibo*. "But they didn't pay any attention to us. We also complained to the Council for the Protection of the Child and Adolescent of Cabimas and we're still waiting for a reply."

Altagracia maintained its innocence, producing affidavits with detailed information about the player's birth date and residence. Altagracia then won the Latin America tournament. Valencia went home, but joined San Francisco's protest.

Altagracia's records for the player were in perfect order. The problem was, they belonged to the player's younger brother.

To settle the controversy definitively, the imposter was required to report to an office of Venezuela's National Office of Identification and Immigration (Onidex). There, he submitted to fingerprint testing. Two days later, Onidex announced definitive proof of the fraud. "The fingerprints that the player that participated in the tournament carried out in Maracaibo is the older brother of the boy that appears as legally registered in the youth category of the Altagracia Little League," an Onidex official said.

But the controversy was even more nefarious than the Venezuelan media reported at the time. Because Little League now requires three documents to verify a player's age and residence, the fraudulent birth document was not enough to get the illegal player in the game. A government official was implicated in doctoring documents to disguise the real age of the illegal player, Little League officials later revealed.

Little League CEO Steve Keener was philosophical about the controversy.

"If somebody really wants to do it, they're going to find a way to do it," he said. "They're going to at least fool everybody temporarily. They may not ultimately [succeed] in the long run, but they can have people forge documents. If somebody is sophisticated enough to do that type of thing, they're going to get away with it."

Part of the problem, Keener said, is cultural. Referring to Latin American teams, he said the scandal pointed to attitudes and practices "that are typical or common in those parts of the world."

People on all sides of the controversy reacted with anger, hurt, and resolve. Lilunia Osorio, president of the San Francisco Little League, criticized Little League officials for not acting sooner. The manager of the Altagracia team maintained his innocence. "They also deceived me," Alfonso Avendaño said. "If they did it, it was because they hoped for extra money or some kind of scholarship that their son would win."

Luckily for Little League's P.R. machine, no American media reported any details of the scandal.

Here's another reality of a big tournament like the Little League World Series.

Any time you stage an international competition, with teams from different cultures and systems, it's going to be a struggle to make the competition fair and equitable. And you're never going to satisfy everyone.

As the teams settle into Williamsport, another controversy simmered. One coach told me he planned to challenge the rules governing Little League's international tournaments. The way things work now, he said, teams like Curaçao and Japan have unfair advantages.

A long summer of baseball brings teams closer together than most can imagine at the beginning of the all-star season.

Shon Muna worked to get his team from Agana, Guam, to Williamsport for almost a year. He took a team to the World Series in 2003 and barely lost out in the 2004 Pacific regional tournament. Guam had the same 2–1 record as the two finalists but didn't play on because of Little League's tie-breaker rule.

Muna, a Rafael Palmiero look-alike with his brown skin and trim mustache, is one of those guys who are so devoted to Little League that he builds his *love life* around it.

Two years before, Muna asked Clarice Briggs to marry him during the celebration of Guam's Pacific regional championship. When the pair arrived in Williamsport, they had an idea: why not get married at Howard Lamade Stadium? Little League officials gave the okay and issued invitations. One of the team hosts, the Reverend Gary Weaver, officiated. One of Muna's sons, Shane, held a bat and flowers. His other son, Shon Junior, held the rings in a red baseball glove. The bride wore a white pinstriped baseball uniform with white baseball hat. Guam's uniformed players made an arch with outstretched bats as the Munas held hands and walked for the first time as a married couple.

That was fun. But Guam didn't last past the first round of games in Williamsport that year, and in 2004 Guam didn't even make it to Williamsport. And in 2005 Muna not only wanted to get back to Williamsport. He also wanted revenge. He was determined to challenge a system that he says discriminates against Guam.

Muna's complaint is that Curaçao and Japan draw from a broader population pool than Guam. Guam, an island of 170,000 people, has four Little League organizations. Curaçao, with the same population, has only two. Japan has an even greater advantage—300 leagues for a population of 127 million—or about one league for every area of 423,000.

"I predict that there will be lots of investigations over the size of the districts," he said. "Curaçao, that's the team I want to beat. They're a very good team, the cream of the crop. But they have an unfair advantage. We just want to play by the same rules. It's got to change."

I asked Lance Van Auken, Little League's top PR man, about the organization's rule that every league should operate in a population area of 20,000 people.

"Each league is considered separately on the basis of available players, demographics, competition from other sports," Van Auken said. "So, for example, a league in St. Petersburg, where the population is 80,000 or more (which should produce four separate leagues), we grant a waiver because that league's elderly population is 50,000." Another example comes from California's Rancho Buena Vista Little League, which was split into two divisions with two all-star teams before the 2004 season but then reunited in 2005 after a direct appeal from the league president.

The inequities remain, but there's probably not much anyone like Shon Muna can do about it. As John F. Kennedy famously remarked, life is unfair.

Through all the controversy, the Little League World Series remains one of the most enticing events in sports today.

Why?

It's not necessarily the quality of play. Even if Little League showcased the best baseball among eleven- and twelve-year-olds—and it doesn't—these kids are not even close to being fully developed athletes. Most of them are still skinny kids with little of the musculature that great athletic performance requires. Everyone on the field is still learning how to play the game— how to pitch and hit, how to pivot on a double play or hit the cutoff man, how to get a quick jump out of the batter's box or on the base paths.

That's the fascination.

The Little League all-stars represent the ultimate works in progress, pieces of clay that are just taking shape. Those pieces of clay might develop into the most beautiful pieces of art imaginable—or they might just look like the odd-shaped mug or vase a second-grader brings home from art class. There's no telling which of the kids playing in Williamsport might turn out to be a great athlete, worthy of a pro contract, a college scholarship, or even a starting position on a high school team. *There is no way.*

Umpires are among the hundreds of volunteers every summer at the Little League World Series.

No twelve-year-old child has developed fully, physically or emotionally. A kid who lords over other preteens in a summer tournament is not necessarily going to lord over the same group of teens. Some of the scrawny kids will grow into sturdy young men, muscled athletes with explosive power, and take over. Even the best teenagers will get left behind as the field narrows to the high school and college varsities and sundry professional leagues. In fact, researchers have found that excelling at an early age can be a handicap, especially for pitchers. If you throw a lot of innings as a teenager, even into your twenties, you are not likely to develop the capacity to throw very well for very long. The best pitchers at elite levels were often second-tier as they grew up.

Crowds of 10,000 or 15,000 or 25,000 fans at Lamade Stadium—and millions more sitting in front of a TV set—watch the games because of the not-quite-thereness of the kids. Watching works in progress has its fascinations. Physically *and* socially, the kids do things today that they couldn't consider just weeks before.

Take Dante Bichette Jr. This rosy-cheeked kid from Maitland, Florida, never threw a curveball before the summer. Then his dad took him and his teammate Skip Kovar aside at a tournament. Dante Bichette Sr. taught the boys how to throw the twelve-to-six-o'clock curveball. In just a few hours, these kids learned enough to baffle some of the best Little Leaguers anywhere. When these works-in-progress took the mound, you could see them getting better—almost inning by inning.

Little Dante's maturation was not just physical or athletic. For the first time, he had to learn how to deal with failure on the field. After a player from Iowa hit a long home run against him in Williamsport, he admitted that his sweet little world just got rocked. "It was killed. I was shocked," he said. "No one's ever hit that far against me." He had to learn how to recover from that setback. And his teammates had to help. After the home run, Tanner Stanley and Florida's other infielders gathered on the mound for a brief pep rally. "We got your back," each chirped to the stunned pitcher—street talk from suburban kids in support of their manchild. Bichette became a better pitcher, a better athlete, because of his mistake.

Another kind of maturity develops during that ten-day tournament. Thrown together in a long festival of baseball, the youngsters learn how to deal with a constant stream of attention. Some never move beyond the short, shy responses to the media but others become poised stars. Dante Bichette Sr. and his wife Mariana taught their son how to handle the media before coming to Williamsport. On the way home from a game in Florida, they asked Dante Junior what he'd say when reporters asked him questions about his feats. In their first mock Q&A, he gave them one- to three-word answers: "Yes," "It felt good," "No," "I guess so." No, that's not enough, his parents said. You gotta *handle* the media, give them polished phrases. They prepped him to expand his answers. In Williamsport, Dante Junior talked like a pro.

And you see it all happening right in front of you, over a period of just weeks.

Games take place morning, day, and
night during the early days of the
Little League World Series.

Aaron Durling, an American ex-pat
playing for the team from
Saudi Arabia, became the biggest
player in the Little League
World Series in 2005.

CHAPTER 2

─────── •◆• ───────

Arriving at the Show

WANT A SYMBOL OF HOW *big* the Little League World Series has gotten? Take a look at the kid from Saudi Arabia who would make Babe Ruth look like a yoga instructor.

Aaron Durling is a fleshy, molasses-skinned boy. He walks shyly, slowly. He speaks quietly, usually only when someone speaks to him. When a stranger approached him in Williamsport and asked if he could call him "Jumbo," Durling softly said yes. The stranger tried it out: "Hi, Jumbo!" Durling smiled, but didn't respond.

As far as anyone can tell, Durling is the tallest player in the history of the Little League World Series. He stands six feet, five inches, and weighs 226 pounds. His size is the early buzz of the 2005 World Series.

As teams from around the world gathered in Williamsport, Durling was the focus of conversation.

From a distance—walking down the long hills to a practice field, gathering for a team photograph, awaiting instructions from coaches—Durling almost looked like an old man. Like all his teammates, he bleached his hair white in a show of unity. But to join his teammates in anything they do, Durling has to lean over. He almost *bows* when he talks to his teammates. When he can, he sits so he doesn't have to stand so high above them.

For the last five years, Durling has lived with his family in Saudi Arabia. His father works for the national oil company. Life in Dhahran is isolated, with a small village of Americans and other ex-pats living among 100,000 people in the heart of Saudi Arabia, but almost completely removed from the Arab kingdom.

The all-star team from Dhahran breezed through the Trans-Atlantic tournament—a contest of ex-pats based mostly in Europe—for the last five years. This year Dhahran outscored its rivals by a combined score of 80–2. But the competition was not very good—teams from Belgium, the Netherlands, Germany, Italy, England, and Spain. The Saudi players and coaches knew they had not faced the same tough competition as Japan and Guam, California and Hawaii, Curaçao and Canada. Their goal was not to win but to "show people we belong here."

As soon as ESPN learned about Jumbo, its producers taped spots of him and smaller players. They got the smallest player on the Saudi team—DeRon Horton, four-foot-nine, seventy-seven pounds—to hide behind Gulliver and then pop out from behind. Then they shot Durling with Curaçao's Rayshelon Carolina. At four-seven, seventy-five pounds, Carolina is the smallest player in the whole tournament (*less than one-third of Durling's heft*). The camera lingered at their shoes, one a size thirteen, the other a size six—and then slowly moved up. Then Carolina played peek-a-boo behind Durling.

Durling comes from a family of big Texas athletes. His father and grandfather played college football. His grandfather went to the Baltimore Colts training camp without ever having played football. He can tell people he once shared a locker room with Johnny Unitis. The Little Leaguer's aunt, Margo Graham, played four seasons in the WNBA and still holds discus and shotput records at the University of Houston.

Two questions followed Durling as he ambled around the complex.

The first question: Was he really just twelve years old? Little League limits eligibility for its summer-long "Major League" tournament to boys and girls who are ten, eleven, and twelve years old. The cutoff date for eligibility has always been July 31—a date selected to conform with the Williamsport Public Schools cutoff date for kindergarten, many generations ago. Little League officials checked Durling's records—once, twice, three times. He was legit. Durling's parents point out that he'll qualify for Little League again next year.

The second question: Can he play?

The conventional wisdom in youth baseball is winning teams need one or two imposing power pitchers and at least one big bopper at the plate. Big kids have dominated play in Williamsport. In 2002, Louisville's Aaron Alvey pitched twenty-one shutout innings and struck out forty-four batters. In 1982, Cody Webster, of Kirkland, Washington, pitched a two-hit 6–0 shutout in the series final to end Taiwan's thirty-one-game winning streak. Sean Burroughs dominated the series in 1991 when he pitched two no-hitters in Long Beach, California's second straight championship. In 1971, Lloyd McClendon of Gary, Indiana, hit five home runs in five at-bats and took a 3–3 tie into the ninth inning of the championship game against Taiwan.

But size does not guarantee dominance.

At the batting cages at the Little League complex, Durling got caught in the black netting as he got in and out of the cage. When he stepped up to the plate, he struggled to coordinate his far-flung body parts. His bat moved slowly toward balls from the pitching machine. He missed more balls than he hit. Other players hit virtually every pitch from the machine. In the World Series games, Durling did not get a hit. He did not get much of a chance, because he did not play much more than the minimum of one at-bat and one inning in the field every game. In short, he's not very good. Not yet, anyway.

Baseball is not Durling's favorite sport. Basketball is. Durling told his teammates and players from other teams that he's going to play Division I college hoops. The University of Texas has contacted the family. *Wink, wink.* Colleges are not allowed to recruit kids at such a young age, but they *can* tell kids they'll be watching the summer tournaments that Nike and Adidas stage to showcase the best teenaged basketball talent in the country.

The value of baseball for Durling is that it forces him to do things on the diamond that can be brought into the flow of basketball—charging forward and moving back, moving to the right and to the left, reacting to pitches sizzling into the plate at major-league equivalents of ninety or ninety-five miles an hour.

"Baseball has taught him coordination," his mother Dana told me. "Before, he was falling up stairs. Basketball is his true love but he kept falling on top of kids. In soccer, he had to stop playing because he kept falling on kids. There's no insurance for broken kids."

———————•◆•———————

One after another, buses carrying boys from all over the world arrived at the Little League complex. The buses came from airports in Harrisburg and Philadelphia, about two or three hours away, after journeys from all over the world. The trips totaled about 50,000 miles.

Lance Van Auken, the public-relations executive of Little League, says his favorite moment of the Little League World Series occurs when the kids arrive on buses.

"I like to stand by the fence and watch them come in," he said. "Their eyes get big when they see the stadium, and they run over to The Hill and just want to slide down. Some of them slide down The Hill before they even get to their dorm rooms."

Throughout the World Series, fans and players slide down the hills overlooking Howard Lamade Stadium.

Players came from all over the U.S.—as far away as Hawaii, California, Louisiana, and Florida; and points closer, too, Pennsylvania, Maine, Iowa, and Kentucky—to play in the 2005 Little League World Series. Foreign teams flew in from Japan and Guam in the Pacific; Arctic neighbors Canada and Russia; Venezuela, Mexico, and Curaçao in Latin America; and an outpost of ex-pats in Saudi Arabia.

The complex sits about 1,000 feet above the Susquehanna River; a nearby lookout provides views of the river, farmland, and an airstrip. Back in the day, the hills cut an even slope from the river to the top of the mountains. But land was scooped out of the hills to make the river dams that protect the area from constant flooding. Little League's stadiums and practice fields are built into those hills.

As they settled into their dorms, players and their coaches and families posed for pictures with Lamade Stadium as the backdrop. They walked down the steep concrete steps that have been built into the hills—a total of more than 120 steps—and milled around the edges of the two stadiums. The two stadiums are as modern and sparkling as the best minor-league ballparks. The infield dirt is manicured perfectly, the Kentucky bluegrass as bright and finely cut as the turf in Fenway Park or Dodger Stadium.

--------------•◆•--------------

After exploring the complex during the day, the players and coaches watched ESPN at night to track the latest regional tournaments. The dorms have cable. Some coaches brought VCRs to record the games to scout future opponents.

By the time these regional championship games take place, teams have advanced through district, sectional, and state tournaments. In the international bracket, teams move through sectional, national, and regional tournaments. The final games of the eight American regional tournaments are televised on ESPN.

In the must-see regional title game, two California teams faced each other for the West regional title, playing in the scorching heat of San Bernardino. The favorite was the Rancho Buena Vista Little League, a team from outside San Diego; the underdog was Tracy, a team from about fifty miles east of Oakland. Vista's Nate Lewis beat Tracy, 7–2, to advance to Williamsport.

But the marquee player for Vista was a goateed young man named Kalen Pimentel. During the season, Pimentel hit more than thirty home runs—no one knows how many exactly because the team stopped keeping track—and batted close to .700. Pitchers walked him in almost half of his plate appearances. At one point, the righthanded Pimentel batted lefty to shame the pitcher into pitching to him.

Pimentel's a quiet kid who's just gotten big before the other kids—and happens to have a top-caliber coach in his father. Like a couple dozen of the players in the World Series, Pimentel's already reached puberty. You can still see traces of the child in his face, but his face is lean and his body well muscled. In the press conferences after games, Pimentel squirms like some of the other players, but more out of bemusement than awe or shyness. He has Derek Jeter's smirk. When he starts to talk about how he hit a home run or racked up all those strikeouts, he suddenly sounds like a man. He explains, better than even the best coaches could, how he hit the ball because of an adjustment in his swing that enabled him to turn on the ball. But just when you start to think he is a man, you see him running around the complex with his teammates. He's the Tom Hanks character in *Big*.

Pimentel's hitting scares other teams, but his pitching *terrorizes* them. If you want, you can pitch around Pimentel when he comes to the plate. Just throw junk, and he can't beat you every time. But on the mound, you can't avoid him. On pitch after pitch, he comes at you with a fastball that sometimes exceeds eighty miles an hour and a curveball that breaks as sharply as a good high school player's bender. And he's just forty-six feet away.

Fear of Pimentel caused one team to purposely lose a game in the West regional tournament. The team from Tracy had a choice in the final game of pool play: win the game and you face Vista and Pimentel in the semifinal. Lose it, and you play an easier team in the semifinals—and a chance to play for the regional championship.

Tracy used its second-string lineup and an inexperienced pitcher in the semis against Chandler, Arizona. Chandler won, 11–10, and so Tracy got Chandler again in the semis. Tracy won this time, 10–0, and advanced to the championship game against Vista.

"I've been coaching years and years and I've never done that in my life and never knew how difficult it would be," Tracy's manager, Emmett Lee, told a fellow coach of his decision to lay down in the semifinal game. "We mixed up the lineup, but the kids just kept hitting the ball. You can't tell them not to swing the bat."

Other wild games took place in the West regional. Peccole, Nevada, beat Snow Canyon, Utah, by the obscene score of 30–3. Peccole took a 9–0 lead in the first inning and manager Bobby Burns told his players to ease up—take only one base no matter what, bunt the ball back to the pitcher. But the assault continued. The game was halted after four innings under Little League's ten-run mercy rule.

The best regional championship game—and the most painful to watch—took place in Indianapolis. In the Great Lakes tournament, the team from Owensboro, Kentucky, survived a punishing last-inning rally to beat Kankakee, Illinois. Owensboro took an 11–4 lead into the bottom of the final inning with its toughest pitcher, Nolan Miller, on the mound. But Kankakee sent ten batters to the plate and came within a run of tying the game.

Miller, a thin boy with his pale face reddened and glazed by exertion on a muggy midwestern night, lost all control of the game. He started to overthrow the ball. Rather than using his whole body to power his pitches, he threw with just his arm. Manager Rick Hale came out to encourage him during the assault. "Just relax, take a deep breath," he said in his long drawl. "You okay?" Hale tried to lock eyes with his exhausted pitcher. "I believe in you, baby," Hale finally said before walking off the mound.

All the while, the parents on the Kentucky side were having fits in the stands. *Bring in a new pitcher, Ricky! C'mon, Ricky, he's too tired to finish it!*

Hale later explained why he left Miller in the game when he was obviously exhausted.

"I didn't think I had anyone else who could have withstood that punishment," he told me. "When [Kankakee] started their move, I said, 'How is it going to be easier to live with yourself if you lose this thing?' My assistant coach was *begging* me to make a move. That's the only game I've watched on tape and it's painful for me to watch it. It was a calculated move. It's not like I was in a coma. Nolan's the only kid I got."

Nolan Miller did, in fact, finish the game. But by the time Kentucky got to Williamsport, Miller's arm was hurting. So were the arms of his teammates.

———————— •◆• ————————

Excitement blends into nervousness in the early days in Williamsport. When they want to win too much, managers can start acting like jerks.

Before leaving for Williamsport, I visited Tom Galla, the manager of the 1989 Little League World Series champions from Trumbull, Connecticut. Trumbull's victory became big news because it interrupted a long period of Asian dominance. The Asian teams were so strong—and controversies over rules violations were so rampant—that Little League banned foreign teams from the World Series in 1975. Overall, Asian teams won championships in sixteen out of the previous twenty years when Trumbull, Connecticut, won in 1989.

But Galla admits now that he almost ruined his team's chances.

"When we arrived in Williamsport, everybody jumped off the bus and looked off the edge of The Hill and saw the stadium: 'Wow!' The next thing, they gave the kids jackets and brought us over to the infirmary. We were in line and the Taiwanese team shows up right behind us. Our kids were dressed like American kids—shorts, T-shirts, sneakers. These guys [the Taiwanese] had their practice uniforms on, they were carrying these bags, brand-new baseball gloves, brand-new spikes, brand-new everything, and they just looked really sharp, really professional."

A newsboy hawking papers is just part of the retro feel of the Little League World Series.

Galla panicked at the display of professional confidence. And he pushed his own players too hard.

"We went down to the field and I was a miserable SOB in practices, yelling at everybody, making a nuisance of myself," he says. "I was nervous that they might think we can't do this. I was putting everyone through their paces, more difficult than ever before."

Then, in a flash, he says he realized that he was sapping the game of its fun, making the players press.

"Then I walked around the practice and talked to each kid individually when they were still on the field and I said, 'You did a great job today, I just want you to know that you guys belong here.'"

The team was loose the whole way, winning four straight games and the title. In the final, Trumbull beat Kang-Tu Little League, 5–2. The starter for Trumbull was Chris Drury, who became a star in the National Hockey League and played for the U.S. Olympic team in Turin in 2006.

———— •◆• ————

For the teams that do not qualify for the Little League World Series, watching the games can produce regrets—and anger—about what might have been.

When a bunch of kids from Paramus, New Jersey, watched the Mid-Atlantic Region championship game on TV, they got upset.

One of the teams in the game—Pennsylvania's Council Rock Little League—was comprised of most of the same players who competed as as the Newtown Blue Dawgs travel team in the Sports at the Beach tournament in Rehobeth, Maryland, over the Memorial Day weekend.

So what?

For weeks, the Paramus Little League tried to get permission from Little League officials to do the same thing—play in both the Little League tournaments and the Sports at the Beach tournament. But Little

League officials told John Tenhove, the coach of both teams, that there couldn't be "too many" of the same players on both teams.

The reason was that Little League bans forming all-star teams before June 15. If a Little League's top players competed together as part of a travel team before June 15, that might be tantamount to creating the all-star team before the magic June 15 date. That rule has a good rationale. Teams competing for a spot in the Little League World Series should play on equal terms.

The Paramus Patriots travel team signed up for the prestigious Delaware tournament before the 2005 Little League season. Tenhove didn't want to get called for breaking the rules later on, so he went to Little League's regional headquarters in Bristol, Connecticut, for clarification of the rules.

"They told me that since we had so many players on the travel team, we were forming the Little League all-star team before June 15, and so that was a violation," Tenhove says. "I kept asking them, how many is too many? Seven? Eight? Nine? I never got an answer."

Since the Patriots already made a commitment to Sports at the Beach, the Paramus Little League pulled all its all-star teams out of Little League tournaments.

"The Williamsport tournament is very attractive; I would have loved to take a shot at that," Tenhove says. "My kids and my whole team watch it every year. When it came on TV this year, I got calls from my players: 'Hey, coach, the Newtown team's on TV.' That's what bothers me. They were allowed to play [in Little League tournaments] and we weren't."

So when the Paramus players saw some of the Newtown Blue Dawgs on TV, competing for a spot in the Little League World Series, they called Tenhove.

Hey coach, those guys from Newtown are playing in the Little League tournament? How come they're allowed to play in Little League and Sports on the Beach, and we aren't?

In fact, eight players on the Newtown Dawgs travel team also played for the Council Rock Little League all-stars.

Bill Hartley, the manager of both Newtown teams, doesn't apologize for having players on both teams. "If anyone tells you they're just playing Little League," he told me, "they're lying."

And he's right. The best players in the U.S. usually want to play on travel teams, and many of them also want a shot at the Little League World Series. Little League officialdom resents travel teams, but wants at least *some* of the best travel-team players involved in its World Series tournaments.

"There are a lot of gray areas," Little League CEO Steve Keener admits. "What the rules say is the local Little League in whatever town cannot sanction, finance, or support Little League participation in a non-sanctioned Little League activity," he told me later. "But the rule is full of loopholes, and this is what the team from Pennsylvania—the way they did it is the way you have to do it to beat the rule. It's the same people, the same coaches, the same kids, but Little League is not paying the insurance, it's not paying the fees, it's done separately. It's how you beat the system."

At times, Little League all-stars play *simultaneously* on travel teams. The Peccole Little League, winners of the Nevada state title, allowed six players to play for the Las Vegas Coyotes in the prestigious Cooperstown Dreams Park tournament during the week of June 25.

"Half of the team went to Cooperstown during all-star practice," said Bobby Burns, the Little League's manager. "It wasn't the best players and they didn't do very well. But it shows that travel teams have become a very important part of Little League."

———— • ◆ • ————

It's probably not a stretch to say that the best teams in the Little League World Series are made up of ringers from travel teams.

The teams from Hawaii, California, Florida, Louisiana, Pennsylvania, and Kentucky all play on travel teams. Every single player on the Maitland Little League all-stars also played for a travel team called the Maitland Pride. Dante Bichette Sr. formed the Maitland Pride the previous year for the sole purpose of getting ready for a run at Williamsport.

Sid Cash, the manager of Maitland's Little League all-stars, told me that "we still honored the Little League because we picked a kid who wasn't on the travel team." That player turned down the all-star spot, to Cash's regret. "He was a black kid named Jason Billy," Cash says. "He was rough but he could run. If we could have had him on the team, he could have put down a bunt and made it every time. He comes from a split family and spent the rest of the summer in Houston. We would have paid for him to fly in for games."

The all-stars from Vista, California, were mostly the same kids who played for the Team Easton, a travel team sponsored by the sporting-goods company. The all-stars from Hawaii also played on a Cal Ripken Baseball team and a travel team called the Paina Boyz. The all-stars from

Lafayette, Louisiana, play in off-season as the Lafayette Renegades. And, of course, the all-stars from Pennsylvania played on the Newtown Blue Dawgs. All but two of the Owensboro, Kentucky, players competed on travel teams when they went to the World Series in 2004, and four of the players were on travel teams in 2005 before playing in that year's Little League World Series.

Steve Keener doesn't like the term "ringers" to describe the travel team players that dominate the Little League World Series. Technically, Keener says, ringers are players who play in a tournament despite not playing for a team all year. Fair enough. But the fact remains that Sunbelt teams often get built around travel-team players who work out for years in preparation for the run to Williamsport.

Somehow, that's not quite fair to the teams from Davenport, Iowa, and Westbrook, Maine.

Most of the Iowa kids play other sports in the winter—wrestling, basketball—and don't have the time or facilities to play baseball. "You don't do a lot of winter workouts in baseball in Iowa," Ed Grothus told me. "Once a week maybe. Our kids are doing other stuff. It's not all baseball, all the time."

The dominance of the Little League World Series by travel-team players troubles Steve Keener, but he says the courts prevent any effective response. "I don't like it, but there's nothing I can do about it," Keener told me. In the 1980s, in a case brought by the Amateur Softball Association, state courts rejected Little League's right to restrict outside participation.

Speaking of Frostbelt teams like Davenport, which do not have opportunities to play all year long, Keener said, "I feel badly for those kids because they're probably at a competitive disadvantage. But [the Midwest and other northern regions] have been at a competitive disadvantage in this World Series since competition began in 1947."

Little League needs to figure out some way to address the phenomenon of travel teams. Some community leagues have experimented with creating teams for both Little League and elite tournament play. The White Marsh Baseball of Perry Hall, Maryland, for example, provides programs for community leagues similar to Little League and PONY baseball, as well as travel teams. Like weight classes in wrestling and youth football, the separation allows kids to compete against their real athletic peers. "Our major goal is teaching the game and having some fun," says Bob Palmer, the head of the program. "There are some kids who want something more. It's the parents who want something more, actually, so they can brag about their kids. But we have programs for them, too. That way we can provide something for everyone."

Blankets claim space for the Little League World Series championship game and make a giant quilt.

The first few days in Williamsport entail a lot of waiting around. The players get fitted for uniforms. Camera crews from ABC and ESPN shoot features and short clips for "bumpers," the transitions from commercials to game coverage. Some teams practice from early in the morning till late at night. Some of the teams occupy the fields and batting cages all day.

Others—like California's Marty Miller—disdain working out too much.

"We haven't taken infield practice in four weeks," says Miller, an Idaho native who owns a construction company and has been playing or coaching baseball for more than four decades. "Give them six or eight balls and they're okay. You can kill them by over-practicing on defense. If you do 200 grounders, you're going to wear your arms off. There are some coaches that can't teach pitching or hitting so they hit ground balls all day long. But fielding is not that hard to teach—butt down, gloves out front, eyes on ball."

When they're not practicing, what can the players do? Most teams don't let their kids swim in the pool because they might overtax some muscles or stub a toe. There's a game room with free video games and pool tables, but eventually even that gets boring. They can roam around the complex and make new friends. Some do, some don't.

"I try to tell the kids don't be overwhelmed, and *I* was overwhelmed," manager Rick Hale of Kentucky told me. "It's a big stage, and there are a lot of people and a lot of attention. There was so much time you had to fill with the kids. We got there on Monday and didn't have a game till Saturday. I wish I had come up with activities like they were in school. You can't practice them to death. It's a carnival atmosphere. I turned them loose, and they ran back and forth to the game room and left the complex and went to fields and the tents. That makes for some locker room rumbles. All because we were cooped up together for too long."

Shon Muna, Guam's coach, balanced baseball and fun with a strict/loose system of discipline. The team practiced many hours a day. And when they practiced, they worked hard. If Muna couldn't think of anything else to have them do, he told them to run "until *I* get tired." The team worked hard on infield drills and hitting mechanics. The Guam kids were usually the last team on the practice fields.

But when they weren't practicing, the players were allowed to roam as far as they wanted—so long as they responded when Muna called.

I was talking with Muna one time in a pavilion as his kids were running around, eating, trading pins, shadow boxing, flirting. The group was wild—all over the place. But when Muna calls, they respond. "Want to see how it works?" Muna asked me. "Watch." He paused for a moment, then called out, loudly: "*Oyyyy!*" Within five seconds, every player on the team surrounded Muna. "What's up, coach?" "What you want, coach?"

———————— • ◆ • ————————

For a town that gets so much of its identity from Little League, Williamsport has not done much to celebrate its event. But in 2005, Williamsport decided to throw a parade. The Grand Slam Parade took place the night before the opening day of the World Series and was followed by fireworks over the Susquehanna River.

Maybe 1,000 people set up butterfly chairs and lawn chairs and laid rugs by the side of West Fourth Street. They sat for almost an hour, listening to music blare on a public address system while waiting. American flags, large and small, were everywhere. Otto's Bookstore set out carts and tables with baseball books on the sidewalk. The city's grand hotel, Genetti's, sold hot dogs and cokes from a pushcart. A twenty-five-foot blow-up baseball took up space on the sidewalk. The Clother, on old-timey haberdasher, put some sale items out on the sidewalk. Aluminum stands provided seats for a couple hundred people. At least a dozen storefronts along the street shut down.

California's Nate Lewis reacts after getting hit with a pitch in a game against Hawaii.

Williamsport had not held a parade for its signature event since the 1950s, and people seemed happy to wait for this one to happen. The start time of 5:30 p.m. passed with nary a word. Then 6 p.m. passed. And people sat and waited.

A group of Mexican women—parents of players on the team from Mexicali—broke the monotony by walking down the center of the street waving green pom-poms. People started cheering. The PA system played "That Old Time Rock and Roll" and "Downtown" and "Dance to the Music." Was *this* the parade?

No. But about fifteen minutes later, the procession finally began. The leader of the parade was Governor Edward Rendell, a man who's still getting used to little town ways after serving two terms as mayor of Philadelphia. Rendell was stuffed into a bright blue suit, the jacket button holding his girth inside. His gray hair matted across his pate, Reddell wore a pol's smile on his ruddy face and waved as his six aides surrounded him on all sides during the promenade.

Then came a Hummer with an Iraq War veteran, followed by the usual small-town figures. The Montgomery High School Red Raiders marching band performed, followed by the Red Raiders cheerleaders, who carried plastic white blowup bats. Antique cars, one carrying Karen Stotz Myer, the daughter of Little League's founder, followed. The Sons of Italy had a car. The Lycoming County Dairy Princess, a blonde in a flower summer dress, tilt-waved at the crowd. Then came teams from the Original Little League, the organization Carl Stotz set up after his bitter split from Little League. And there were a couple of furry cartoon characters—Little League's mascot, a huge furry rodent named Dugout, and Puxatawny Phil, the symbol of Groundhog Day. Finally, on flatbed trucks, all sixteen teams in the Little League World Series arrived. The players, dressed in their uniforms, tossed candy and waved.

———————————— •◆• ————————————

Before the Little League World Series starts, all the teams are undefeated—and they all have a chance to go home as champions. It's a time of optimism. All but about a half-dozen teams know, deep down, that they're not going to win. But like a governor from a farm state who gets mentioned as a long-shot VP candidate, they all have elegant scenarios in which they could win, if only…

Waiting for the games to start, the reporters hunt for stories.

The big story in baseball in the summer of 2005 was the steroids scandal shadowing the major leagues. In the first year of regular testing for the drugs, a number of major leaguers got caught taking the performance-enhancing drugs. But as much as they tried, there wasn't much of a story to be gotten in Williamsport. I saw repeated variations of the following conversation:

Reporter: There seems to be a problem in the major leagues with steroids. What do you think?

Player: Well, I guess it's bad.

Reporter: Do you think major leaguers should be role models?

Player: Yeah, I guess.

Reporter: Who's your favorite ballplayer?

Player: Barry Bonds.

At this stage of their development, players are not going to have the kind of layered political opinions that the reporters were seeking. They like to play the great game of spotting contradictions when it suits their immediate interests—*Why does he get to do it and I don't?*—but they're not interested in cross-examining players to the nth degree. Logic and consistency are not the ultimate values of childhood.

I spent about a half-hour one afternoon hanging out with the players from Kentucky as they waited on The Hill for the bus that took them to the parade in downtown Williamsport. We talked at length about their favorite players and teams, what they want to do for a living, and what they think of steroids and greed and other flaws of modern major leaguers.

They alternated between saying what they thought I wanted to hear and defiantly sticking to their guns, no matter what the evidence.

I asked them to name the greatest living ballplayer. One said Barry Bonds, which was a reasonable pick, but then he backed off when I mentioned steroids. I suggested Willie Mays and Henry Aaron. Politely, they agreed. *Yes, that makes sense. Mays and Aaron it is.* But I sensed they were just being polite with an adult.

Then one of them renominated Bonds. "You know, I don't care about steroids," he said. "Just look at the way he *hits* the ball."

These kids are not going to agonize over the misdeeds of major leaguers. They get an image of what they like, mostly from TV, and they idolize it. They don't want to be critical of salaries or steroids. They don't want to talk about who's a selfish player and who's a team player. They just want to fasten onto an idol and forget about the rest.

———— • ◆ • ————

Every year, ESPN shoots short instructional clips for use during the week and a half of games. Harold Reynolds, a twelve-year veteran of the major leagues who now works as a broadcaster, guided a bunch of Little Leaguers through the paces before the TV cameras at Lamade Stadium.

Reynolds is a trim and outgoing African American man with a short haircut and a wisp of a goatee, and he wears a powder blue golf shirt with an ESPN logo, baggy khakis, and white sneakers. He moves easily around the field. He hasn't exercised seriously since ending his career but says he's going to start running again. "I just got so burned out after playing all those years," he said.

He pointed to a couple of players who were recruited to star in the instructional spots. "Here's what we're going to do," he told them. "You guys are going to be first basemen. There are two ways of scooping up the ball. Are you good at the stretch? Let me see."

Andrew Stevenson, who played for the all-stars from Lafayette, Louisiana, and Paul Kelsch, who played for the Saudi Arabia team, listened and followed his motions. Oleg Khudyakov, one of the all-stars from Moscow, Russia, stood nearby. Reynolds tried talking to him, then started to motion, but gave up quickly. "Can anyone translate for Oleg?" No answer. "Oleg, I'm going to use you to hit. Okay?" No response. Reynolds gently pushed him back to the dugout.

Three girls watch the game from The Hill.

Reynolds tried to chat up Mitch Burns, a player for the team from Surrey, British Columbia, in Canada. "I'm from Spokane. You know where that is? Washington State. Washington State?" Burns shook his head. Then he walked over to Zachary Ranit of Ewa Beach, Hawaii: "Hey, you hit a home run the other night? Yeah, you did!" He hit the bill of his cap.

The camera people set up a light screen to do the spot. "*I'm* here with Andrew and *Paul*," Reynolds said to the camera. "As you can see, they're *different sizes*. It doesn't *matter* how big you are. What's *important* is you catch the ball." Cut! The players were distracted and didn't know where to look. Reynolds walked over and hugged them. "Re-*lax* and have some *fun*," he said. They got the spot right in four takes.

The other players waited to play their parts. Zachary Ranit demonstrated Hawaii's shaka sign, which can be translated as "Hang loose" or "Aloha." The thumb and pinky extend outward, and the other fingers close in a fist. Dylan Demeyer, who plays for the Vista, California, team, played hackey-sack with a ball. Ranit and Stevenson played catch for the camera.

Once the camera stopped shooting, they stopped playing. Little League in the age of TV.

Throughout the Little League
World Series, fans slide down
the hills overlooking
Howard Lamade Stadium.

For decades, boys and girls have gathered at the Original Little League Field to try out for the new season.

CHAPTER 3

————— •◆• —————

The Rise of Little League

*O*N ONE OF THEIR OFF DAYS, the team from the Brateevo Little League in Moscow took a pilgrimage to the Eden of Little League Baseball.

They went like they were visiting the Hermitage in St. Petersburg or Red Square in Moscow. They took cameras and walked around, inspecting the objects in the museum and looking over the field as if it was hallowed ground.

To get to the heart of Little League, you drive up West Fourth Street from downtown Williamsport, beyond the elegant mansions and into the territory of auto parts stores and check-cashing outlets and a struggling residential area. Finally, right across the street from Bowman Field, the home of the Williamsport Cutters of the New York-Penn League, you find a bright greensward and a small stone building.

Carl Stotz Field is where Little League staged its World Series games before Howard Lamade Stadium opened in 1959. It's a smaller, cozier version of Lamade Stadium, nestled into a small hill on the other side of the Susquehanna River. Like Lamade Stadium, it has a hill just beyond the outfield fence. The seating is mostly standard-issue aluminum benches. The stone building houses the Original Little League Museum, as well as the scorekeeper's booth and a place for players to change clothes. The museum is usually open when Little League games are under way, but otherwise you have to make an appointment to see the collection of old uniforms, scorecards, photos, bats, and balls.

A couple blocks away, on the other side of Bowman Field, is the place where Carl Stotz had the brainstorm that led to the creation of Little League in 1939.

Outside the museum, just feet away from a symbolic lilac bush, a plaque honors the man who revolutionized youth sports in America. The plaque reads:

A PROMISE KEPT

LITTLE LEAGUE'S FOUNDER GAVE PART OF AMERICANA TO THE WORLD.
THOSE WHO KNEW HIM SAW A MAN OF PROFOUND INTEGRITY AND CHARACTER,
TRULY ONE OF THE GREATEST MEN OF ALL TIMES.
THE IDEALS BY WHICH HE LIVED ARE THE ULTIMATE MEASURE OF
THIS EXTRAORDINARY MAN.
HE REMAINS MR. LITTLE LEAGUE.

Those words are over-the-top generous to Little League's founder. Honestly, "one of the greatest men of all times"? But when you know the history, the words have an edge to them.

To many people's way of thinking, this is not only where Little League was born. It's also where the soul of Little League died.

———————— •◆• ————————

Every great organization—nations, corporations, religions, movements, and even sporting events—nurtures a powerful mythology of its founding.

The founding myth gives people a reason for elevating their activities above others and commanding the allegiance of new generations. At the center of the myth stands a figure who embodies both humility and transcendence. He touches people emotionally, but often stands aloof. He considers his followers to be his children, who must obey and honor him without question.

The founding act usually results from some moment of revelation, a sudden flash of divine inspiration that even the founder cannot fully explain. That moment of inspiration—that eureka moment—lends an air of inevitability and transcendence to the organization.

Ultimately, the founding myth includes a tale of betrayal, the moment when the forces of greed and egotism try to steal the empire from the founder. This betrayal often creates a great civil war, which leaves everyone damaged. If they're lucky, new generations come along to heal the wounds of that battle—and bring the organization to new levels of glory.

———————— •◆• ————————

The founder of Little League Baseball—now the largest amateur sports organization in the world—was a twenty-eight-year-old clerk at Pure Oil Company named Carl Stotz.

Carl Stotz was a thin man with thin black hair, combed back in the severe style of the time. His face was long and his body was lean. His efforts to bring baseball to kids took him all over the world. In the beginning, he used his own money, even when he was unemployed, to spread the gospel of Little League. When I spoke to some of the men who played on the first Little League teams back in 1939, they alternated between the honorific "Mr. Stotz" and the friendly "Carl" when they talked about him.

A one-room museum next to the Original Little League Field in Williamsport honors Carl Stotz, who founded the organization in 1939.

Carl Stotz told the story of Little League's founding the following way.

One August day in 1938—a couple months after the National Baseball Hall of Fame in Cooperstown enshrined its first five members—Stotz was playing catch with his nephews, Jimmy and Major Gehron, in the yard of his house on Isabella Street. The house was not far from Bowman Field, the home of the Williamsport Grays, the Eastern League affiliate of the Detroit Tigers. A ball got away. As Stotz ran after the ball, he brushed his leg on a lilac bush.

When he sat down to nurse his scrapes, he had a revelation which "is hard to explain unless you have experienced it yourself sometime in your life, where all at once something comes to you that they call a flashback...There it is in one scene."

In that one pivotal scene, Stotz asked his nephews a series of questions:

How would you boys like to play on a baseball team? How would you like to play in uniforms, just like major-league players use? With real equipment— a fresh supply of balls and bats, with catcher's gear. Umpires would call the games, so arguments about balls and strikes, catch or no catch, fair or foul, would not interrupt play. Coaches would teach players. Someone would keep score. At the end of the year, the best teams would play for the championship of the league. What do you think of that, boys?

Jimmy and Major Gehron nodded enthusiastically and set out to tell their friends about a new baseball league. Within days, the boys gathered a group of friends and they practiced at a nearby field. But the real league wouldn't begin to play until the spring of 1939.

Stotz recruited boys to play in the new league. He went to schools and churches and asked boys the same question he asked his nephews: *how would you like to play in a league just like the major leagues?* As the spring of 1939 approached, Stotz and his followers cleared a vacant lot owned by the Williamsport Textile Company, graded the surface, marked out a baseball diamond, built a backstop behind home plate, and planted grass.

The lilac bush would remain the symbol of Little League inspiration. Stotz preserved the bush for posterity. In 2005, a local artist claimed he got a piece of the bush and mixed it in with the paint he was using to create a mural depicting the influential people in Williamsport's history. The portion of the mural depicting Carl Stotz was painted with the lilac-laced paint.

Stotz also asked local businesses for support. As he went from business to business in Williamsport—once the center of the lumber industry, now a city in decline—he received blank stares and polite rejections. Finally, three local businesses agreed to help. Lundy Lumber Company, Lycoming Dairy, and Jumbo Pretzel Company pledged to spend a few hundred dollars to establish "midget" baseball teams.

No one had ever organized kids that young—eight, nine, ten years old—to play in organized baseball leagues. Until then, kids couldn't play on teams until they were in high school. Churches and boys clubs organized occasional games, but most youngsters learned baseball on the streets and in the fields. They played pickup and sandlot games. If they didn't have money for equipment, they made bats and balls from whatever materials were available. They argued frequently over rules and calls. The bigger boys dominated the games, sometimes bullying younger kids and sometimes looking out for them. If they couldn't get enough players for a game, they improvised.

Adults rarely intruded on this world. A few zealous adults—like Carl Stotz—played catch or pitched to their boys. The most contact that most kids had with adults in Williamsport at this time came near Bowman Field, the home of the Williamsport Grays minor-league team. Neighborhood kids met players before and after games, and the pros gave away broken bats and played catch.

A loose model for Little League emerged a decade before, in 1929, when a YMCA employee in Chicago named Joseph Tomlin started a football league for boys in Philadelphia. Tomlin organized the league to combat an outbreak of delinquency. Boys were breaking factory windows all over the city, and Tomlin wanted to fill their time. Since it was fall, Tomlin organized a four-team Junior Football Conference. Over time the new league set up weight classifications to make sure that kids played with their physical peers. Coaches taught the game's basics—passing and catching, blocking and tackling—and offered special recognition to kids who did well in school. In 1934, the organizers renamed the league for Pop Warner, a college coaching legend whose players included Jim Thorpe. By 1938, 157 teams competed in Pop Warner leagues.

Before Little League's first season in 1939, Stotz devised new rules for baseball appropriate to small boys. He decided right away that batters shouldn't take first base on called third strikes or take leads to steal bases. He also experimented with different field sizes before settling on a diamond two-thirds the size of a regulation field. He describes his experimentation with field sizes in his memoir, *A Promise Kept*:

"After I placed the papers around the field to represent home plate and each base, I positioned the boys around the infield while I served as pitcher. From time to time, I changed the distance between the bases. I was trying to find out what distance would enable the boys to throw a runner out from third base or shortstop while still giving the batter a fair chance to beat it out, depending on where he hit the ball...Each evening I continued experimenting with the distance between bases. When I finally had what I thought was the ideal distance, I stepped it off and used a yardstick at home to measure my strides. The distance was so close to sixty feet that I set that as the distance we would use thereafter."

The pitcher's rubber was placed forty-four feet from home plate; it was later moved back to forty-six feet when the shorter distance was considered too dangerous for pitchers and hitters alike.

Stotz could not have known the long-term impact of his decision. The small field would enable little guys to play the game with ease. Over the years, the smaller field would also produce a game long on power and short on finesse. To win the Little League World Series, you have to strike out batters and hit home runs. That style of play contributed to a crisis in pitching injuries that reverberated all the way to the major leagues.

———————•◆•———————

Long before Ray Kroc franchised McDonald's hamburger joints across the world, Carl Stotz had the idea of creating a franchise system for children's sports.

After Stotz started Little League Baseball in 1939, he decided to spread it as far as he could take it. He proselytized community leaders from other towns—teachers, preachers, fathers, businessmen—to start their own leagues using Little League's rules. Stotz traveled first around central Pennsylvania, then all over the eastern United States, to preach his gospel of wholesome play for boys. He went to Sunday school classes, Lions Club meetings, school boards, YMCAs, and other organizations that gathered together boys and their fathers.

At one point, Stotz considered adding other sports to Little League. But he decided that if he was going to grow his organization, he had to focus on the sport he knew best.

Everywhere he went, his message was the same: Boys should be able to play in a miniature version of the major leagues, with all the trappings of the game. But the game should always be local. Dads should organize and coach teams. Neighbors should help out. Fans should pitch in with donations. Local merchants—owners of dairies, lumberyards, newspapers, hardware stores, restaurants—should sponsor teams.

To get a Little League charter, local organizations had to abide by simple rules set by Williamsport, but otherwise they were free to administer their leagues as they saw fit. To keep the experience as local and intimate as possible, Little League required all leagues to operate in a geographic area containing a population of 20,000 people. In such a small community, everyone would know everyone. And with tryouts and drafts, the teams would have comparable talent. Unlike high school sports, which were always dominated by the biggest schools with the most dominant players, Little League would be competitive for all. The point was to get as many kids involved as possible and have fun.

For years, Carl Stotz worked on his own time. He was lucky to have bosses who appreciated his league, so he left work early and took long summer vacations. In 1949, Little League's first major sponsor, U.S. Rubber, gave Stotz a ten-year contract to work full-time for Little League.

With its franchise model, Little League grew fast. By 1947, Little League had seventeen leagues in Pennsylvania and New Jersey.

In 1947, Little League's board of directors decided to hold a tournament to determine a "national" champion. The tournament gave Little League a spotlight that eventually helped it to become the biggest youth sports organization in the world.

Newsreels produced by the maker of the classic film *Lost Horizon* carried an account of the second tournament in 1948. Eighty million Americans saw the newsreel. A feature in the *Saturday Evening Post* in 1949 brought hundreds of requests for information on forming leagues. An article in *Reader's Digest* in 1951 produced another avalanche of inquiries. In 1953, CBS televised a tape of the World Series championship game and ABC broadcast a radio account with a young play-by-play man named Howard Cosell.

By 1952, the organization had 1,500 leagues. The league attracted the effusive praise of notables all over. Former president Herbert Hoover called Little League "one of the greatest stimulants of constructive joy in the world." The other Hoover, J. Edgar, the director of the Federal Bureau of Investigation, called Little League "the greatest deterrent to crime that America has ever seen." Arthur Daley, a sports columnist for the *New York Times*, said Little League was "the biggest thing in the sport since Abner Doubleday outlined his baseball diamond in Cooperstown in 1839."

Little League helped to define the emotional geography of American suburbia. As G.I.s returned from World War II and Korea, they settled in housing tracts and shopping malls rising on the crabgrass frontier.

The affluence of the postwar era created new opportunities for learning and play—and more often than not, these new opportunities took on a structured form. As succeeding rings of suburbs filled with single-family homes and "pods" of activity centers—clusters of separate activities, like office parks, shopping centers, schools, theaters and arts centers, playgrounds—children's activities operated with formal rules and organization. As consumerism spread into every crevice of everyday life, people paid for goods and services that they once made for themselves. Little League was at the leading edge of this new age of organized play.

Over the years, Little League expanded beyond its early program— boys eight to twelve years old—to offer programs for boys and girls of all ages. Partly to head off the drive to allow girls to play baseball, Little League created two softball programs in 1974. Over the years, Little

League added baseball programs for thirteen- to fifteen-year-olds in a Senior League (1961) and sixteen- to eighteen-year olds in a Big League (1968). In 1979, Little League created a Junior League program for thirteen-year-olds.

Little League provided the perfect vehicle for keeping kids busy under watchful eyes of dads and other trusted adults. In fact, if a small-town man like Carl Stotz did not invent Little League, someone like William Levitt or Ray Kroc would have had to do it.

———————•◆•———————

Like the rest of America, Little League struggled to confront the major social challenges facing the United States. On two issues—race and gender—Little League attempted to avoid the bitterness of the struggles.

The 2005 Little League World Series closed a sorry chapter on racial exclusion. Before the game between Florida and Iowa, an all-black team from Charleston was proclaimed the South Carolina state champion. Six of the surviving players from the 1955 Charleston team walked onto the field, lined up along the first-base line, and accepted a plaque and banner celebrating the team's achievement.

On the field, they wore the kinds of broad smiles that you usually see after the tournament is over. When they walked off the field, they were surrounded by TV reporters who wanted to know what it felt like to be champions.

In 1955, the year Rosa Parks refused to move to the back of the bus in Montgomery, Alabama, racial politics created a deep split in Little League.

South Carolina in those days had sixty-two Little League organizations—all but one of them all white. Rather than playing in a tournament with the black team from Charleston, the Cannon Street YMCA all-stars, the white leagues boycotted the tournament. Little League executives wouldn't intervene, so South Carolina got shut out of a possible berth in the World Series. Little League's split-the-baby solution was to allow the Charlestown kids to stay in Williamsport dorms while other teams played in the tournament. Just as segregationists established private academies rather than enroll their kids in integrated schools, they also created a new league. Hundreds of leagues dropped out of Little League and formed Dixie Youth Baseball.

The saga of the Cannon Street YMCA all-stars is vintage Little League. Since its earliest days, Little League has avoided controversy. A small-town organization that targeted its growth efforts to suburban communities, Little League was not going to get into the middle of a growing crisis over race relations and civil rights. Little League's executives were not going to try to force white teams to play with black teams or to award the black team a forfeit victory in the state tournament.

But at the same time, to its credit, Little League did not endorse the bigotry of South Carolina's all-white leagues.

Blacks have never had a huge presence in Little League's biggest stage. Over the years, few black teams have competed in the Little League World Series. The best team came from Gary, Indiana, in 1971. Led by a future major-leaguer named Lloyd McClendon, Gary took Taiwan beyond the regulation six innings in the championship game before losing in the ninth inning. The other successful black team came from Harlem in 2002.

The underrepresentation of black kids in Little League is mirrored at higher levels. Only about 9 percent of major leaguers today are black, down from a high of 23 percent in 1984. Only 6.1 percent of Division I college baseball players are black. Many inner-city neighborhoods don't even have Little League or other youth baseball leagues. Blacks have come to favor football and basketball.

———————— • ◆ • ————————

After Little League confronted the race problem—or at least put the problem aside—the question of the rights of girls moved to the fore.

Girls were always excluded from Little League for the same reason they were excluded from Boy Scouts. It was just *assumed* that baseball was a boys' game, period. A girl named Kathryn Johnston became the first girl to play in Little League in 1950 when she dressed up as a boy and called herself Tubby. But most leagues banned girls, and most girls didn't care enough to fight.

By the 1970s, though, girls started to demand to play Little League. In 1973, Maria Pepe played three games in the Hoboken Little League before Williamsport intervened to bar her from the league. Essex County's branch of the National Organization for Women (NOW) took the case to New Jersey's Civil Rights Division, which ruled in her favor. At the urging of officials in Williamsport, most of the state's 2,000 leagues postponed registration to avoid complying with the ruling.

"The girl is more likely to get hurt," Little League's CEO Creighton Hale argued. "From the time boys are six years old, they have more muscle fiber than girls." The controversy, Hale sighed, was political. "Most girls can play softball and I think more girls can benefit from a good softball program. Too much emphasis is placed on the game itself rather than what you get out of the game."

The New Jersey Superior Court supported the state's ruling. Seeing that it had lost its fight, Little League dropped its resistance. President Gerald R. Ford signed a 1974 law rewriting Little League's special federal charter by changing the word "boys" to "young people." In 1975, Amy Dickenson became the first girl drafted for a Little League team in New Jersey. She became a minor celebrity, appearing on *Wonderama* and sitting in the Mets dugout.

The controversy never disappeared. Girls have always had to deal with isolation on the team and stupid indignities like being ordered to wear a cup (it happened in Michigan's Romulus Little League in 1974). But there have been triumphs. Twelve girls have played in the Little League World Series. In 2004, two girls pitched against each other in a friendship game at the Little League World Series—and, Little League flak Chris Downs says, "one of them was actually a legitimate player." In 2005, when a girl named Katie Brownell pitched a perfect game in upstate New York, it was big news. She was everywhere in the media, met President George W. Bush, and had her jersey displayed at the Baseball Hall of Fame in Cooperstown.

————————•◆•————————

Over the years, Little League faced a number of critics. But the biggest critic turned out to be Carl Stotz, the founder of the organization.

From the beginning, educators worried that Little League put too much pressure on kids.

Charles Bucher, professor of education at New York University, thought Little League rushed boys out of their special dream world.

"The drive to win is traditional in America and must be preserved," Bucher wrote in 1952. "But a boy will absorb that lesson soon enough in high school. In his grammar school years it is more important that his recreation is guided toward other objectives: the fun of playing rather than winning, the child rather than the game, the many rather than the few, informal activity rather than the formal, the development of skills in many activities rather than specialization."

Others endorsed Little League as long as it stayed true to its roots, but resisted the national tournament and corporate sponsorship. "There's nothing wrong with Little League Baseball as long as it is confined to local competition and as long as exploitation and commercialism are avoided," said George Maksim, chairman of the school health committee of the American Academy of Pediatrics. "Competition is part of the growing child that should be recognized, accepted, and directed."

The criticism that Little League professionalized childhood would be heard more insistently over the years. When the Little League World Series became a major event—with days upon days of television coverage, parades, and scholarships and thousands of dollars worth of booty for the champions—Little League would become the target of stinging critiques from psychologists and educators.

By the 1990s and 2000s, it wasn't just Little League that seemed to pose such troubling questions. In other youth sports—soccer, basketball, football, lacrosse, hockey, gymnastics, and a dozen other sports—parents pushed their kids hard. Parents wanted the kids to qualify for competitive tournaments, win scholarships, and even get pro contracts. Cheerleading, once an innocent realm for boosters of sports, became so competitive that parents started gaming the system. One notorious Houston mother conspired to kill one of her daughter's classmates to ease the way for her child to make the squad.

Whatever you think about organizing kids to compete for glory, Little League was the model that everyone else followed. The uniforms, standings and stats, the adult supervision, the thick nest of rules, the drafts and trades, the international tournaments, the media glare—all were pioneered by Carl Stotz, who had this idea about creating a game where kids would dress up and act like adults.

Like all charismatic visionaries, Carl Stotz got caught between his desires to keep his organization small and under his own control, and his dreams to make Little League big.

Stotz loved the national attention and corporate support of the Little League World Series, but he also worried about Little League losing its local character. Coaches were starting to pay so much attention to building a national-caliber team that they neglected their lesser players. Stotz also feared that coaches intent on winning the championship would be tempted to cheat or bend the rules to win.

With its World Series as a headline event, Little League boomed. By 1948, the organization had ninety-four leagues; the next year it was 309 leagues. In 1950, Little League incorporated as a nonprofit organization.

Stotz made Little League's first efforts to globalize the organization. He traveled to U.S. military bases overseas to introduce Little League to the children of servicemen. The first Little League franchises overseas were set up in the Panama Canal Zone in 1950; other foreign programs soon followed in Canada, Cuba, Hawaii (then a U.S. territory), and Puerto Rico. The following year, foreign teams were competing to play in the World Series.

In 1952, U.S. Rubber wielded its power as Little League's major corporate sponsor and engineered the appointment of a public relations executive named Peter McGovern as Little League's president. McGovern had a corporate mindset. He helped to pack Little League's governing board of directors with businessmen, celebrities, and other well-connected men.

The year McGovern started his twenty-one-year reign, 1,500 leagues played games in forty-four states. Ten years later, in 1962, Little League Baseball had 5,500 leagues. By 1978, it was 6,500 leagues—plus 4,150 leagues for boys in other age brackets.

With every major growth spurt, Stotz grew more uncomfortable. He argued against inviting international teams into the World Series and, in 1955, the board voted him down.

As Little League's founder, Stotz thought he should have the major say over day-to-day management. He held the title of commissioner, which he thought gave him control over baseball operations while McGovern tended to the business operations. In fact, Stotz had a gentleman's agreement with a U.S. Rubber official that gave him final word on issues like new league charters, game rules, and management of the office. Problem was, the U.S. Rubber official died.

At a meeting after Thanksgiving Day in 1955, Stotz confronted the board of directors. He demanded that his powers as commissioner be recognized and that McGovern be removed as president. Neither of Stotz's motions was seconded. Stotz left the meeting an outcast from his own organization. After he departed, the board voted to remove him from his position as commissioner.

Stotz, meanwhile, got a local sheriff to padlock the Little League offices under an order from the county court official. The order shut down the offices to prevent the corporation, legally based in New York, from removing equipment from the Williamsport offices. Stotz then filed a breach-of-contract suit to take back control of Little League. By the time the 1956 season started, Stotz and the board settled out of court.

Bitterness lingered. While Little League continued to grow, Stotz supporters never forgot.

"We are fighting for an ideal," one supporter told the *New York Times* in 1956. "We can see nothing ahead under the present system except numerical growth that will be followed by dissatisfaction and deterioration." Stotz formed a rival organization that he called Original Little League. Ultimately, though, Stotz decided that he couldn't beat the Little League heavies. He surrendered.

Before he died in 1992 at age eighty-two, Stotz and Little League reconciled. The league honored Stotz and rewrote its documents, once scrubbed like a Soviet history book, to acknowledge the old man's authorship of Little League. Since then, Karen Stotz Myers, the founder's daughter, has been the honored guest at all major functions of the organization.

———————— • ◆ • ————————

Ask any baseball fan about a man named Creighton Hale, and you're likely to get a blank stare. But Hale has had a greater impact on the game at all levels than many Hall of Famers. Bruce Sutter? Dave Winfield? Rollie Fingers? Please. Compared to Creighton Hale, they're as important as the guys who put out the deli spreads in clubhouses.

Creighton Hale was an academic by training, but one of the more energetic and affable figures in youth sports. During his reign as CEO, from 1973 to 1994, Little League expanded from 10,006 to 21,711 leagues, from 90,000 to 198,347 teams, and from 370,000 to 3 million players. Little League also expanded internationally, and now includes over 100 countries.

Hale also invented the tools that have shaped the game at all levels. Many of Hale's patents made Little League a small fortune.

A former professor from Springfield College, this conservative Nebraskan first got involved with the organization when he analyzed the physiological effects of Little League on its players. For years, Little League struggled with academic claims that games put too much stress on kids. Hale devised a study. He recorded the pulse rates of kids during and after games. He found that kids *do* get aroused—but the arousal quickly disappears after the game. Adults, on the other hand, took hours to restore their equilibrium.

Another study found that more batters got hit by pitches in Little League than in the major leagues. So Little League moved the mound from forty-four to forty-six feet to give batters more time to react.

Another study revealed that most injuries occur when players slide into bases that are bolted to the ground. Hale's research shop led the effort that produced "break-away" bases that are held loosely to the ground with a grid of snaps. Research on injuries also prompted Little League to ban headfirst sliding for twelve-and-under players and to eliminate the on-deck circle.

Little League's ubiquitous mascot, a rodent named Dugout, dances with players from Guam before a game.

Hale headed up an effort to improve the baseball helmet. The helmet that Little League mandated in 1961 had earflaps and was made of materials that protected the head. Everyone wears those helmets now.

Hale was also part of the R&D effort that produced the aluminum bat. Wood bats splintered and broke, endangering kids. They were also expensive to replace all summer long. The aluminum bat, developed with Alcoa, was first mandated for Little League use in 1971. Today, virtually every amateur league and tournament uses aluminum bats. Aluminum bats pose their own dangers—balls fly off faster, making pitchers want to blow the ball past hitters—but no one can doubt their importance.

The list goes on—the one-piece catchers mask and helmet, the chest protector with a throat guard, portable plastic outfield fences that reduced collision injuries, rubber spikes.

Under Hale's leadership, Little League's research established an extensive database to safeguard the safety of players.

Then there was Hale's empire-building. In 1964, President Lyndon B. Johnson signed Public Law 88–378, which gave Little League a congressional charter of federal incorporation. Other organizations with the charter include the Red Cross, 4-H Clubs, the Boy Scouts of America, and the Boys and Girls Clubs of America.

Little League created a thriving business in memorabilia—hats, T-shirts, uniforms, publications, videos. Little League expanded its roster of official sponsors (it was sixteen in 2005).

In 1959, Hale opened a massive international headquarters in South Williamsport (which was expanded in 2001), as well as regional headquarters in California, Florida, and Canada (other regional headquarters would follow in Connecticut, Indiana, and Texas, as well as overseas). The regional headquarters brought the organization impressive real estate holdings at almost no cost.

———————— • ◆ • ————————

When Creighton Hale retired in 1998, a longtime Little League employee from the nearby town of Lock Haven took over as CEO. Steve Keener has spent his whole adult life at Little League, starting with a summer internship when he was a student at Westminster College in 1980. He worked his way up through the media relations department. For five years, Creighton Hale groomed Keener to take over as CEO.

Keener, a boyish looking forty-eight years old, has strived to keep Little League the dominant youth sports organization in the nation. Keener takes two approaches, which sometimes work at cross-purposes. Keener works to strengthen programs to train coaches, mandate greater playing time, initiate programs for handicapped children, and adopt programs to protect player safety. "There is no other sports organization that can compare" with Little League's advocacy of safety and open participation, Keener says.

At the same time, he has aggressively expanded Little League's television presence, which critics say feeds the competitive frenzy that makes Little League more than just a kid's game.

———————— • ◆ • ————————

From the second year of its World Series, Little League has used the dominant media to broadcast at least the championship games across the U.S. and the world. The media blitz started in 1948 with newsreels of the championship game between Lock Haven, Pennsylvania, and St. Petersburg, Florida, which were eventually seen by eighty million moviegoers.

Little League CEO Steve Keener awards participants in the Challenger Game for handicapped children.

For years, ABC's *Wide World of Sports* aired the championship game of the Little League World Series. The event became a late-summer ritual. Old ballplayers like Mickey Mantle, Sandy Koufax, and Jim Palmer provided the color commentary for the games. Grown Little League alumni relived their own days playing ball on sixty-foot bases. More than anything else, the game was an exercise in anthropology. Viewers would get exposure to the way baseball got played someplace else in the world— usually Asia, since Taiwan and Japan dominated the event for more than two decades.

The Little League World Series got on TV not because it was the best brand of baseball— it wasn't—but because it was a small sample of the "constant variety of sports." That's what *Wide World* was all about, providing a broad buffet of sporting events you don't ordinarily watch. It was TV's original "reality" programming. Anything that could be turned into contest—not only minor sports like ski jumping and gymnastics, but also contrived events like Evel Knievel's motorcycle jumps or climbers scaling the Eiffel Tower. So why not broadcast kids' baseball?

Over the years, the broadcasts expanded. In 1984, an upstart cable network called ESPN started to televise the two semifinal games. Year after year, ESPN expanded its Little League lineup. By 2000, ESPN broadcast twelve games from the World Series. By the 2005 event, ESPN and ESPN2 carried all eight U.S. regional championship games and twenty-seven World Series games, while ABC carried the U.S. and World Series championship games. Hundreds of hours of Little League games are shown on TV.

Year after year, the ratings for the Little League games are high. Most championship games attract bigger audiences than many major-league and National Hockey League games. The highest rating was a ten, which translates to almost ten million households. More typical ratings are five or six for the championship games broadcast on ABC.

In America, once you have a chance to be on TV, everything changes. The stakes get higher. When you're on TV, you become a celebrity. People shower you with gifts and adulation. People ask for autographs and invite you to big-league parks and resorts. You actually hear people say, "Your money's no good here."

Wander around the practice fields at the Little League complex, chat up the kids while they're waiting for their turn in the batting cages. Find them in the pin-trading tent or on The Hill. Ask them why they have worked so hard to be in the Little League World Series.

"To be on TV."

"ESPN!"

"I want to be on *SportsCenter!*"

Everywhere you go at the Little League complex, people mug for the TV cameras. At one game, a girl brought a huge piece of cardboard marked up and colored to look like a TV. The middle—the screen—was cut out so she could put her face inside. "Put Me On TV," the sign beseeched. When *SportsCenter* set up a temporary booth on top of The Hill, hundreds of kids gathered. Like ancients drawn to statues of idols given mystical powers, players are drawn to the power of the televised image.

Not like the TV people were ever going to give the players any distance. Everywhere, ESPN and ABC crews followed players and put their cameras just feet or even inches from their faces. They arranged the players and fans to dance and jump and cheer. *Live, from TV Nation . . .*

I asked Little League CEO Steve Keener whether televising all those games might be overkill.

"No," he said quickly. "Overkill for who? Overkill for what? If it's overkill, then one [game]'s too many. You either object to it being televised or you don't."

But televising more games creates the incentive for hundreds of teams to push aggressively in the state and regional tournaments. The more games are televised, the more teams do whatever it takes to win. "There may be that desire to be on TV, and obviously everyone enjoys being on TV," Keener acknowledges.

The bottom line, Keener says, is that "TV is very important because the World Series is really the strongest marketing vehicle we have. I'm not denying there are problems from time to time, but 95 percent of what comes out on TV is very positive and that's a great marketing vehicle for our program."

What would happen to Little League if its TV coverage disappeared?

It's reasonable to expect that many of the best players would leave Little League to compete exclusively on travel teams. For the kids still interested in playing in community leagues, the Cal Ripken and PONY leagues would be more attractive. The Little League World Series would be just another tournament in a beautiful rural setting. Not much hoopla, just pretty good baseball.

Actually, it's not hard to imagine the Little League World Series without TV. Because it happens every summer.

Little League runs international tournaments in three other age divisions. Ever hear much about the Junior League World Series, Little League's tournament for thirteen- and fourteen-year-olds, in Taylor, Michigan? Or the Senior League World Series, the tournament for fourteen- to sixteen-year-olds, in Bangor, Maine? Or the Big League World Series, for sixteen- to eighteen-year-olds, in Easley, South Carolina?

Didn't think so. No one pays much attention to these events. ESPN2 broadcast the final game of the Junior League's tournament, on a tape-delay basis. But besides that, TV ignores the organization's other baseball tournaments. And the rest of the media follow. The *New York Times* never sends anyone. The teams' hometown papers occasionally give them a few paragraphs, but not the hundreds of column inches and commemorative sections that local teams get for advancing to Williamsport. The Little League organization itself does little to publicize its other divisions. Go to Little League's website, and you find a vast trove of current and historical information about the Little League tournament in Williamsport—but almost nothing about the competition in its other divisions.

In the classic *Calvin and Hobbes* comic strip, Calvin tells his pet tiger that no reality exists outside of TV. He might have been talking about the impact of TV on the Little League World Series.

————— • ◆ • —————

To understand the soul of Little League—and all sports—you have to go back to its early days. By looking at before and after pictures, you get a sense of what Little League has done for baseball in America—and what has gotten lost in the process.

To do just that, I met with a group of retired men who were present at the creation of the Little League World Series.

About two dozen players from the first Little League World Series—then called the Keds Little League National Tournament—gather every month for breakfast at the Summervale Diner in Enola, eighty-two miles south of Williamsport. A couple days before the start of the 2005 World Series, I joined the group as a guest.

The diner—a squat, faux-stone building nudged between an Advantage Auto Parts and a Quality Inn—lies along Route 15/11, about a two-hour drive from Williamsport.

To get there, you meander on a road along the Susquehanna River. The road tells the story of small town America's rise and fall. Route 15/11 is flat and nondescript, with gas stations and adult video shacks, fireworks outlets and car dealers, malls and motels. Homemade quilts and furniture hang on the railings of a porch on an old house. An Amish woman in a bonnet rides on a horse-drawn carriage. Old farms survive along some stretches; signs beseech motorists to stop to buy fresh corn. Occasionally an old village center—like Liverpool—rises up from below. Even more spectacularly, the Allegheny Mountains and the Susquehanna River come into view when the road bends.

Little League was still new in Perry County when these men played the game back in '47. Teams didn't play in preliminary tournaments to qualify for the Little League Baseball National Tournament. The coaches picked all-star teams, the boys practiced for a few days, and then they traveled to Williamsport.

The players occupied a much smaller, more isolated world in those days. TV did not bring the rest of the world home and chain stores did not equip households with the same basic goods. In fact, Little League was one of the first organizations that provided the same recreational activities to communities across the country. Others were the YMCA, 4-H, and Pop Warner.

"That was the first time I was ever away from home," says Dick Cullen.

"I remember when our coach, Claude Smee, asked me if I wanted to go to Williamsport to play," says Bill Seitz. "I asked my parents and they said, 'Why do you want to do that? You can play right here in the back of the church. You don't have to go way up there to play ball.' We had no idea."

Uniforms have always been part of the Little League's appeal. "We had woolen suits and they were scratchy and hot," says Jack Wagner. "But it didn't matter because we were just so pumped up about playing baseball." Earl Stoltzfus says he was so small that he had to fold the uniform in the shoulders and legs so he could avoid tripping on his trousers while playing.

Those early players might as well have been wearing armor for all their discomfort and restricted movement. But wearing the uniforms made them bigger than the game. They represented their hometowns when they wore the scratchy threads.

The events of those early games remain fresh on the players' minds. The players recount the game life like golfers fresh off the links, detail for detail.

In 1947, the team from Perry County took an early lead against Lock Haven. Perry led by 5–0 going into the bottom of the third inning, but Lock Haven scored twice in the third, twice in the fourth, and four times in the fifth.

Bill Seitz contributed to Perry County's attack with a home run that almost didn't count.

"Coming around, I didn't touch home base," Seitz said. "And the coach grabbed me quick and I went back and touched it, so it did count.

Dugout dances with an umpire.

I know we scored a lot of runs that day. But we lost the game."

He paused for effect and raised his voice above the diner's noise. "I know the pitcher said he didn't get any support. Who *was* the pitcher?"

The former Little Leaguers chortled, for the hundredth time. Charlie Sheaffer, that pitcher, sat silently and smiled.

Lock Haven later played in the first championship game, losing to the Maynard Little League of Williamsport, 16–7.

Like me, the original Little League World Series contestants loved playing the game in uniforms on a formal diamond. But playing the game away from the structure of Little League was great, too—even better in some ways.

"We never went anywhere without a baseball," says Gene Hammaker. "If you rode a bicycle, the baseball glove was hanging on the handlebars. When we went to Williamsport it was just another baseball game."

You didn't need two teams of nine players apiece to play baseball. Variations on the game let you play with four or five players. "We called it Scrubbie," says Bud Whitaker. "You had a pitcher and a catcher and whatever else you had."

"You didn't have computers, you didn't have the things that occupy kids' time now," says Frank Reidinger. "So you were playing baseball all the time—from the time you got up in the morning to the time it was too dark to play. When we played sandlot, we played with baseballs with tape around them and string coming off of them and we made our own bats."

The best bats came from the railroads. "If you were lucky you got a brakeman's club," says Sheaffer. "The brakemen would carry it with them, it was a portable thing. Brakemen would ride in the back and get up on the top to turn the wheel and put the breaks on manually. It was made out of hardwood and they were maybe thirty-six inches long. But if all we could find [was] a two-by-four, we worked with that. We used anything. And of course you had to mend your own glove."

For all the boys, baseball was its own country, a land with its own common-law constitution and power structure and foreign policy. As long as it was light outside, you could find refuge in baseball, whether the game was played under the rules of kids or the rules of adults.

The refuge was especially important for a scrawny kid named Earl Stoltzfus, whose father's alcoholism created chaos and pain in the household. The Stoltzfus family never found stability. The best the family found was an apartment near an Amish farm. Young Earl did not do well in school and did not know much about the wider world.

"I didn't have too much of a life when I was a kid," he now says. "My father was an alcoholic. He died while I was in Little League. He was what you call a whiskey alcoholic. In his last years he'd work a week and then he'd go on a binge. And he was very mean when he was drunk."

Claude Smee, the coach of the Enola Little League team, provided what little direction and discipline Stoltzfus got as a kid.

"He treated me well, why I don't know," he says. "He treated all the guys well. He was strict. I stole a lot of bases and one time I stole when I wasn't supposed to and I sat on the bench."

The child of an alcoholic desperately craves consistency, reliability, and predictability—even if it comes in the form of punishment. All these years later, Stoltzfus cherishes even the scolding he got from Smee.

As the team's smallest player—he would not reach five feet until the year he graduated from high school—Stoltzfus had to hustle for any success on the field. That hustle was an outlet for the anger that he felt over his home life. Stoltzfus remembers slamming into infielders when he was running the bases and intimidating baserunners while playing shortstop.

"Baseball meant a lot to me. I slept with my glove. I was Charlie Hustle, that's it, because I didn't have the ability that a lot of kids have. I used to go all summer and my left hand swelled up and my knuckles. And I had strawberries down both hips from sliding. That was another thing that amazed us—we saw that field in Williamsport and we said, 'Wow, look at that field.'"

Stoltzfus watches Little League games on ESPN and ABC. As an adult he has seen the World Series in person just once—when he was in town to work on a project at the local Sylvania plant—but he holds fast to his own memories.

He shakes his head at today's players' athleticism and skills. But today's kids have advantages he could never imagine. They play on groomed fields, practice in batting cages, and shape their bodies in gyms with trainers. "These kids today would play circles around us," he says. "Back then anyone who had a Little League team could go to Williamsport. They were *looking* for teams to go there."

It was a rougher game, but baseball was more meaningful for Little League's early generations. When his son played Little League, Stoltzfus coached for two years. He got frustrated with the kids' attitude.

"An awful lot of those kids don't want to play. Their parents made them join. They didn't want to sleep with their gloves. We really loved the game."

Little League baseball has come a long way—
from a game played only in small towns of
Pennsylvania to a league played in thousands of
American leagues and hundreds of international
organizations. Guam's Sean Manley scores in a
game against Mexico.

Many of Hawaii's players were
teammates for years before switching
from PONY League to Little
League—and a chance to play
in the most famous tournament
in youth sports.

CHAPTER 4

Working Class Champs from Paradise

*T*HE SUREST WAY TO FIND ONE OF THE FATHERS from the West Oahu Little League all stars is to look inside a truck. Those men are always in trucks. Five of them drive trucks for a living, and others use trucks in their construction or manufacturing business or their work in the Marines. As they drive around, they talk with each other on cell phones. They make plans for their kids' sports teams, set details of the next family reunion, or discuss how to get their kids into prestigious private schools. Only a couple of them spent any time in college, but they all want their kids to go.

I found Layton Aliviado driving in a truck. Aliviado was the manager of Hawaii's all-star team in the Little League World Series. He was one of the people I needed to see when I visited Hawaii. I wanted to find out how this group of families built the team that won the Little League World Series in 2005.

The morning after I arrived in Hawaii, I was eager to explore the island. But first I had to trade in my rental car, a big and boxy Chevy with huge blind spots. I was driving back to the Hertz franchise at the airport and approached a fork in the road at a traffic light. I rolled down the passenger window to ask the guy in the truck beside me if I was going the right way.

"Hey, you're here! When did you get in?"

It was Aliviado, sitting high in the truck he drives for the U.S. Postal Service. He was wearing his crisp USPS uniform, hat, and sunglasses. He was driving back to the main distribution center at the end of his shift.

As if we were old neighbors, I asked him about the weekend's football and baseball games. He told me where to go and when. Then I asked if another dad, Jesse Aglipay, was around. "Yeah, I just talked to him a minute ago. He's got to pick up Alaka'i but they're going to the field later. Meet them there."

And then the light changed and he went one way and I went the other. I learned my first lesson about life in Hawaii. The islands are very small, and even strangers run into people they know.

———————— •◆• ————————

We live in a time when baseball has become dominated by two extremes—the affluent American suburbanites who spend tens of thousands of dollars on private coaches and travel teams, and the poorest of the poor in places like the Dominican Republic and Mexico and Venezuela.

The team from Ewa Beach lives in a place that looks a lot more like the old blue-collar communities of New Jersey celebrated by Springsteen. It's a place where people get married early, take jobs in factories and construction sites, drive trucks, and struggle to survive economically. It's a place where sports and family milestones structure the calendar. It's also a place where one generation is always trying to find ways for the next generation to have a better life.

In a way, those families live in paradise. They have great weather all the time. They play sports year round. They have family reunions and parties every time their kids play in a game. When they're not on a field outside, they're hunting wild pigs in the mountains or surfing in the ocean. They even have their own language. Hawaiian, once a dying tongue, is a part of the everyday chatter. The way they blend fragments of Hawaiian into English—"Eh, brah, da guy wen quit his job"—both widens and tightens the circles around them.

The most common tourist image of Hawaii is Waikiki Beach, the stretch of white sand and blue waves not far from the high-rise hotels and apartment buildings and expensive department stores in Honolulu. Waikiki is the place of surfers in buff bodies, Don Ho singing and playing the ukulele, bonfires and celebrations. That's Hawaii's glamour. Then there's the other famous image of Hawaii, the underbelly seen on TV shows like *Hawaii Five-O* and *Magnum, P.I.*, which show haoles—white guys, outsiders—chasing down murderers, pimps, drug dealers, money launderers, kidnappers, and other lowlifes.

But most life in the Pacific paradise is more ordinary than all that. For most people in Hawaii, including most of the Little League families, life is about just getting by—holding a job, making huge house payments, finding a good school for the kids, keeping kids away from the lazy ways of the beach bums and the rough ways of the street.

When I watched the Hawaii players in the Little League World Series, I was impressed with how strong and focused they were—but also how loose they could be, too. The players knew each other and played together most of their lives, starting at age four or five. Three of them were related—two were first cousins and the other was a second cousin—but all of them might as well have been related. There was one haole and two white-collar families on the team. But such distinctions didn't seem to matter much.

Until 1890, Ewa Beach was nothing but a fetid swampland. It was damp and dirty and filled with disease, with no real benefits to the island's economy or population. Then the Dole family decided to raze the nearby hills to harvest pineapples. The dirt cut out of the hills got moved to the fens. Suddenly, it was land, and it could be harvested for something.

Then along came a railroad magnate named B. F. Dillingham who was looking for a reason to build a railroad circling Oahu. Dillingham leased land to the Ewa Sugar Plantation, knowing that a thriving plantation would create steady business for haulers. If the sugar plantations moved in, population would fill in the rest along the rail ring.

Within a generation, the Ewa Plantation became one of the biggest in all of Hawaii. By the time of the Great Crash, the plantation produced more than 60,000 tons of sugar a year.

At its peak, 2,500 workers labored in the fields. They came from all over the world—from China and Japan, the Philippines, and other islands of the Pacific. And they lived in workers camps segregated by nationality into three main areas—Varona, Tenney, and Renton Villages. Living in single-wall houses built by the plantation, they maintained their native customs while sharing the fields, schools, churches, and local stores with everyone in the area.

In its own way, Ewa Beach provided one of the most compelling models anywhere for multiculturalism. If you want to see a place where American immigrants held tightly to their heritages, while at the same time lived and worked closely with people from other backgrounds, get in the time machine and go see Ewa circa 1920 or 1930.

Like plantations everywhere, the Ewa Sugar Plantation imposed harsh conditions on its workers. Even though workers were paid substantially more than the industry standard, they gave up control of their own lives. Any sign of resting or socializing was met with physical intimidation. A Japanese worker in 1906 described the discipline in the Ewa plantation: "The *luna* [boss] carried a whip and rode a horse. Up until our time, if we talked too much the man swung the whip. He did not actually whip us but just swung the whip so that we would work harder."

Renton Road had everything a self-contained community needed— primary among them, the mill where sugar cane was processed and the warehouses where the sugar was stored before getting sent by rail to market and ports, but also to schools, churches, stores, a bicycle repair shop, and the mansion of the plantation manager.

Plantations once covered about 20,000 acres on Oahu. But the industry declined in the years after World War II. Latin America took over the international sugar markets. Even when the federal government spent billions on subsidies for sugar industry, it didn't help. Foreign sugar was still a bargain. When sugar prices got too high, manufacturers of soda and sweets turned to sugar substitutes. From 1941 to 1995, the number of sugar companies on the island declined from thirty-one to five.

The Ewa Plantation ceased operations in the 1980s, long after it was sold to the Oahu Sugar Plantation. Few signs of the old sugar economy remain. But a lot of the old buildings are still there—a few churches, the Ewa Preservation Society, and the Easter Seals. The liveliest institution in the area is the Lanakila Baptist School, a Bible-based school of about 100 children in grades seven through twelve.

A native Hawaiian named Lance Arakawa, who took piano lessons in the area in the 1960s and 1970s and waited for his ride home at the manager's mansion, has a dream of making the road a beautiful homage to the days of the sugar plantation. Arakawa leads a group of a dozen volunteers to restore the elegant mansion to its past glory—and, some day, to restore the decaying mills and warehouses nearby.

When tournament games were broadcast on ESPN—the championship game of the regional tournament, and then six games in the World Series in Williamsport—the mansion became a gathering place. Arakawa set up a big flat-screen TV and neighbors and friends watched games in the neighborhood where the team's journey began.

Layton Aliviado, the man in the truck, put together the first pieces of his Little League World Series team almost eight years before.

Layton Aliviado is a small man—five feet, four inches—but powerfully built. During the run to Williamsport, he was forty-one years old, with two grown children and a twelve-year-old, but he looked like he could be thirty.

He has brown skin and a thick mass of hair as black as newspaper ink. Outside, where he spends almost all of his days, he shields his eyes behind sunglasses. He speaks in a staccato voice, his words sometimes rising to a squeak as they tumble out, quickly, in short phrases. He gets embarrassed when he has to talk publicly. "I'm not a speaker," he told me. "I'm just a local guy who speaks Pidgin."

Aliviado works the night shift—from 1 until 9:30 in the morning—so he can be available to coach baseball and football in the afternoons. After he gets home—sharing family news with his wife, grabbing a bite to eat—he naps until the early afternoon. Then he gets ready to coach. He's lucky if he puts together five hours of sleep every twenty-four hours. "Hey, you do what you gotta do, you know?" he says.

The time in the truck gives Aliviado plenty of opportunity to plot his moves on the field. He talks on the cell phone with other coaches and parents about the best way to train kids, how to teach pitching and hitting motions, the best lineups, the recruitment of players for the team and league. For years, Aliviado's truck talk has focused on how to create a team that could win the Little League World Series. He and the other dads studied tapes of past World Series championship games, and then they talked about what they saw. *What did they do to win? Can we do it too?*

When Aliviado's son was four years old and his two cousins were five, they played T-ball together. The cousins had to battle to win infield positions. But once they got inside the diamond, they were there to stay. His son Layson, usually known by his Hawaiian name of Kaeo, was the smallest of the three cousins but he was also lefthanded, so he played first base. Myron Enos Jr.—known as Kini—was the swiftest and the most athletic, so he became the shortstop. Sheyne Baniaga—nicknamed "Bubbles" by his mother because of the shape of his ample posterior—was the strongest, so he became the second baseman.

That first T-ball team was awful. The kids lost game after game. But the cousins kept playing together, Tinkers and Evers and Chance, and developed together. Because they were relatives, they saw each other all the time. They developed a pattern of caring for each other. When Hawaiian families gather, everyone takes off their shoes at the door as they're entering a house. Denise Baniaga, Sheyne's mother, remembers Kaeo gathering his cousins' shoes so they wouldn't have to search for them at the end of the evening.

With the core set, the team added one or two players every year until it was one of the best for its age group on the island.

As the team grew, the families grew closer as well. After every game—and many practices—the team held potluck dinners and stayed an hour or more socializing and analyzing the game. Each time, a different family was responsible for bringing chicken and rice, vegetables, beer and soda, cookies—and the island's favorite delicacy, SPAM. If you don't go, you're considered suspect.

"It's a big social thing, and if you don't participate people are like, 'What's your problem?'" says Mark Milton, a New Jersey transplant who coaches youth sports and paid the airfare and lodging costs for many of the team's families to travel to Williamsport. "It's a bonding thing. People love the game and their kids. They want to savor the experience. That's what the potluck is about."

Over the years, the families decided that the kids were good enough to compete in national tournaments. At first, the core of the team played in the younger age brackets of the PONY League. Over time, the PONY all-star team from Waipio (near Ewa) developed into a powerhouse. The families also formed "weekend" or travel teams, and they played for a year in the Cal Ripken League. In 2003, the PONY League team won the Hawaii state tournament with a surprise victory over Mililani, which had long been the best league in the state.

But the bitter events of that tournament prompted Layton Aliviado to consider moving the team out of the PONY League and into Little League.

Before the state tournament in Hilo, teams in the district tournament complained that Kini Enos did not belong on the team, that he lived with his parents outside the league's geographic boundaries. The director of the state organization investigated and found that the address listed on official forms was inaccurate. That was the address of his uncle, not his parents.

After an investigation, the state administrator declared Enos ineligible to play in all-star games and suspended Aliviado as manager of the team.

All of Hawaii's families attended the World Series almost 6,000 miles from home.

Gwen Earll, the state director of the PONY League, delivered the news to Aliviado.

"We found that he was playing out of the boundaries, living in another area," she told me. "He kept insisting that he does live there and whatever. But if you [can qualify for a league] because your uncle lives there, anybody can do it. His parents were saying that he lived with an uncle. But you have to go by where the parents live, otherwise everybody does it."

The PONY League's office gets a smattering of complaints every year about teams using ineligible players. The complaints don't usually start until the tournaments, when opponents have a greater stake in the competition. Teams that win the state tournament win the right to travel to the mainland for the West regional tournament. In her decade running the state PONY organization, Earll says, she has disqualified only three or four players.

Aliviado was angry. He claimed that the league betrayed him and Kini Enos by allowing them to participate in the league and the first round of tournament play, and then turning them away.

"With all the paperwork they had, they qualified the kid," Aliviado says, his voice rising to a singsong. "And all of the sudden, the [state organization] said he was illegal, he wasn't in the district. But I told her, 'You know what, you qualified him and now you're going to take that away from him. Why did you qualify him in the first place?'"

Aliviado says the incident brought home how resentful other teams would be because of the team's success. "You know what, there's a lot of jealousy for the kids who make the all-stars," he says. "That's why I was pissed off. You're taking the kid out of the game—if the paperwork wasn't good enough, you shouldn't qualify him. When Kini was crying, I was sad. 'Why you do this to this kid?' She couldn't say nothing. It's all jealousy."

Aliviado doesn't dispute that he was using an illegal player. His complaint is that all of his players were cleared before tournament play began and only challenged when another team filed a protest.

The Waipio all-stars—minus a manager and a star player—won the state tournament and advanced to the West regional tournament in Chino Hills, California. In Chino Hills, the team lost two one-run games and was eliminated.

In both the state and regional tournaments, Aliviado managed the team from the stands—an easy feat in Hilo, but harder to maneuver in California. As he sat in the stands, frustrated because he had to let go of his play-by-play control of the team, Aliviado started to think about the future.

The tournament in Chino Hills taught important lessons about winning and losing. Even though the team played well, the players and their parents were distracted. The team took a trip to Disneyland before play began. At the hotel, the players exhausted themselves swimming in the pool. Meanwhile, the parents drank into the night and bickered among themselves. Factions developed, often over which kid got to play what position. Aliviado did not want to repeat the experience.

Next time, Aliviado told other parents as they stewed over the events of 2003, *we're going to play to win*. It's not enough to beat Mililani. The point of playing in these summer tournaments is to win and advance to the next level. The families have to commit to doing everything they can to go all the way—even winning a national or international championship. No sports team in Hawaii had ever won an international championship before.

"We had to all be focused on one thing," Aliviado says. "They had to trust me to do the right thing and forget about anything else."

Not only because of his vision and toughness as a coach, but also because of his blue-collar background, Layton Aliviado is the emblem of the West Oahu all-stars.

The son of a cop, Aliviado lived on both the islands of Oahu and Maui as a kid. His favorite sport was basketball, which he played for a year in high school. Baseball was not fast enough for him. He also boxed and surfed. He met his future wife when he was a sophomore in high school and she was a freshman. Layton and Debbie met at Skate World, a roller skating arena on the other side of the island, where she lived. "I used to try to hang out and act cool," he says. "I saw her skating and wondered who she was and asked my cousin for her phone number." When he was eighteen and she was seventeen, they had their first child, Layton Junior. "Her dad wanted to kill me," he laughs. "But if he did, his grandson wouldn't have no father. And everybody saw that we stayed together, so that's good."

After graduating from Waipahu High School in 1981, Aliviado enrolled in the National Guard and started loading trucks for Magnum Transportation. At twenty-one, he qualified for his trucker's license, and he's been driving ever since. Four years after the arrival of Layton Junior (who now works for a cement company), Debbie gave birth to Lacie (who now works as a real estate appraiser). Eight years after that, Layson Aliviado—Kaeo is his Hawaiian middle name—was born.

Aliviado first started coaching baseball when his first son started playing. He coached him all the way through high school. A couple of years after that, he started coaching Kaeo in T-ball. The cycle started over again. The whole time, he has played for a men's softball team. "He just loves his baseball, you know?" says Debbie, a personal financial advisor.

Jerome Williams, now a starting pitcher for the Chicago Cubs, is Aliviado's most famous player. As Williams watched the games on ESPN, he recognized the same coaching style he experienced in PONY baseball under Aliviado. He saw how strong and thick the Hawaii players were, and he knew why. Aliviado made his players run sprints and long distances, up and down hills. The more they complained, the more he made them run. Running made them stronger than they ever thought they could be.

"When we're young, we didn't want to work, we just wanted to play and have fun," Williams tells me. "If you're strong in the legs, everything will come after that. At that time I didn't realize how important it was. I was throwing the ball hard. Why did I need to run? We started pouting, 'Aw, coach, come on.' But we can't say nothing because we're only eleven years old. Some parents didn't like it. They'd say, 'No, my child is coming home, his body is sore.' But we discovered that when you do something a lot, you get used to it. The parents changed their mind in the middle of the season when they could see us get stronger and better. Then they're all, 'Oh yes, you have to listen to the coach.'"

I asked Williams if he gives Aliviado any credit for his success as a major leaguer.

He paused for a moment. Learning to work hard was a great lesson, he said, but lots of coaches could have taught him that. Something else made the difference.

As the only black player on the team, Williams endured racist taunts from other teams in the league. His father, Glenn Williams, told him to ignore the ugliness and just work hard. But he needed to hear it from someone else. When Aliviado talked to him about race, he listened.

"Other coaches at that time didn't like me because I was black," Williams says. "Kids at that age are calling me names and I couldn't take it. Layton knew I could play and gave me a chance. He said, just do like your dad did, never mind what these guys tell you. Let your talent take over everything else. I actually listened to that. I took that from when I was ten until now. The first time I heard that it was from my dad and I didn't believe it. But when you hear it from another adult, someone you look up to, you listen."

Actually, what Aliviado taught Williams he learned from Williams's father. When Aliviado played basketball as a kid, *his* coach was Glenn Williams.

May the circle be unbroken.

————— • ◆ • —————

For years after the sugar plantation closed in the 1980s, Ewa was a fringe area. It was hard to reach because of poor roads. The houses were cheap and unattractive. Even the beaches were run down, lacking all but a few modest amenities.

Leon Edel, the literary critic who lived his last quarter-century in Hawaii, dismissed the old sugar town: "There is no particular reason to go to Ewa, no shops, no businesses, no famous views, no place to eat or even walk far; there is only the fact that the place is there, intact, a plantation town from another period."

That was then, this is now. Ewa's population has increased from 5,000 to 50,000 in a generation. Off Fort Weaver Road, the north-south artery that leads to the H-1 Freeway, housing developments and shopping and office parks are blooming everywhere. Every year the developers increase their prices—from under $300,000 for a three-bedroom home five years ago to $500,000 for the same house today—and each year the houses sell out before they're built.

In the last decade, developers have built thousands of units of new housing. With every expansion of housing—660 units here, 400 units there—the prices leap. Getting into a modest three-bedroom town-house now costs more than a half-million dollars.

The U.S. Census Bureau calls the area Ewa Villages, a euphemism for spurt of uncoordinated growth. The housing developments carry names grander than their construction—Ewa By Gentry and Ocean Pointe.

Tesha Malama, a member of a community advisory commission and candidate for state Senate, pushed for a resolution calling for a moratorium on development until traffic and infrastructure issues could be addressed.

"I have seen Ewa Beach grow from a two-lane, dark, winding road lined with sugar cane to a parking lot four-lane road lined with houses," Malama tells me. "Our schools are bulging at the seams, our roads are like parking lots, and our cultural resources are like limu seaweed, which was once abundant on our beaches until people from all over the island came and picked it until it was almost extinct."

———————— • ◆ • ————————

The sprawling growth played a critical role in the making of the Little League World Series team of 2005. In 2002, the population in the Ewa Beach Little League's territory grew so fast that it had to split into two to conform to Little League boundary rules. The spinoff was called the West Oahu Little League.

Like all new organizations, the West Oahu Little League was open to being shaped and molded by anyone who wanted to take over and make it their own.

Which is exactly what Layton Aliviado did when he moved his PONY League all-star team before the 2004 season.

When the Waipio PONY League all-stars got home at the end of the summer of 2003, Aliviado and the other parents decided to pull their kids out of the PONY League and put them into Little League.

Jumping leagues came at the perfect time. The new West Oahu Little League was such a small, fledgling organization that it could only field two teams. Aliviado managed the Red Sox, the team that won the championship in the next two years. Tyron Kitashima managed the Cubs. The two teams practiced together both summers, with the sole goal of developing a team capable of winning the Little League World Series in 2005.

Because the league boundaries for PONY and Little League were different, the move allowed Aliviado to bring new players into his all-star team. Aliviado started with his core of players—Kaeo Aliviado, Kini Enos, and Sheyne Baniaga, the three cousins who started playing together on a T-ball club. Vonn Fe'ao joined the group when they were eight years old. The others came along over the next couple of years.

With the move to Little League, the boys could continue to play on a field with sixty-foot bases. In the PONY League, eleven- and twelve-year- old boys move up to play on seventy-foot bases. "Our kids were getting bigger and stronger and would be more dominant with the smaller field sizes," says Clint Tirpak, one of the team's coaches. "If you're playing the odds, that's what to go for."

Another advantage of Little League was that they could play against lesser teams from Hawaii. The powerhouse for youth baseball in Hawaii was the PONY team from Mililani. Aliviado's team beat Mililani in the state championship in 2003, but it was easier to advance to the mainland without Mililani in the way.

A final advantage was TV. Players and coaches freely acknowledged that the chance to play games broadcast on ESPN and ABC—starting with the regional tournament in San Bernardino, California—made Little League more attractive than the PONY League.

When the 2004 season arrived, the teams set a simple goal: Win the district championship and advance to the state tournament.

No one cared much about what happened during the season. The primary focus was training the kids for the all-star tournaments. They set their sights on the mainland. They wanted to qualify for the Northwest regional tournament in San Bernardino, where they could win a berth in the Little League World Series in Williamsport.

"We knew we had a good team, but we never [thought] about other teams," says Aliviado. "We didn't care if we won or lost because our goal is to go to the all-stars and see how far we can go. We beat everyone, and every game we hit one or two home runs. But we never cared. The goal was to work the kids hard, and if we lose one or two it doesn't matter. I wasn't worried about that. Still, we went undefeated."

Long before the season started, Aliviado and Kitashima agreed to hold intensive workouts all summer long to prepare for the all-star team's effort to play in the Little League World Series. All twenty-four players from the two teams would train together. Only half of them would make the all-star team; everyone would share the commitment to get the all-stars ready for tournament competition.

And the all-star team was more successful than anyone imagined. West Oahu Little League won the 2004 district tournament and advanced to the state tournament in Hilo. The team lost both games they played by one run, 1–0 and 4–3. Not bad for a bunch of eleven-year-olds in a tournament dominated by twelve-year-olds.

───────────── • ◆ • ─────────────

Wherever they played—the PONY League, Cal Ripken League, Little League, or tournaments for travel teams—baseball was always the top sport for Layton Aliviado's players.

But other sports—especially football—gave the team the toughness it needed to survive a long and grinding summer of tournaments.

A bunch of the players—Vonn Fe'ao and Alaka'i Aglipay, Sheyne Baniaga and Kaeo Aliviado—played football in the fall.

Aglipay's mother kept him out of football until he was eleven. She was worried he'd get hurt and wouldn't be able to play baseball. But she finally said okay and Aglipay became an instant football star. He got bigger and stronger and tougher, qualities that served him well in baseball.

Football gave the Little Leaguers a strategy for training and conditioning. Football also made them tough in combat. In tackle football, every play has the potential to break a bone or pull a muscle—or just rough up a kid so he can't move much the next day. No matter how big or small they were, the kids who played football learned how to be more aggressive than most baseball players.

"On almost every play, something hurts when you're playing tackle football," says Darryl Stevenson, a retired army guy who coaches youth football. "There's no way you can't get hurt. Every play, you get hit. Football is a straight contact sport. You're hurling the body. You have eleven other guys trying to hit you."

Knowing that "you have a target on your back all the time" teaches these kids to be aggressive all the time. You can't avoid injuries by holding back.

So you charge forward as hard as you can, and you get strong enough to survive some hits and nimble enough to avoid other hits.

In football, you build their bodies in different ways than most baseball players. You build for toughness and endurance. You build lower body strength. You build explosive power. You develop lateral movement. And you do it all with a set of boot-camp drills that would make most young baseball players wilt.

--------------------◆--------------------

As the Ewa families plotted their course to the Little League World Series, they also gave themselves a backup plan.

Since 2001, Cal Ripken Baseball has staged a World Series of its own in Aberdeen, Maryland. That's the town an hour north of Baltimore where Cal Ripken, baseball's all-time iron man, grew up. The Ripken organization has combined forces with Babe Ruth Baseball in an effort to transform baseball in America from the ground up.

Ripken Baseball offered two major advantages for Aliviado's bunch. First, the league plays three seasons. Each season's top two teams can play in state and regional tournaments and have a shot at the World Series. Second, many of the Ripken all-star teams were better than the Little League all-stars. They draw from broader geographic areas, so they can pick and choose the best pitchers and other star players. So the Ripken teams would make strong opponents.

The Ewa all-stars played in the winter league of Ripken Baseball and qualified to play in the all-star tournaments the following summer. That provided an alternative to the Little League marathon, if they wanted to use it.

--------------------◆--------------------

When the West Oahu Little League all-stars met for the first time in 2005, Layton Aliviado invited the parents of the players to the scraggly old field near the old Ewa Sugar Plantation. While the kids played on the fields below, Aliviado lectured the parents and set the rules for the team.

Aliviado needed all the parents to contribute to the team throughout the summer. All the parents had to make sure the kids got to practices on time, six days a week. If they were not carting equipment or manning workout stations on the field, they had to make the potluck dinners that followed games and practices. Parents also needed to monitor their kids' schoolwork, so that they would not feel extra pressure on the playing field. All a little backwards, that last thought, but essential to make a winning team.

"I'm just a simple guy and all I wanted was to work hard," Aliviado says. "We had to agree that if we were going to do it, we had to do it the right way. If we go to the mainland, if we make it to San Bernardino, we go for baseball—no swimming, no distractions—because I don't want to go back and say we should have done this and we should have done that. No regrets."

The parents had to accept every single decision without complaint. The first time a parent complained about playing time, the more difficult it would be to deal with the other parents. Every kid and every parent had to accept his role, even if it meant playing the league-mandated minimum of one at-bat and one inning in the field. If someone was sitting on the bench, it was his job to win more playing time by playing well.

Later that night, with both the parents and players sitting on the hill, Aliviado reached into a cardboard box and pulled out T-shirts for everyone. The T-shirt read "One Team, One Dream" on the front and "Work Hard, Play Hard" on the back.

Aliviado gave each of the parents one shirt and each of the players three shirts.

"If you accept this shirt, you have to be devoted," he told them. Then he spoke to each player separately, in front of the group. He turned to Vonn Fe'ao. "Vonn, if you accept this T-shirt, you accept this goal that we're going to do. If you take these T-shirts, you have to be completely on board, you have to do everything my way." One by one, the players surrendered themselves to whatever Aliviado said to do for the sake of winning the Little League World Series. It was like they were all wading into a river to be baptized and born again.

Aliviado told the players to wear a team T-shirt for every practice. "I give you three shirts. On the fourth day, if you never wash it, you wear it dirty."

"He was the captain of the militia," says Ed Javier, one of the parents. "Everyone agreed and said they would help as much as we can. That's where I give Layton kudos—telling parents that they have to accept whatever he decides about who plays."

The West Oahu all-stars faced little real competition on their road to Williamsport.

They went 3–0 in the district tournament, winning by a combined score of 30–1. Then they went 3–0 in the state tournament. Here's where they faced their first real competition. Pearl City is a longtime Little League power in Hawaii. In fact, the Pearl City Little League went to the championship game of the 1988 Little League World Series. But the West Oahu kids beat Pearl City 4–0 in the opening game and 5–2 in the championship game.

Cell phones were constantly buzzing during the World Series.

Then it was on to the Northwest region tournament in hellishly hot San Bernardino, California. Only one of the six games there was close. The Hawaiians beat Murrayhill, Oregon, 17–1; Ada, Idaho, 16–5; Heights, Montana, 26–7; and Diamond, Alaska, 10–0. Idaho gave the Hawaiians a one-run game, 6–5, in the semifinals, but then Hawaii crushed Idaho in the final, 12–1.

Hawaii outscored its rivals in the regional tournament, 87–19.

The best sign for Layton Aliviado's team going into the Little League World Series was that every player on the team did something big at some point in the long run of tournaments. One day it was Vonn Fe'ao or Alaka'i Aglipay hitting a towering home run. Another time it was Harrison Kam making a diving catch he had practiced endlessly on his living room carpet. Another day it was the cousins turning a double play or getting a critical base hit. Or Quentin Guevara pitching a shutout. It was the ultimate cliché—everyone contributed—but it was true.

———————— • ◆ • ————————

When it came time to play in Williamsport, the Hawaiians were determined to scare the other side before the games even started.

Opening Day of the Little League World Series attracted a big crowd because Hawaii's opponent was a team from suburban Philadelphia. Fans came from all over the state to cheer for the Council Rock Little League. On the hills, placards spelled out the team's hometown, Hollywood style: N E W T O W N. The air buzzed.

The Hawaiians lined up along the third base line for a game of synchronized catch. First, they were forty feet apart. They threw the ball hard, as if they were pitching or throwing out a runner. They moved to about sixty feet apart and snapped the ball harder. Then they threw from about ninety feet, and they snapped the ball harder than ever, their bodies turning over with every throw. Finally, they moved further back—100, 110, 120 feet—for long tossing. The arcs of the balls crossed each other.

Layton Aliviado then shouted and the players started moving together again, in stages, for the original game of snap catch.

The players then broke into two groups. Aliviado hit hard grounders to the infielders, who then threw hard to the catcher. On the outfield grass, Clint Tirpak sent players out for football-style pass patterns. The players darted this way and that, moving out and then cutting over for the catch. Then Tirpak hit them balls that take short, hard skips in the outfield.

Hawaii's pregame drills sent a message. In San Bernardino, one opposing coach told his players to turn their backs to the field when the Hawaiians practiced. He didn't want them to see just how good the kids from Ewa Beach were.

Pennsylvania's boys did standard fungoes and grounders before the game. Their infield tosses were lobs. They knew they were outmatched right away. They wore grim faces.

"There was a real lot of butterflies," Pennsylvania's manager Bill Hartley told me later. "Us guys coming off that big win over Toms River [the New Jersey team that Pennsylvania beat in the championship game of the Mid-Atlantic regional tournament], it was hard to keep that emotion level up. Then we saw their ace and the kid with the long hair who threw rockets up there. It affected us."

Little Harrison Kam made a crucial diving catch for Hawaii—and saw his catch replayed on ESPN *SportsCenter*'s "Web Gems" feature that week.

———————— •◆• ————————

With Aglipay on the mound, Hawaii defeated Pennsylvania in the first inning.

Keith Terry, the starting pitcher for Pennsylvania, has a near-perfect delivery. Just one problem: as he moved into his motion, his foot shuffled along the rubber. The rubber shuffle unsteadied his body, which undermined his pitches' movement and location.

To beat Hawaii, Terry needed to bring the ball inside once in a while. Hawaii is a team of hackers, with enough power to hit the ball out of the park. Most teams pitch Hawaii outside. But the Hawaiians then just move up and hang over the plate and reach those outside pitches. You can't be scared against Hawaii. You have to burn inside and then get them to chase pitches outside.

Alaka'i Aglipay stepped up with a man on base. Terry got ahead 1–2. But Aglipay hung tough, fouling off three straight pitches. Terry came in again. This time, Aglipay got around on the pitch and sent a parabola down the left field line. The ball wrapped around the left-field pole for a home run.

Terry came in again on Michael Memea, who dumped the first pitch into shallow right-center field. Terry decided to come in again to the next hitter, Vonn Fe'ao. But the pitch was flat and Fe'ao took an extreme uppercut, smacking an arc over the center field fence.

Give Terry credit for the guts to go inside.

Bill Hartley regrets using Keith Terry against Hawaii. "I had more confidence in Darren Lauer," he says. But Lauer's father Robert convinced him to use Terry because he thought Terry could pitch harder and longer than his son. "Keith is not a real emotional kid," Hartley said. "He goes out there like a robot."

Thanks, coach.

———————— • ◆ • ————————

Alaka'i Aglipay started on the mound for Hawaii. Manager Layton Aliviado started Aglipay in as many games as possible.

"The first inning is the most important," Aliviado says. "We want Alaka'i for that. And then we can use him again against Iowa. And then we'll pitch him the whole game against Florida—that's the good team. That's when we need him the whole game."

Aglipay had no trouble with Pennsylvania. The first hitter, Ryan Hartley, dribbled back to the mound. The next hitter, Dave Pine, struck out on a check-swing. Then the team's power hitter, Blaise Lezynski, hit a grounder to second base. A one-two-three inning.

Exeunt Aglipay, enter Quentin Guevara.

Pennsylvania played a desperate game all night. Hawaii scored three more times in the third. With two baserunners, Pennsylvania's Daniel Denton leapt and caught Aglipay's drive—but coming down, dropped the ball. A good throw to second base would have gotten Aglipay, but the throw was off-line. Then, with two men on base, Michael Memea hit a screaming line drive over the right-center field fence.

In the fifth inning, Pennsylvania fans tried to gin up enthusiasm. "Let's go, Newtown! Let's go!" they shouted. But they sounded desperate. Not fun.

Against Vonn Fe'ao—Hawaii's hardest and wildest pitcher—Darren Lauer dropped a perfect bunt down the first base line. The next batter, Ryan Hartley, also decided to bunt when he saw the infield play back.

After taking a ball, Hartley got ready.

A fastball burned inside but Hartley kept his body inside. He stuck out his bat, his fingers wrapped near the thick part of the bat. The sound of the ball hitting his hand cracked throughout the stadium. In pain, he ran around in circles, turning his face upward and downward in gri-maces. When his father came over, he was crying—and with his father miked for national TV, his cries were for all the world to see and hear.

The Pennsylvania side sucked its collective breath.

The younger Hartley moved slowly to first base as a hit batsman.

Mike Ludwikowski, the trainer, trotted to the field to look at his hand. Ludwikowski held his hand, turned it over, asked when it hurt, felt for broken bones. He felt swelling, but not a break. Bill Hartley wanted his son to run the bases, and Ryan Hartley wanted to stay in the game too.

Hawaii manager Layton Aliviado waited for the moment's anguish to subside. Then he walked to the home plate umpire, Bob Claton. Aliviado pointed to his hands, making a bunting movement with an imaginary bat. The umpire nodded. He motioned to Hartley at first base and made a strike sign. Hartley's dad came out again. Claton explained. Hartley argued. The umpire shook his head.

Hawaii's Kini Enos, Hawaii's shortstop and a team leader, swings at a pitch.

Claton ruled that Ryan Hartley should not get a free base but a strike call instead. When he was bunting, Hartley offered at the pitch. That's a strike, whether the ball hit the batter's hands or not. Hartley had to come back to the plate, with the count 1–1.

Panic and anger rose from the Pennsylvania parents. "That sucks, ump!"

"Go home, ump!"

"Get another umpire!"

Hey, blame Layton Aliviado.

Hartley could run the bases, but he couldn't swing the bat. Michael Tentilucci came in to finish his turn at the plate and walked. The crowd came alive again. Blaise Lezynski laced a ball over Zachary Rosete's head in right field, but Rosete reached over his shoulder and caught it—and then he threw a strike to second base for a double play.

That was the last rally for Pennsylvania.

After the game, Bill Hartley pleaded with the trainer to find a way to get Ryan back on the field. Ryan nodded quietly as the doctor showed him the broken bone on the X-rays. But his dad didn't want to give up.

"His dad would say, 'Jeez, isn't there anything we can do to get him going again?'" trainer Mike Ludwikowski remembers. "When the X-rays came back, I put them on the board. I showed them where the fracture was, and he asked if there's any chance. I said, 'No, a fracture is a fracture.' Then he was fine with it, but as time went on, people started talking and getting in the coach's head, trying to intervene and ask for other possibilities."

———————— • ◆ • ————————

Of all the teams in Williamsport, Hawaii makes it hardest to pick out the stud player, the one player who's going to overwhelm other teams with power. Vonn Fe'ao is imposing. Michael Memea, the catcher, is a big, strong kid, but he moves slowly and he swings and misses a lot. Pitcher/infielder Quentin Guevara looks like he's going to fill out, but he's a bean now. Sheyne Baniaga is small but has a powerful lower body. Kini Enos is wiry, quick. Others are tiny.

If anyone's the team stud, it's Alaka'i Aglipay. In the last year he put on twenty pounds and became more physically imposing. He plays football and has started to work out with weights. His father Jesse has made him into a project. They're talking about playing pro baseball and training hard to make it happen.

Aglipay was one of just a few pitchers in Williamsport who could locate the ball within a baseball's width of his target. Coach says throw an outside and low fastball a baseball's width off the plate, and Aglipay throws it right there. Coach says throw the ball in on the hands, and the ball's there. Coach says waste an 0–2 pitch, and the ball's not going to slip across the middle of the plate.

Alaka'i Aglipay's light brown face is soft, his almond eyes alert and relaxed. Even more impressive, his body flows effortlessly on the field.

His legs and arms move like liquid, whether he's pitching the ball or swinging the bat. In his practice swings at the plate, he scrapes his bat just above the plate as if practicing a golf swing.

Until two years ago, Jesse Aglipay drove a truck for Coca-Cola. Then he started having trouble with his heart and took time off. The doctors decided he had congestive heart failure and that he couldn't come back on the job full time. Too much stress. So he's out on disability, permanently.

"So now I have all the time in the world for these guys," he says. The guys, besides Alaka'i, are twin sons Kana'i and Po'okele, who have just started to play baseball.

More time with the kids does not mean picking them up after school and watching practices. For Jesse Aglipay, it means taking Alaka'i out of school altogether and bringing him down to the field for practice every day.

For two years, Alaka'i Aglipay has been homeschooled. He sees a private tutor named Linda Sofa twice a week, for periods usually ranging from one to three hours. He spends the rest of the time working on his computer and with his books. Before he got the tutor, Aglipay struggled in school. He couldn't keep his attention on what was happening in the classroom.

"When I started seeing Alaka'i, he was so undisciplined," Sofa told me. "He had the worst study skills I ever saw. He didn't have any idea what a due date was. He forgot his books. He forgot his assignments. I just wouldn't let him leave until he got it right. I tried to use baseball to show him how to do things: 'Listen, what if you went to the practice field and didn't have your glove?'"

Aglipay still struggles with his work, but he shows more interest in studies than ever before. He says he's fascinated by Greek mythology. His writing is getting better. Math and science remain a challenge, but even they are getting better.

The most important thing is that Aglipay has a goal. He wants to attend the Punahou School on a sports scholarship. Punahou is the ultimate sports school on Oahu. It's golf phenom Michelle Wie's school. *USA Today* has ranked Punahou the number four sports school in the United States, on the strengths of its many after-school sports and unmatched state championships won by those teams.

Aglipay played an important role in every one of Hawaii's wins in the World Series. He pitched in four games, more than any other player in the event. He started the first three games of the series, going one inning in the first two and then shutting out Florida in the third game. And then he beat California in the U.S. championship game. And he was one of

Vonn Fe'ao launches his body toward second base to break up a double play.

the leading hitters in the series, finishing first in home runs (three), second in runs scored (eight), and fifth in slugging percentage (1.133).

He wasn't perfect. In his win against California, he walked five batters and left the game in the fifth inning. He was tired from the long season and lost about five miles an hour on his fastball. Still, he surrendered only one run and got the win.

After the game, he broke down crying. His mother took him to the parking lot to console him. The next day he was embarrassed at his outburst. It became a family joke. "I'm glad you weren't crying on the mound," Jesse teased him.

Everything Alaka'i does, the family is involved.

Before the state championship game, his arm was hurting. His aunt massaged him to get him ready for the game. "He had these muscle spasms that could have gotten really bad," says Dawn Aglipay. "She told me, 'I don't see this in kids. It's unusual. You better be careful.' She took care of it. She used a Hawaiian massage called Lomi Lomi and he hasn't had any problems since then."

———— • ◆ • ————

As much as things fell apart for Pennsylvania in the World Series opener, they came together for Hawaii. Aliviado was chipper after the game. He bounced off his chair in the front of the media room, directing questions to his players sitting behind the table.

"We never did scout the other teams," he says. "People said they were good but don't worry. But we always worry." Aliviado is pleased that he can replace his ace pitcher early. "We knew we would have a right-hander then a left-hander and then see what happens."

Aliviado was gentle toward the injured Ryan Hartley, but doesn't want to get caught up in the collective hurt and anger on the Pennsylvania side. "I just told him [Bill Hartley] it was sad that that happens but what can I say? I feel bad too, but that's baseball."

Aliviado took issue with a statement that his Hawaii boys are bigger than Pennsylvania's players.

"Maybe we're more thick than they are, but size-wise and height-wise we're the same."

He was right. On average, the Pennsylvania players stood just under five feet, four inches and weighed just over 115 pounds. Hawaii players stood, on average, five feet, two and a third inches and weighed just under 113 pounds.

More thick.

For decades, boys and girls have
gathered at the Original Little League
Field to try out for the new season.

All-stars from the Pabou
Little League of Curaçao listen for
instructions from their manager,
Vernon Isabella.

CHAPTER 5

————————————— ◆ —————————————

Little League Dynasty in the Caribbean

*M*OST DAYS AT FRANK CURIEL FIELD IN WILLEMSTAD, on the Caribbean island of Curaçao, boys play baseball. Even when school is in session, boys gather at the field for practice. The field is the home of the Pabou Little League, the winner of the 2004 Little League World Series and a favorite to win again in 2005.

As Little League complexes go, it's not much. The field itself is a jagged plain of dirt, with rocks and pebbles mixed into the dry soil everywhere. In the rainy season—the off-season for baseball—dampness holds down the soil. The rest of the year, the dirt kicks up any time a player or ball bounds across the ground.

The organizers of the Pabou Little League—which has sent all-star teams to the Little League World Series four times—plan to cover the infield with an artificial surface. But the rocky terrain of the infield has always helped to train young players. Every ground ball on the dirt surface bounces differently, and the kids learn to field even the strangest hops with ease. Good reflexes are made, not born.

Behind the plate, a cinderblock structure painted sea blue serves three purposes. Right behind home plate, a booth provides a perch for official scorers. Behind that booth, a small kitchen provides space for cooking barbeque chicken and pork and for storing concessions. On the second floor is the home of Frank Curiel, the founder of the Pabou Little League—potentially the biggest dynasty in Little League since Taiwan dominated play in the 1970s and 1980s.

Nearby, on the wall of the equipment shed and bathrooms, a poster exhorts the youngsters to play hard: "With the Lord's blessing, we will achieve our GOAL." The author of that message is Yurendell De Caster, a Curaçaoan who was once a prospect in the Pittsburgh Pirates organization.

———————— • ◆ • ————————

Curaçao, one of the five islands of the Netherlands Antilles in the Caribbean Sea, might be the perfect place for Little League baseball to thrive. Warm climate? Check. Social stability? Check. Disciplined players? Check. Parents committed to winning? Check. A passion for the game? Check. Role models who set high goals? Check.

The 171-square-mile island that the Pabou Little League all-stars call home—not much more than a few piles of prehistoric volcanic ash spewed from the northern coast of South America—is one of the more obscure places in the world.

Curaçao has no resources to speak of. It doesn't have the great expanses of white-sand beaches of Aruba or other Caribbean havens. There's no land worthy of agriculture. The only real city, the capital of Willemstad, is small. But the island's location at the intersection between Europe and the Americas has fostered a culture of trade and diversity. Its openness to outside influences has always given it a small but meaningful place in world affairs.

In 1776, when Adam Smith published *The Wealth of Nations*, he praised Curaçao's virtues as a place of open trade. Centuries before NAFTA and CAFTA, Curaçao created wealth by taking goods made elsewhere and transporting them to someplace new—a radical idea in those days. "This freedom, in the midst of better colonies whose ports are open to those of one nation only," Smith wrote, "has been the great cause of the prosperity."

By opening itself to the world, an island with no great natural resources became a major center of commerce between the new and old worlds.

Colonial powers didn't see much worthwhile in Curaçao. Inhabited for centuries by tribes called the Arawaks, the Spanish colonized the island in 1499. They left after a generation because they couldn't find any raw materials—no precious metals, timber, agriculture, nothing. The Dutch West Indies Company—dedicated to colonization, slavery, and trade— took over and installed Peter Stuyvessant as governor. And in 1675, the capital city of Willemstad was declared a free port. The island used its strategic location to serve as an intermediary for trade. The goods to be traded included slaves, oil, financial assets, art, and booze.

Trade brought a dazzling range of people to the island. The Dutch arrived from the Netherlands to tend to public affairs and business. Jews came starting in 1649 and established businesses from street peddlers to bankers. Africans arrived, in steerage, to be sold as slaves. Latinos and Europeans moved on and off the island while doing business with each other.

The city's architecture and street rhythms, schools and arts, reflect its mixed heritage. The capital city of Willemstad presents a jaunty parade of gingerbread architecture painted in vivid pastels. Music and food come from Africans. The legal and educational systems have a European cast. Curaçaoans speak two, three, four, even five languages. Dutch is the official language, but English, Spanish, and Portuguese are spoken there, too. Some speak French. And almost everyone speaks Papiamentu, a Creole language originally developed as a secret way for slaves to communicate freely.

Over its history, this obscure and complexly beautiful isle has operated—usually—above the poverty and strife and militarism that often characterize other nations in Latin America. Curaçao's history contains its share of inhumane and exploitive moments. But mostly, the place provided a laboratory for diversity. Operating with the strong European ideals of the Dutch, people from all over the world found ways to live together like almost no other place on earth.

"The Dutch influence is so strong," says Randy Wiel, one of the island's great athletes. Wiel left the island to play basketball for Coach Dean Smith at the University of North Carolina in 1974. He's been to the Pan-Am games and the Olympics in track and field. When I talked with Wiel, he was coaching a Dutch basketball team called the Eiffel Towers. We talked on the phone as he caught up with sports news on ESPN.

"You don't have discrimination there the way you do other places. People never talk about race, if you're black or white. If there's prejudice, it's about class and education. People care about education. If you don't graduate, people look down on you, like you're a dummy."

Early in the twentieth century, after the discovery of vast oil reserves in Venezuela, Curaçao built refineries that provided the island's main employment for generations. Like other extractive industries—Williamsport's timber industry, for example—oil took the edge off the creative and competitive spirit that Adam Smith celebrated. Getting a job in the refineries reduced the incentive to seek out niche industries and seek an education. But it also provided stability, a rarity in Latin America.

Shell Oil sold its refineries to the Dutch government in 1985. Venezuelans now run them. The refineries still hum, but other parts of the economy are getting bigger. Industry makes up about 15 percent of the economy, services the other 85 percent. Drug trafficking and money laundering make up the economy's underbelly but do not dominate the island like they do in, say, Colombia.

Now, the Pabou Little League plays a small role in the island's economy. With its victory in the Little League World Series in 2004, international attention on the island increased dramatically. People who never heard of Curaçao wanted to take vacations there. The island's tourist bureau is doing everything it can to leverage Little League into a new tourist boom.

———————— • ◆ • ————————

The godfather of Little League in Curaçao, Frank Curiel, has lived all his sixty-two years in the neighborhood of Santa Maria in the capital city of Willemstad.

Curiel is a strong man made soft by the years. His brown skin is topped by close-cropped gray hair. He moves slowly, especially in the evening. But he talks with animation. He gestures the way he teaches kids to hit a baseball, with short, strong movements. He tailors his words and gestures to connect with whoever he's talking with—the women who sell refreshments, the five-foot infielder, the twenty-three-year-old manager, the thirty-year old parent.

Growing up, Curiel played soccer, tending goal. He eventually took up baseball. At the age of seventeen, he organized a team. Occasionally watching games on TV, he became a passionate fan of Roberto Clemente, the graceful right fielder for the Pittsburgh Pirates. So he named his team the Santa Maria Pirates. In 1969, Clemente organized a baseball clinic in Puerto Rico. Curiel went. The event changed his life—and baseball in Curaçao.

"That's when I decided there needed to be a Little League for boys," Curiel told me as we watched a game from the field's aluminum stands in the middle of December. "He gave me the feeling to go back to my country to start a league for little players. We started with four teams in 1970." The league did not succeed right away, but "we came back in 1974 and had six teams."

Over time, the league developed into one of the most successful anywhere. The Pabou League first won a spot in the Little League World

Series in 1980, when Curiel was the coach. Pabou also sent teams to Williamsport in 2003, 2004, and 2005. The rival Pariba League—the only other Little League on the island—participated in the Williamsport tournaments in 2001 and 2002.

Curiel spent his career working for SEDREKO, Curaçao's sports and recreation agency. That job allowed him to build Little League throughout the year. The field that bears his name was once a junkyard. He organized families to help him clean it up, level the ground, mark out the field dimensions, build the fences, and install the lighting. "I pay the light bill for this park," he said. I asked other people about that and they rolled their eyes. No, sponsors and government grants pay to put the beams on at night. But allow the old man his pride.

On a warm evening during my visit in December 2005, the stands filled with about 200 fans. A tar-like stench from a nearby oil refinery soaked the still air. A PA announcer called the play-by-play. The fans screamed loudly, shouting advice and criticism of the manager's field strategy. It's the kind of noise you don't hear in the U.S. until a district championship.

Curiel sat on the aluminum stands for a while, and then walked around to greet people. He watched the game for a while with the men perched on folding chairs near the scorer's booth. Then he drifted over to a table where women sell candy and chips. As the game progressed, fireworks twice filled the sky a half-mile away.

Children ran up to Curiel to ask for money to buy candy. In return, he asked them to get him a can of Red Bull energy drink and a plastic cup filled with ice. From that he makes his own cocktail. "I mix it with Dewar's," he tells me. "Want a cup?" Curiel mixed new drinks during the game as he made the rounds in the ball park.

Everyone associated with Little League in Curaçao says Frank Curiel is the wisest and most important figure, still, in the island's baseball life.

Curiel takes a special interest in players whom he thinks could grow into Little League all-stars or coaches. He knows every kid who plays in the league, and his mind constantly sorts the players by age and position and strength. When he saw Rayshelon Carolina play in a game for Marchena Hardware one day, he decided that the small child needed a new approach to hitting. He took the four-seven, seventy-five-pounder aside and taught him how Ichiro Suzuki swings—as the pitcher delivers, take a shuffle-step forward, drop the bat on the ball, and start running to first base at the same time.

About fifteen years ago, Curiel saw a lanky kid in practice and took a liking to him. He was an infielder and he wanted to stay at the park all afternoon, into the dusk when he couldn't see the ball anymore. And then he stopped coming for a month. Curiel found out his name and where he lived—it turns out that he came from a broken family and he lived with his grandmother—and went to his house to find out why he didn't come to the park anymore.

Curiel talked with the kid's grandmother to find out if she had any problem with him playing baseball. She said no. Then he talked to the kid alone, and told him he wanted to see him playing at the park again.

That kid was Vernon Isabella, who is now the twenty-three-year-old manager of the all-stars from Pabou Little League.

After that, "I didn't want to ever leave the park," Isabella says.

Curiel helped guide Isabella through a long career as a Little Leaguer and then to an internship as a gym teacher with SEDREKO. He gave him the position as manager of the Pabou League's premier team, the Refineria Isla.

Most of the boys who play baseball on this tiny island—and their parents—dream of becoming the next Andruw Jones. The graceful centerfielder for the Atlanta Braves is the island's great success story. Images of Jones look beneficently from billboards, telling players: "*Ku esfuerso i determinashon bo tambe por*" ("With effort and determination, you can too"). Every player on Curaçao's team lists Jones as his favorite player. Jones has emerged as one of the handful of premier players in all of baseball.

But when Frank Curiel walks around the baseball field that bears his name, in the shadow of the short cinder block structure where he sleeps at night, he's not thinking about finding another Andruw Jones.

He's always looking for the next Vernie Isabella. Or the next Jonathan Schoop. Or the next Jurickson or Juremi Profar or Darren Seferina. These are the child stars of Curaçao.

———— •◆• ————

When I was in Curaçao, I asked my guide, a Little League father named Vico Rojer, to show me as many of the fields and neighborhoods as possible. We passed through Brievengat, the neighborhood where Andruw Jones grew up. (Brievengat means letterbox, which refers to the hiding places for pirates' notes in the island's early years.) I asked to see Andruw Jones Field, which the major league star has paid to fix up. The field was still a mess, overgrown. It was the off-season, so no one was playing baseball.

But across the street, at the Sentro Deportivo Korsou, hundreds of kids and adults were on hand for swimming and soccer. This was a modern facility, filled with kids of all ages. It's active all year long. Maybe baseball has become the most visible sport in Curaçao because of the Pabou Little League's 2004 championship. But it's still just one of many sports on the island.

Like the rest of Latin America—and the rest of the world—soccer has always been the favorite sport in Curaçao. But because Curaçao has no professional sports leagues and its culture is dominated by the Netherlands, most kids don't gravitate toward only one or two sports. Kids sample a wide range of sports—baseball, soccer, basketball, swimming, gymnastics, and track and field.

To understand how baseball developed in Curaçao, I called Darren Van Tassell, the technical commissioner of the International Baseball Association. Van Tassell works with amateur and professional leagues outside the U.S. to develop training programs, league organizations, rules, and protocols. He also teaches at Georgia Southern University.

Van Tassell first went to Curaçao in 1991 to teach in a clinic sponsored by SEDREKO, the national sports agency. Andruw Jones was one of the players in the clinic. What he remembers most was the quickness of the players.

Christopher Garia bears down in a game against Saudi Arabia.

"Great infielders is what I remember," he says. "The playing surface was so difficult, they had to be quick. There were rocks all over the field, so the ball always took bad hops. I saw them practice with a bouncy rubber ball."

Back then, he says, baseball was not a central part of Curaçao's sports culture—but it is today.

"It's no longer something they're borrowing," he says. "They've made it their own. It's like many things there, a blend of Caribbean and French and Dutch and American. Almost every night of the week, there are games being played. Baseball is usually only big where there's a big enough population, so you can have [a critical mass for both] soccer and baseball—places like Venezuela and Mexico. But even though Curaçao is small and soccer is still popular, baseball has become part of the culture."

Randy Wiel returns to the island frequently to put on baseball clinics. He says Little League has separated itself from other sports in one important way. In most sports, he says, "There is a great sense of discipline. Kids listen to what their coaches tell them to do. But we have a problem with punctuality. There's always an excuse. That's a problem they don't have with baseball. One of the reasons is the baseball coaches are adults. In soccer and other sports, the coaches are often the players' friends." Kids don't dare to show up late for practice or games in baseball, because they feel a keen sense of competition and know that someone might take their place on the field.

Despite the island's enthusiasm for Little League and Andruw Jones, Curaçaoans still place school ahead of sports.

"The last time I was in Willemstad, a lady came up to me and asked me if Andruw Jones finished his education," Wiel says. "I told her that he got to the Braves awful fast, that he was very successful as a baseball player, that he makes millions of dollars. She said, 'Yeah, but why didn't he finish school first?' In Curaçao, if I don't graduate, people think I'm a dumbo. That comes from the Dutch. Education is big, big, big there. You can't say you're going to be a professional athlete."

That attitude melts a little bit every season as Andruw Jones excels in the major leagues and the Willemstad Little Leaguers make appearances in Williamsport. But the schools remain the center of children's lives outside the family.

If the United States is a vast melting pot, a great cauldron that brings together people from all over the world and makes them American, Curaçao offers a different model of culture-building. It's more like a smorgasbord in which the foods can be mixed together or taken separately.

More than anything, Curaçao is about accommodating many different cultures and religions. The one way to do things in Curaçao is to do it *many* ways. It's how the island established a major international port that would be celebrated by Adam Smith, and it's how the island accommodates tourists and nurtures niche industries like liqueur and offshore banking—and it's how the island builds baseball players.

The symbol of the island is Papiamentu, the language that holds the many pieces together, loosely. Only about 200,000 people speak Papiamentu worldwide. Papiamentu began as a Pidgen language—a way for natives to speak pieces of the colonizer's language. But over the years, it's become a language of its own, an amalgam of Dutch, English, Spanish, Portuguese, French, and various African dialects. The language's polyglot character makes it ever accessible.

In recent years, Papiamentu has become a more central part of the island's life. One experimental school uses Papiamentu as the primary language of instruction and has seen performance improve significantly. But unlike Quebec or Spanish-speaking parts of the U.S., where a native language becomes a means of separation, Papiamentu always invites its speakers to use other languages too. Papiamentu is, after all, just a collection of those other languages.

Speaking a language like Papiamentu becomes a way of life and a metaphor for how to do other things—how to build a small business, how to keep families and communities together, even how to play baseball. Papiamentu reflects a different kind of diversity and toleration.

Sorick Liberia stands on base.

Papiamentu has become the foundation for the island's modest culture—a way of remaining apart from the homogenizing world, but also for maintaining the ability to range far and wide in the world.

Baseball has started to play the same role on the island. Because of the success of the Little League teams, Curaçao has yet another language, yet another way of life. More people across the world now know about Curaçao because of its Little Leaguers than its oil industry or tourism or polyglot language. Baseball is now Curaçao's reference point for the world.

———————— •◆• ————————

When Carl Stotz created Little League almost seven decades ago, he wanted all the kids to have an equal chance to win, year after year. So Little League established a draft system to spread the talent evenly.

But in the Pabou Little League of Willemstad, playing a competitive season is not the point. The point is to create a baseball program that sends teams to the Little League World Series every summer—and, eventually, produces major leaguers.

The teams in the Pabou Little League do not participate in a draft. Instead, the coaches actively recruit the best players. Two teams—the Refineria Isala team from the Santa Maria neighborhood and the Marchena Hardware team from Marchena—dominate the league every year.

"During the regular season, we have a farm system that [places] players according to their abilities," says Vernon Isabella, the manager of the Pabou all-stars in 2004 and 2005. "Players who want to play for me can find a spot on one of the teams. There are nine teams in the Pabou League, and Santa Maria has three."

In addition to the three twelve-and-under teams, Isabella oversees six teams from ages five through nine, two junior league teams (mostly ages fourteen and fifteen), and one senior league team (mostly ages sixteen and seventeen).

"I am the main instructor for kids ages five to sixteen. The kids start at five, learn how to catch the ball. And they go all the way to the older boys…Before the tournaments begin, there are about 200 kids involved in the team's farm system."

Isabella works with coaches throughout the league to establish common approaches—strength training, fielding drills, hitting mechanics—to coaching the kids. The coaches regularly share information about rising stars, teaching strategies, and game performances. During the season, Isabella spends most of his time at Frank Curiel Field, teaching and getting to know Santa Maria players of all ages.

The difficulty, Isabella says, is turning away boys from his team.

"We have to disappoint some children," he says on a warm December afternoon at Frank Curiel Field. As he is talking, a worker uses a leaf blower to direct trash into a pile, and day laborers snore in the midday sun.

"The problem is, at one point you have to stop accepting them or else you have to start a new league. The league can have only ten teams. It doesn't matter to me if the league is split up, because the two top teams will stay in the league where I'm coaching. But it's more of a challenge for the others involved with the league. We don't turn them away; if they want to come and practice, they can do it. You get a fair chance if you perform."

In 2005, the Pabou League's all-stars came mostly from two teams. Seven players represented Michelangelo Celestina's Marchena Hardware team: ace pitchers Sorick Liberia and Jurickson Profar, catcher Willie Rifaela, and four other players. Vernon Isabella's Refineria Isla team had four all-stars: pitcher Naeem Lourens, future shortstop star Darren Seferina, and two others. Jeep of Jandora had two stars, including Christopher Garia, and UTS of Buena Vista had one. The other four teams had no representatives on the team.

When I visited Curaçao, Isabella and Michelangelo Celestina, the manager of the Merchena Hardware team, were enthusing over rising stars in the Pabou Minor League. Everyone in the league was watching Puremi Profar, the younger brother of two-time World Series star Jurickson Profar. As we discussed the younger Profar, the guy blowing trash came over and pointed to a glossy brochure that features the past, present, and future stars of Little League. In 2005, the younger Profar—like his brother, a shortstop—batted .444 in the regular season and .300 in the all-star games.

When Isabella went to the Little League World Series in 2005, he took four players from the 2004 championship team. In 2006, seven of the 2005 players will be eligible to play in Williamsport.

As far as Isabella is concerned, the question is not whether the Pabou League all-stars will advance to Williamsport in 2006 and beyond. The question is which of the seven potential returnees will make the team.

———————— • ◆ • ————————

Curaçao sent teams to the Little League World Series four times before the Pabou Little League won the championship in 2004. The players who won that series—Jonathan Schoop, Carlos Pinada, and Jurickson Profar—have become examples of how everyone else should play the

Jurickson Profar pitched Curaçao to the international championship.

game. Curaçao did not dominate the series the way other teams—especially Asian teams—have in the past. But no matter. They won.

Schoop was the best of the group. Standing five-foot-eleven, Schoop won two games on the mound and supplied power hitting. After getting hit in the arm with a pitch—at first, everyone feared he'd broken his arm—Schoop returned to the lineup and went two for three against Saudi Arabia. Then he had two big RBIs in a big win over Japan and another win in the title game against California.

But it's Schoop's toughness that everyone remembers now.

"He could do anything," Vernon Isabella says, longingly. "No matter what happened, he did not break down. He was tough. He had a look in his eye. He was stubborn. Some of these other guys aren't like that. Jurickson, I don't know. . . he's not tough like that. He can back off. He doesn't want it as bad."

Carlos Pineda gave up just two hits in the opening-day win over Mexico and then won the championship game against California. In that title game, he struck out eleven batters in five innings. Called "Big Papi"—the nickname of David Ortiz, the bearlike slugger for the Boston Red Sox—he also hit three home runs in the first five games of the series.

Profar also won a name for himself in 2004, pitching a one-hit shutout and striking out twelve batters in the international championship game against Mexico. He also starred in 2005, winning two games on the mound and playing flawless shortstop. Profar thinks about situations two or three plays in advance. When a ball comes to him, he knows what to do, how much time he has. He almost never rushes his throws.

His regular-season manager, Michelangelo Celestina, says he's the best Little Leaguer he's ever seen. He thinks he has the potential to follow Andruw Jones to the major leagues.

"Jurickson is not like anything I have ever seen," Celestina tells me after a game at Frank Curiel Field. Celestina is driving me back to my hotel so we can keep the baseball talk going. "He is one in a million, maybe more. He has a chance to be like Andruw Jones if he continues to have the attitude he has. He's very smart on the baseball field. He knows what's going on all the time and knows how to prepare and tell his teammates what to expect. He's just like Schoop, except that he's much more powerful."

When I talked with the players and coaches in Willemstad, everyone agreed that Jurickson Profar was the class clown. He prances around with his uniform pants up by his armpits and jokes all day during practice. He's nicknamed Chokoi, after a local comedian. Sometimes the coaches get frustrated that he's not tougher or more focused. Then you remind those adults that he's just a kid, and they're fine again.

———————— •◆• ————————

Baseball's turning point in Curaçao, an event everyone remembers the way a generation of Americans remembered V-J Day, was the 1996 World Series when Andruw Jones hit a pair of home runs at Yankee Stadium. With those two swings of his shiny black bat, the nineteen-year-old Jones created more instant excitement than anything else in the modern history of Curaçao. Houses and sports clubs exploded in celebration, thousands of people spilled onto the streets for a spontaneous party. Fireworks went off. Car horns blared for hours. And the next year, Little League tryouts that once attracted hundreds of boys now attracted thousands. "I can still look back and remember what it felt like when Andruw hit those home runs," Michalangelo Celestina told me. "It changed everything. Everyone who loved baseball, now we were the center of attention."

But baseball was already growing on Curaçao when Andruw Jones hit those two home runs at Yankee Stadium.

The two Little League organizations in Curaçao have traveled to the U.S., not only for the Little League World Series in Williamsport, but also for the

Senior League World Series in Bangor, Maine (2003). Curaçao has sent five players to the major leagues. Besides the great Andruw Jones, Curaçaoans in the majors have included Hensley Meulens (1989–98), Randall Simon (1997 to the present), Ralph Milliard (1996–98), and Ivanon Coffie (2000). And there are some good prospects in the minor leagues for the Baltimore Orioles, Los Angeles Dodgers, and Atlanta Braves.

The best baseball factory anywhere in the world—the Dominican Republic—also plays in Little League's Caribbean region. How does Curaçao beat the Dominicans at baseball, again and again?

No one I talked with really has a definitive answer. But they offer theories.

The first theory is that, because the Little League organization is so strong in Curaçao, kids learn to play together as a team earlier. Curaçao does not have the abject poverty of the Dominican Republic, so kids have the luxury of playing on organized teams for years. And with the Dutch approach to instruction, coaches teach and kids learn to execute as a

Curaçao's Sorick Liberia at the plate

team. People like Frank Curiel and Vernon Isabella have made a long-term commitment to winning the Little League World Series every year. If the Dominicans had that same commitment and resources, they would have more success.

Everyone I talked with in Curaçao offered a second theory, impossible to prove or disprove: the Dominicans were strong in Little League before 2001, but got scared away by the fallout from the Danny Almonte scandal. Since then, Curaçao has gone undefeated in the regional tournaments.

"They were bigger, older kids," says Vernie Jenson, a coach for a Junior League team whose brothers, Ardley and Kaenley, play in the Dodgers and Braves systems in the U.S. "They used to cheat. That's how it went every year. They made fake papers. The controls of Williamsport were not strong like they are now."

But both theories pale next to a third factor. By the time the best Dominicans are twelve or thirteen, they're already playing under the watchful eyes of professional scouts. Major league teams can't sign foreign players until they're sixteen years old, but agents can. And they do. So by the time some players move into puberty, some agents are managing their playing time.

Once they sign, the Dominican players are put on strict regimens for exercise, nutrition, and playing time. Most American and Japanese franchises have established "academies" in the Dominican Republic where young players live together in dorms and play ball. Those organizations have scoured the landscape for promising baseball talent, leaving few kids in the neighborhoods to concentrate on Little League. Even so-so players get brought into the academies. Someone has to take the field to give the true prospects competition, after all.

In Curaçao, Little League dominance has not translated into a steady stream of major-league prospects. Once kids get past Little League, they don't have as much opportunity for instruction or league play as do the best of Dominican kids.

Norval Faneyte now coaches some of the players who played for the Little League champions

Christopher Garia pitches.

from 2004 and 2005. It's his job to keep developing them so they can remain the elites of their age groups. I asked him to call a practice session so I could see how he works with his kids. On short notice, a dozen players showed up and went through all their paces—long tossing, running, lifting small weights (plastic Coke bottles filled with sand), batting practice (hitting to the opposite field), fugoes, and situational fielding drills.

"Scouts start to look at them in the Junior League," explains Faneyte, "and our job is to teach them so they can climb to higher and higher levels. But we haven't always done a good job."

Hensley Meulens, a Willemstad native who once played for the New York Yankees, is back on the island working with the older teenagers—the ones

who might have a chance to sign pro contracts. But finding good competition for those boys can be difficult. Teams can travel to other islands for games, but they don't have the critical mass of players on Curaçao—or the hunger to escape the island that impoverished communities have—to create a farm system like the Dominican Republic or other Latin hotbeds like Venezuela.

Curaçao's Raysheldon Carolina gets advice before stepping to the plate. Carolina's home run in the fifth inning gave Curaçao a 6-3 lead over Hawaii in the championship game.

Even though Curaçao has produced only a handful of major leaguers, baseball has become a marketing tool for the island's tourist industry, thanks to the Little League's 2004 championship team. The tourist bureau's website gives as much prominence to Little League as it gives the beaches, hotels, shopping, and museums.

Tourism has never been the major economic engine in Curaçao as it is in nearby islands like Aruba. Oil refineries, shipping, and international finance have always been a cornerstone of the economy. But developers and tourist officials are working feverishly to bring more outsiders—and their money—to the island. And they are eager to use whatever means they can to advertise the island to the world.

About 250,000 visitors come to the island annually. But Curaçao's business leaders want more. Curaçao now has a national master plan to build tourism. Two major hotel chains now serve the island, and two more are under construction in downtown Willemstad.

Before the Willemstad all-stars left the island, the island's tourist agency gave them a party. They all gathered at a restaurant for a pep talk. They were reminded of Curaçao's championship in 2004 and told to go out there and win another.

"Our Curaçao website doubled in hits last year when you boys won the series," the bureau's top man told them in Papiamentu. "Now it is up to you to win again and triple our website visits, and help us increase our tourism. It is up to you, boys!"

The players mostly ignored the win-one-for-the-Gipper pitch. An Atlanta Braves game was on TV and the boys craned their necks to watch the action in Atlanta.

The tourism official then announced a surprise guest. Miss USA 2005, Chelsea Cooley, stopped by. The five-foot-seven brunette from North Carolina came to wish the Curaçao kids good luck.

Cooley had visited Curaçao once before—to participate in the 2001 Miss Teen Universe pageant—and accepted the tourist bureau's invitation to promote the island as a vacation spot. She has been a baseball fan since she was a little girl and calls herself a tomboy. She watched games on TV with her father and collected baseball cards. And now she has a younger brother playing in Little League.

"I thought it would be neat to meet them," said the veteran beauty contestant, who has taken a year off her studies in fashion school. "I just wanted to share and express my congratulations for what they accomplished."

It's hard to say whether seeing a gorgeous young woman can inspire a bunch of eleven- and twelve-year-olds to greatness. But Curaçao's tourist people were determined to do everything possible to inspire the kids.

I asked Cooley what lessons her own years as a beauty queen might offer to the Little Leaguers. "Just be proud of yourself, who you are, and where you came from," she said. "It has to come from deep down inside."

Finally, after days of media interviews and photographs, Team Curaçao got on a plane in Willemstad's Hato Airport to begin the defense of its Little League World Series championship.

But disaster almost happened right away.

Curaçao ran into trouble in the very first game of its championship defense at the Little League World Series in Williamsport.

Curaçao took an early 3–0 lead against Venezuela and its powerful starter, Richard Alvarez Jr. The Pabou Little League scored once on a solo home run by Sorick Liberia and two more on four walks and a hit batsman. Then, in the second inning, they increased their lead to 4–0 on a fielder's choice. So far, so good.

Curaçao's Denjerick Virginia stretches his body back to prepare to hit against Guam.

Jurickson Profar looked unhittable most of the way. He struck out eleven batters in six innings. But Venezuela tied the game in the fifth inning when Richard Alvarez hit a dramatic grand slam.

The game went into extra innings and Curaçao loaded the bases in the eighth. Sorick Liberia lifted a high fly ball to left field that scored the winning run. "I thought it was a home run, but I uppercut it too much," Liberia said.

So the Willemstad all-stars won. And a good thing, too. Because Japan demolished them in the second game of the World Series, 9–0.

The early line on the all-stars from Chiba City, a suburb of Tokyo, was: good pitch, good field, no hit.

But Japan looked like a team of Godzillas against Curaçao. The early scoring was a gift from the Caribbean team. Japan took a 3–0 lead in the first inning when Curaçao's starter, Manuela Dienston, walked four straight batters and threw three wild pitches before leaving the game with only one out. Yusuke Taira hit a two-run homer in the fourth inning and Yuki Mizuma hit a three-run shot in the sixth.

Taira gave up only three hits and had two walks and a home run to lead Chiba City. Taira threw Japan's patented wicked curveball all day, reducing Curaçao's biggest hitters to futility.

After the game, the players looked loose and confident—especially considering they could have lost their first two games and been eliminated already. But their third game of pool play was against Saudi Arabia, one of the weaker teams in Williamsport. And they already saw the best that Japan had to offer.

"We'll be ready for Japan next time," Vernon Isabella said.

Most teams that advance to the Little
League World Series spend years in
training. The team from Guam was one
of the most energetic teams, and they
advanced to the semifinals in the
International division of the tournament.

CHAPTER 6

Training to Win

JOHN BANIAGA WAS ONLY KIDDING, but he was trying to make a serious point. Baniaga was recalling the way the team from Ewa Beach marched powerfully and confidently through all of the qualifying tournaments for the Little League World Series—and then, suddenly, started to feel weak and homesick.

When the Hawaii players arrived in Williamsport, they discovered that breakfast on the mainland meant eggs, bacon, and grains. They couldn't stand it. They hated the taste, they hated the texture, and they hated the way they felt after eating any of it. It was as if Sam I Am showed up and was trying to force green eggs and ham on the islanders.

The Hawaiians complained. "They were craving SPAM," Baniaga, one of the truck-driving dads on the Ewa Beach team, told me. "They just weren't right till they had their SPAM."

So the team's family members, thirty of them packed into an eight-room bed-and-breakfast outside of town, bought a rice cooker, a big supply of SPAM, and made the kind of breakfast the kids got back in Ewa Beach— SPAM Musubi. It's a roll of rice, grilled SPAM, and nori seaweed. It was the official food, the fuel, of the Hawaii team.

SPAM was once the ultimate food of the postwar era. Originally sold in 1937 as the first canned meat not requiring refrigeration, SPAM has become disdained on the mainland, a symbol of suburban blandness. But SPAM has a mystical hold on Hawaiians. SPAM recipes are a favorite of Hawaiian homes, and SPAM meals are served in restaurants all over the islands. Even McDonald's serves SPAM.

During the games in Williamsport, Baniaga and others held up signs that proclaimed the power of SPAM:

The Hawaiian families cooked SPAM for the team from Ewa Beach.

EWA BEACH ALL-STARS: POWERED BY SPAM MUSUBI

SPAM was Hawaii's power food. SPAM calmed down the Hawaiians physically, making them stronger, so that they could then settle into their baseball routines in Williamsport and win.

Something similar happened a quarter-century before. The all-stars from Taipei, Taiwan, got to Williamsport and could not handle the American food—especially cheese, milk, and other dairy foods. They had stomachaches and diarrhea and couldn't concentrate in practices. So the team's manager called the embassy in Washington, and the embassy's chef came to prepare Chinese food for them. Taiwan went all the way, winning the Little League World Series with a 5–0 victory over Santa Clara, California. That was the beginning of Little League's greatest dynasty. Teams from Taiwan won seventeen Little League championships between 1969 and 1996.

A few years later, the chef decided to move to Williamsport. Yu-Cho Yen, known as Charlie, had the option of signing on for another tour with the embassy but declined. He remembered the small town in Pennsylvania where he became a hero for his cooking. He opened Yen King Chinese Restaurant in Williamsport in 1972.

Yen King is still in business. The eighty-five-year-old Charlie Yen is retired these days, but he comes to the restaurant every day to cook for the family.

———— •◆• ————

The real answer to Hawaii's powerful play was less about diet and more about punishing work. The West Oahu Little League all-stars won because they trained hard, for two solid years. The coaches took a bunch of skinny kids and ran 'em hard, every day except Sunday, until it hurt, until they doubled over with cramps, until they vomited and begged to stop. They hardened up those soft bodies—especially the lower bodies. Those workouts made the legs strong and quick. The Hawaiian players developed explosive power. They could throw hard, hit hard, run the bases hard, and go after grounders and pop flies hard.

By the time they arrived in Williamsport, Hawaii was the strongest of all the teams in the Little League World Series.

Months after the series, I was talking with former major league star Dante Bichette, one of the coaches of Florida's team. He asked me about my visit to Hawaii and what the team did to prepare for Williamsport. He listened and then turned silent for a moment. "Oh, no wonder," he said. "Of course they were so strong." Another pause. "Really? They did all that?"

———————•◆•———————

This is what the all-stars from the West Oahu Little League, from Ewa Beach, did to prepare for their run at the Little League World Series.

Six days a week, a group of men gathered at that unkempt Little League field near the old Ewa Sugar Plantation to set up machines and equipment for practice.

Located on the bottom of a fifty-foot slope off Renton Road, the plantation's old main street, the field had a dirt infield and overgrown outfield. During the peak months of summer, the sun beat down hard, even in the late afternoon.

The men—fathers of the players in the West Oahu Little League— brought two portable backstops, two portable pitching machines, PVC pipes, bats, helmets, balls, and catcher's gear. They unloaded the equipment from pickups and set up different stations around the field. As they worked, the first players arrived for practice, which lasted from 4:30 until the sun went down on weekdays. On Saturdays, they worked from nine in the morning until three or four in the afternoon, with a break for lunch. On Sundays, they rested.

The all-stars started their workouts in the spring, long before the all-star team was selected. In fact, every player in the league participated in the boot camp drills. The league came into being in 2004—it was created when the Ewa Beach Little League was forced to split because of a population boom in the area—and still had only two teams.

The managers of the two teams—Layton Aliviado of the Red Sox and Tyron Kitashima of the Cubs—shared the goal of reaching Williamsport and agreed to work out together all summer long. Aliviado had already managed most of the boys in the PONY League, so he knew them well. He also knew he would be the manager of the Little League's all-star team. So he designed training drills and got the players' families to commit to training year-round for the run to Williamsport.

Baseball boot camp started in 2004, helping Aliviado's band of eleven-year-olds to advance to Little League's state tournament. And then boot camp started again in 2005.

The goal was to make the players strong enough to endure a summer of daily baseball without getting tired. On most other teams, over the long summer of baseball, players hurt their arms, lost their focus at the plate, got lazy during games, struggled to maintain good pitching form, lost a step on the base paths or in the field, when it mattered most. The road to Williamsport was a long, grinding, tiring process.

If the kids are not strong in their lower bodies, they will weaken by the time they make it to the World Series. They start to look like the survivors of a dance marathon. But if you're strong—especially if you have strong legs—you can last all summer long without getting tired.

Another goal was to burn good athletic technique into muscles and bones. Like other activities—driving a car, playing golf, building furniture—baseball requires doing countless actions perfectly without thinking. The goal of good training is to make those actions part of the muscle memory. Then everything becomes a matter of reacting. Thinking in a game is just a matter of getting ready, being alert, to let loose with the automatic physical movements demanded by the situation.

In the West Oahu Little League's early training drills, players ran through rope ladders and in and around cones. Aliviado had his kids lift their legs high, running hard through the mazes until they collapsed. And then he had them do it again.

The maze began with a vertical leap. A parent would hold a bat high in the air and the player would jump up as high as he could, using his glove. Because you never know when you need to leap for a ball, in the infield or outfield.

After the leap, the players did ladder drills. Using PVC piping or ropes, Aliviado set up two rows of ladders along the ground. Players would have to run through the twenty or so rungs, about a foot and a half apart, on each ladder. Each time through the course, the players would use different footwork. Sometimes the object would be to lift the legs high. Sometimes the goal was to twist the body while running. Sometimes the object would be to move fast. Always, the goal was strength and agility in the lower body. "Sports is all footwork," says Aliviado. "You got to always move your feet." A drill favorite was the karaoke, in which the players advanced through the ladder by swinging one leg over the other into the next rung space.

Once the player reached the end of one ladder, he would run to the beginning of the second ladder, placed alongside the first.

After running through both ladders, the young athletes were confronted by a set of highway cones.

The players ran from cone to cone, working on the quick stop-and-start movements required on the field. After dashing to one cone, the player crouched down as if he was getting ready to field a grounder—butt down low, hands grazing the ground, head looking forward at an imaginary ground ball. Sometimes, the coaches told the player to "circle around" to the ball. When you come around on the ball, rather than coming to it directly, it's easier to set and throw. The body's movement provides momentum and direction to the throw.

From cone to cone, the players burned the essential movements of fielding into the memory of their muscles.

Burn, baby, burn.

In another drill, the player ran toward the cone looking over one shoulder at an imaginary line drive, then reached up to catch it. He looked over his other shoulder on the next cone. Then he ran with just a glance at the ball, ran full-speed with his eye off the ball, and then looked up again to regain his sights on the ball.

Burn, baby, burn.

After the cones, the players did long jumps—again, strengthening the whole lower body and making movements from a set position ever more explosive. Then there were lunges and duck walks (walking forward while in a crouch with the feet pointing outward). Then jumping rope.

Then they started over and did it again, two or three or even four more times.

Then they took laps and a water break.

"We timed these and tried to get them to go faster and faster," says Clint Tirpak, one of the team's coaches. It was as if the efficiency expert Frederick Winslow Taylor came to Little League. The trick of Taylorism is to get the best workers to set new standards and then apply those standards to everyone. "We always told the players that in the end, it was going to come down to who was conditioned the most to make it. If the players slacked off, I would yell, 'You're just cheating yourselves.'"

The players accepted the routine—they had no choice, since they and their parents had accepted the T-shirts reading "One Team, One Dream"—but they were not always happy.

"Especially when we had to do it again," Ty Tirpak says, "we would get really mad and sometimes swear. And the cousins, and Kini [Enos] especially, would be really mad. I kind of got it because my dad was explaining it to me, but some of the other kids thought it was stupid. Why do we have to do this stuff? Vonn Fe'ao would say we shouldn't have to do it so much."

When the players got sloppy, when they complained about the drills, they got more. Just when the workout seemed like it was over, they'd be told to run back and forth from one baseline to the other, touch the line with their glove hand—to simulate picking up a ball—shouting "We love coach!" every time. Anyone who didn't actually touch the line would have to start over again.

"Kini would be murmuring, grumbling, and we'd say, 'What's that? We'll do it again!'" says Clint Tirpak.

———————— •◆• ————————

After two weeks of drills, Aliviado was satisfied that the players were getting strong enough to survive a long series of tournaments. Then he put them through a series of skill drills—bunting, hitting to the right side of the diamond, double steals, turning double plays, making pickoff throws, hitting the cutoff man.

The oldest and truest critique of Little League practices is that there's a lot of standing around. Players are waiting to hit. Players are waiting for the grounders or fungoes to come to their side of the diamond. Pitchers are waiting for their turn. But not on Aliviado's fields. He always had four, five, even six stations set up. Everyone was in a state of animation.

After basic drills, Aliviado organized simulations of game situations.

Sometimes, the players lost their concentration on specific skills and game situations. Getting tired can cause sloppiness. But getting tired is not an excuse. Anytime the team looked sluggish, Aliviado went back to basics.

"If we go into a slump, we go back a stage to the fundamentals. We have to do the skill things right. You have to concentrate on them, get each one right, before you use it in game situations." It's like the South

Beach Diet; when you start to put the pounds back on, you return to the more restrictive Phase I of the diet.

The fundamentals always go back to the legs.

"The legs are the most important part of being in shape to play baseball," Aliviado says. "I needed to know that they could last the whole summer. We practiced constantly. I tired them out until they weren't tired any more. They got stronger, and so they didn't get tired so easy.

"In anything you do, you always have to set your feet. If you don't have good footwork, you're not going to be good. You got to get them drilling real fast. You have to get to a point where you can do it automatically, where you can do it blindfolded. The feet are always moving. Throw the ball, catch it, set up, and throw the ball.

"You need to move quickly. Without a fast break, you're not going to be able to get where you need to be in time to make the plays. You also have to be balanced, and you're going to be balanced with strong legs and with a quick start."

Aliviado teaches his players to catch with two hands. Yes, it's true that fielders have a greater reach with one hand—and in games, they reach out with the glove hand to catch balls just barely within their reach. "But it's important to get in the habit of catching with both hands, the old-fashioned way," he says. "It's about using your whole body, getting the whole body moving [toward an object]."

Before games, when they need a way to diffuse their nervousness, the Ewa Beach kids play Wiffle ball. Sometimes the coaches throw Wiffle golf balls to players with broomsticks. The kids hit off tees and do soft-toss hitting, too. Someone kneels before a batter and tosses balls—quickly, one after another—in front of the hitter.

It's a system—from the grinding footwork drills to the loose Wiffle ball hitting—that makes the long summer a single, seamless experience.

———— • ◆ • ————

When he's teaching technique, Layton Aliviado keeps his message simple.

If you're strong in the lower body, and if you can concentrate and count to three or four, Layton Aliviado can teach you how to hit and throw.

"If you can see the ball good, you can hit them. But to hit the ball right, you have to work on the footwork. To me it's repetition. In beginning of the season, I do the one-two-three drills. I keep it simple for the kids. The fundamentals, don't try to give them hard words. Everyone can count. Just count out what to do and explain by showing. Then they have it stuck in their heads: 'One, two, three.' I do the same thing with throwing and pitching. Every kid can count, right?"

I talked with Aliviado in the living room of his home in one of the housing developments that have made Ewa the fastest growing community in Oahu. He was surrounded by baseball and football equipment—bats and balls, helmets and shoulder pads—and by pictures of his children playing sports and hula dancing.

He jumped up to demonstrate.

"You got to keep the head down and follow through," he says, slowly moving a bat across the zone, his head still and his eyes trained on the bat as he holds it still over the imaginary plate.

"It's simple: *set, shift, hit.* The hips are leading the hands. *Hips, hands.* Stay on top of the ball. You're doing a few things almost at the same time—stepping down with the forward foot, turning the hip, and moving hands into the hitting zone, with the head down on the ball.

"One: stride forward, at the same time moving the weight back.

"Two: get the hips going, get the hands going.

"Three: snap everything forward, bring the hands around into the zone, snap everything forward."

———————•◆•———————

Three time zones and half an ocean east of Hawaii, almost 3,000 miles away, the all-stars from the Rancho Buena Vista Little League took a drastically different approach to training.

The Californians don't believe in doing a lot of infield drills. They prefer to spend as much time as possible in batting cages, swinging away while oldies music plays on a boom box. Marty Miller, the team's manager, says infield and running drills would wear down his team. Because they have played together for years on travel teams, they already work well together on the field. Miller prefers his players to work on hitting.

A native of southern Idaho, Miller moved to southern California a quarter-century ago because that's where he found customers for his construction business. He speaks with a slight drawl, like the cartoon character Huckleberry Hound. Miller has worn a mustache for thirty years, and the last three years he's sported a wide, white handlebar mustache. It's so big you'd think you could steer it. That mustache has become an emblem of the team.

Sports have always dominated Miller's life. Until recently, he played in men's softball leagues all summer—usually sixty games a year. Miller built his summer days around the softball team's travel schedule. Miller's kids also play sports. His son Brad plays at Oklahoma Baptist. His daughter Kerri also played sports through high school and college.

And Miller knows what works—at least for his bunch of players, most of whom have played on the same teams and practiced together, from January to December, for the past three years.

When the all-star team from Rancho Buena Vista gathered for its first meeting—with all the players and their parents—Miller told them that success depended more on their hitting than pitching or fielding.

"My experience in all-star tournaments told me that if we didn't put up five, six runs, we got beat," Miller says. "Pitching is important but who you have is pretty much already set. If you don't have good fielders on an all-star team, someone screwed up. So we had to make the goal to score five or six runs every game. I told them that if we did that we had a chance to win every game."

Miller sees little need to practice fielding. His players all play on elite travel teams and have worked together for years. If they can't field yet, they don't have much chance of winning. But hitting is such a difficult and complex skill. Even the best players develop bad habits, so Miller pushes his players to work hard in the batting cages. "I want them getting as much hitting as they can stand," he says. "So we use the cage a lot. It's a good way for them to get a lot of swings, and work on specific problems that they have—things that can be fixed."

Joe Pimentel is the man that Marty Miller told to fix whatever doesn't work with the R.B.V. bats.

Throughout the Little League World Series, the Californians worked in the batting cages with a strange laid-back intensity. As the bats made their clanking sounds, hour after hour, a boom box played "Light My Fire" by the Doors, "Stairway to Heaven" by Led Zeppelin, "When I'm Sixty-Four" by the Beatles, "Born to Run" by Springsteen. Song after song, an oldies station played the stuff Marty Miller and Joe Pimintel grew up with.

In one cage, a pitching machine delivered the pitches. Miller or coach Randy Rezniecek held the ball up to the hitter—*get ready to swing*—and then put it on the wheel that snaps the ball forward. The machine is a tool of efficiency. Hitter after hitter steps up to the plate and takes cuts. But the balls sometimes wobble. And the machine can't mix up fastballs, curveballs, and changeups. And hitters can't see different pitches coming out of the pitcher's hand with a machine—the most important split-second moment for the hitter, when he has to decide what kind of pitch is coming from what angle. Only live pitching can really teach hitting and prepare players for game situations.

For live pitching, California uses Joe Pimentel, a former minor-league pitcher who threw batting practice for the San Diego Padres in 1985, 1986, and 1992. Pimentel is the junior-varsity coach at Rancho Buena Vista High and the founder and coach of the travel team called Team Easton. Pimentel also runs a small hitting school at Miller's construction company. One of his former students is Troy Glaus, now a major league star, whom he coached during his tour as Carlsbad High School's coach from 1987 to 1991.

Pimentel is a tanned, strong man with an inexhaustible arm. He wears a Padres hat and a tuft of whiskers below his lower lip. He throws forty or fifty pitches to all twelve California players, each one, every batting practice. Every pitch is a purpose pitch. No lobs. Only hard pitches that challenge the hitters to develop and maintain good mechanics. With every pitch, Pimentel teaches fundamentals—plant the feet, keep the head steady, watch the ball come out of the hand, power the swing from the ground up, keep the swing compact, follow through smoothly.

When he teaches kids to hit, Pimentel breaks his lessons into catch phrases that players with a kid's attention span can understand and remember.

Remember Mom's cooked spaghetti—Relax the arms and shoulders. Make them loose, like limp pasta.

Holding a baby bird—Grip the bat loosely, so that you can maintain a free and easy swing and avoid hitches that slow down the bat.

The dog wagging his tail—Snap the bat when you bring it across the plate. Hitting a ball far requires getting good bat speed, and that requires bringing all the force possible to the end of the bat. As the bat moves through the zone, all of the energy moves to the end of the bat.

Sway like a dancer—Wave the bat over the plate, pushing foot to foot, swaying a little and working off the balls of the feet. The only time a player should be on his heels is when he's backing up on a deep fly ball to the outfield.

Pimentel throws behind a L-shaped screen. On a day when I watched, Johnny Dee stood at the plate. Pimentel threw perfect instructional pitches. They were all near the plate—some right over, most on the corners, some a little high and inside, all pitches that an aggressive batter has to be ready to hack. After every pitch, after every swing, Pimentel had something to say—words of encouragement, reminders of past lessons, challenges and questions, exhortations to stay focused. It's baseball poetry:

Step into the ball. Shift your hips.
You're looking at your girlfriend? You gotta look here.
Roll over. Excellent, Johnny! Roll over those hands!
That's your old swing. Flush it down the toilet!
You're late. Come up with that left hand. That's better!
What pitch was that? Where was it coming from?
That's it! Way to pick it up out of the hand!
That was a foul ball.
Where's the ball going off your bat? It's going off that way.
Make the adjustment!
Way to recognize it!
That ball's gone!
That's right! Way to pick it up out of the hand!
Let it get to you. Stay compacted.
It's all about quickness and speed.
Come on, get extension!
What do you feel?

After pitching batting practice, Pimentel feels physically wasted. Every day in Williamsport, he threw more than 400 pitches. He then went straight to the trainer's room for treatments.

During his time with the Padres, Pimentel sought out the best players, past and present, and quizzed them about the mechanics of hitting and pitching. He talked with Tony Gwynn, the best singles hitter of the last two decades. He sought out Galen Cisco, the veteran pitching coach. But Pimentel learned the most from Merv Rettenmund, a 1970s star with the Baltimore Orioles and Cincinnati Reds. Rettenmund helped

Greg Vaughn and Reggie Sanders have their best years when he was the Padres' hitting coach.

In their conversations, Rettenmund emphasized the need to keep the hands close to the body during the swing. "He started by noticing how Tony Gwynn could move his body and yet hold his hands back," Pimentel says. "That was key for me because I realized the kids don't have the strength to do that. They have to do something else to drive the ball."

A familiar sight throughout the long summer of baseball: California's Kalen Pimentel rounding the bases after a home run. The team was tutored by Kalen's father Joe, a former prospect in the San Francisco Giants chain.

Pimentel turned hitting mechanics upside-down. The classic hitting theory of Ted Williams holds that the batter creates energy from the ground up. But that's not always easy for young hitters. Few kids have the strength—like Tony Gwynn or Barry Bonds—to drive the body forward but also hold the bat back to gain a split-second more of time.

So Pimentel has his hitters throw their bats out at the ball, like snapping a whip—or, in his terms, a dog wagging his tail.

"In my way of teaching the kids, the hands and arms set up my body. I want to get hands and arms and throw them at the ball. Then I add my pivot, which allows me to drive any pitch that is thrown. If you spin [drive the hitting process from the ground up], you're predetermining which way your hands are going to go.

"It gives any kid a chance to drive the ball, even little guys. It starts with the arms, not letting the body [determine too soon] where the hands are going."

———————•◆•———————

Travel eastward another 3,000 miles and a continent, another three time zones, to a suburb of Orlando, Florida. Head to the house owned by Dante Bichette. Stop by almost any day and head for his garage.

That's where Bichette, a big power hitter for thirteen years in the major leagues, conducts his own lessons on hitting and life.

Bichette hit 274 home runs for five major league teams from 1988 to 2001. In the summer of 2002, he was in spring training with the Los Angeles Dodgers when he got word that his son and namesake hit a home run in his first Little League game. That's when he decided to stop playing. Bichette could still hit—in 2001, his final season, he hit twenty-three home runs, batted in ninety runs, and had a .294 batting average—but he had had enough of the itinerant life in the major leagues. He had already made more than $35 million in baseball and never needed to work another day in his life. Now it was time to come home.

And time to teach Dante Junior to hit like his old man.

On the Maitland all-star team—the first Florida team to advance to Williamsport in forty-one years—Bichette was one of two former major-leaguers to serve as coach. Mike Stanley, who played for five teams from 1986 to 2000, helped at the batting cages but focused on teaching fielding and baserunning. The team's manager, Sid Cash, a bank executive who has coached Little League teams for twenty years, taught pitching.

The real signature of the Florida team was hitting. Everybody on the team hit like Dante Bichette Sr.

Throughout his career—which included stints with the California Angels, Milwaukee Brewers, Colorado Rockies, Cincinnati Reds, and Boston Red Sox—Bichette hit with a distinctive toe step. As the pitcher goes into his motion, Bichette would lift his front foot like a ballerina, touch the dirt with his toe, and then land back on his back foot and launch into a swing.

Toe touch, lean back, and whack the ball.

Dante Junior is a rosy-cheeked kid who sometimes wears a scowl to look the way pitchers are supposed to look these days. He is Florida's best pitcher and best hitter. Young Bichette has his father's athletic genes, and those genes are trained by playing baseball all year long. He is probably one of only two or three players in the Little League World Series who absolutely expects to be a major-league player some day.

Before they can refine their stance and swing, the players have to learn how to hit a seventy-mile-an-hour fastball from forty-six feet away. It's all about repetition. Swing and miss. Swing and miss. Swing and come a little closer. Swing and get closer still. Swing and finally hit the ball.

Step two is teaching them how to hit curveballs. That requires getting away from the pitching machines and using live arms for batting practice.

"A curveball comes into the plate like a fastball comes to the plate," Bichette says. "It's just coming in slower, at an angle, and you can learn how to hit that. You have to learn to pick it up out of the pitcher's hand. So we spend all kinds of time working on that."

Maitland's appearance in the Little League World Series was a small miracle. Against other travel teams, the Maitland Pride can be competitive. But other teams around Florida are much better. Mike Bono, one of the pioneers of travel baseball in Florida, calls Maitland's ride a "one-year wonder."

Maitland got past a passel of better teams, not only in Florida but in the baseball-rich Southeast regional tournament as well. With some of the best teachers around, the Maitland team managed to hit and pitch just well enough to succeed.

Sid Cash, a veteran of forty summers of Little League coaching, is still amazed at how much the team learned in a short period.

"I don't think ten years ago you could do that," he says. "I'm still amazed, and I've been doing this a long time. You *can* teach kids to do things that they don't think they can do. It's all repetition. And even though other teams might be more athletic and savvier, you can get them to make adjustments too. You just tell them, and they do it. That was our strength—the adults calling pitches and telling the hitters what's coming. I never knew how much you could do before."

One team—Canada's representative from Surrey, British Columbia—places fun over winning in its workouts.

I wandered over to Canada's practice not long after watching Japan's team work out like a bunch of soldiers. The contrast was huge.

Some players ambled around the infield and outfield. Others clustered behind the backstop. One player kneeled on the mound, next to the manager, delivering balls from the fielders to the pitcher. Manager Glenn Morache and his coaches moved around from the mound to the infield to the outfield to the bench.

The only player who got any real practice or instruction was the batter.

The team from Canada took a loose approach to training, but was all business on the field.

None of the players moved much in the field. More than once, I looked out and saw the second baseman sitting on the bag while two coaches played catch. The outfielders kneeled for a while, and then just sat—until a fly ball came their way. And then they trudged after the ball as if it were an awful chore, like taking out the garbage.

Fielders let the balls fall. Only Nathan de la Feraude chased after any hits. "Hey, only Nathan's getting any fly balls out there!" Morcahe yelled. But even de la Feraude got tired. On one fly, he threw his glove at the ball. Morache cried: "Hey, how come you guys can't shag balls out there?"

Morache did most of the BP pitching.

The batters shuffled to the plate, took their cuts, and shuffled away.

At one point, a batter asked what pitch the coach was going to throw. "What, you think a pitcher's going to tell you what he's throwing? You have to be ready for everything."

"But you were saying what pitch you were throwing before."

Point, counterpoint.

Kristopher Robazza stepped in, alternating his attention between the balls wobbling into the plate and the catcher chattering about pin trading. "Get in a rhythm. Get in a rhythm, Kristopher," Morache said.

But Matt Catano had the hitters' attention as he crouched behind the plate. "I'm going to get all the ring pins," Catonio told Justin Atkinson. "There's a great Tony the Tiger pin." Atkinson nods.

One of the more enthusiastic pin traders was Mitch Burns, a utility player with a mop of blond hair. After getting hit in the ribs with a pitch, he walked slowly over to the bench and nursed his bruise. And talked, at length, about pin trading.

Three or four players sat on a wooden box behind the backstop. They took turns chasing after foul balls. In between, they talked about pins, uniforms, hitting, and life on the road. "The coaches are always mad at us because we keep asking them questions," one tells me. They ask all kinds of questions about the book I'm writing. Finally, I move away. I don't want to get them in trouble.

Later, John Atkinson came over by the fence and talked about the weeks he's spent living with the kids. He rolled his eyes. "One of them says, 'When are we going to eat?'" Atkinson says. "Ten minutes later, everyone is asking, 'When are we going to eat? When we gonna eat?'" Atkinson sighs and wanders off.

One hitter hesitated to get into the batter's box. "Hey you gonna hit or..." Morache shouts.

"I'm going to play with my batting glove all day," the kid mutters.

After a while, Morache tired of the player who's been helping him retrieve balls. "Go! I don't need you!"

Coach Joe Burns played third base when a pop fly came his way. "I got it!" he shouts. He grabbed the ball and flipped it to the mound. Then: "Hah! I think I farted! Sorry!"

A couple pitches later, Glenn Morache let a lazy pop fly fall behind first base. "In your younger days, Coach Glenn?" a player shouts out. "You would have had that in your younger days?"

After everyone's taken BP, Atkinson told Matt Catonio to block some balls in the dirt at the plate. But the drill didn't really work. Some balls dribbled in, some didn't get near the plate. Catonio was too tired to pounce at the balls.

It was hot—in the nineties, hotter and more humid than they're accustomed to in Canada—and everyone was tired.

"Yeah, we're tired from the travel but so is everyone else," John Atkinson said. I told him that the Japanese team practiced at 8:30 in the morning after arriving in Williamsport late the previous night. "Yeah, see, but they want to play and work out the rust."

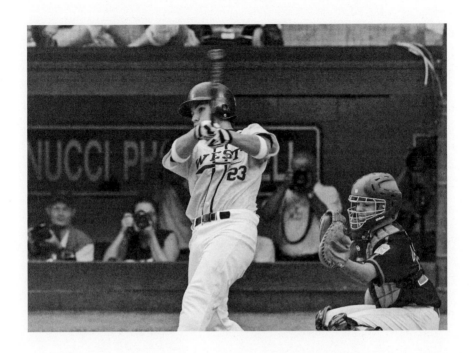

Kalen Pimentel hit two grand slams
in two games to lead the all stars
from Vista, California.

Nathan Lewis of the Rancho Buena
Vista Little League of California was
just one of many pitchers with
injured arms in the 2005 Little
League World Series.

CHAPTER 7

———————— ◆ ————————

Now Pitching for Faust . . .

*L*IKE ALL BASEBALL FANS, I have wondered about why major league pitching isn't as strong as it used to be. When I was a kid I rooted for the New York Mets, a team with pitchers like Tom Seaver, Jerry Koosman, Jon Matlack, and Nolan Ryan. I came to appreciate a 1–0 or 2–1 game more than a 14–10 game. A pitching duel creates the game's greatest tension and suspense.

But reliable, durable pitchers are rare these days. Why? Theories abound. Hitters have bulked up. Ballparks have gotten smaller, with shorter outfield fences and less foul territory. The strike zone has shrunk. Pitchers aren't allowed to throw inside anymore. Hitters wear too much body armor. Hitters stall, ruining the pitcher's rhythm. Specialization prevents young pitchers from developing fully. In amateur ball, hits go so far with aluminum bats that pitchers throw for strikeouts rather than grounders and popups. The designated hitter robs pitchers of first-hand knowledge of their foes. Scouts only care about giants and ignore smaller athletes. Pitchers use bad mechanics.

All very good thoughts. But I was struck by another theory, offered by Dr. James Andrews, the preeminent sports doctor in America.

"The best pitchers in the country never make it to the majors because they're the ones in youth leagues and high school who are overused," Andrews says. "We're seeing more injuries now because these kids are having more pressure to throw at higher velocities. They're throwing more sliders, more stress pitches. But the crux of the problem is we don't have enough quality pitchers to go around because the good, quality pitchers are being hurt in the youth leagues."

We ruin our pitchers when they're young. The pitchers who *would* be major league stars never make it because they blow their arms out in Little League, PONY League, AAU, USSSA, Cooperstown Dreams Parks, and hundreds of summer tournaments. If Andrews is right—and he's someone who should know—then maybe the Little League World Series is the best place to look for the future of pitching.

——————— •◆• ———————

When I was in Williamsport, I talked with dozens of people—coaches and trainers, parents and players—about how they approach pitching.

How many pitches do coaches allow their pitchers to throw? Do coaches let their guys throw curveballs? What kind of curves do the kids throw? Is it safe to throw any curveball? How much rest do pitchers get? Do teams depend too much on the bigger, beefier pitchers? What do coaches know, and what do they teach, about pitching mechanics? Can coaches tell if a pitcher's mechanics are off? When? What happens when pitchers get in trouble on the mound? What's the parents' role in deciding how to use young arms?

When I got home, I had an email from Rick Hale, the manager of the all-star team from Owensboro, Kentucky.

Hale was wracked with guilt about the way he treated pitchers in the long summer of Little League. The pressure to qualify for the Little League World Series—and the pressure to win in Williamsport—was so strong that no team could avoid overusing his top one or two pitchers.

"They are being abused and everyone who has ever coached an all-star team is guilty," he said.

——————— •◆• ———————

Rick Hale is an amiable and animated electrician who has lived his whole life in Owensboro, Kentucky. He was one of the most thoughtful characters I met in Williamsport. We talked for two hours one day—mostly about his players, but also about the larger trends shaping baseball and the best strategies for teaching young players.

Hale seemed conflicted by the whole scene in Williamsport. He loved being there. He was proud that the Owensboro Southern Little League was making its second straight appearance in Williamsport under his command. He loved his players, and he felt good about the support parents gave him. But at the same time, he was already feeling pressure to win. His team lost all three games in the 2004 Little League World Series and folks back home were calling him on his cell phone, prodding him to make sure the team won a game or two.

A longtime employee of Commonwealth Aluminum, Hale has coached Little League for twenty years. Gray and plump, his face stretches as he talks, a thin layer of gray whiskers widening and narrowing as the topics and expressions change. Did I say he loves talking about baseball? Little League is such an important experience for Hale that he named his baby daughter after Meghan Sims, a girl who pitched for his team in 2004.

Most Little League organizations select the manager of the championship team to coach the all-stars. But Hale's team, the Braves, had a record of 0–20 in 2005. The Braves not only lost every game, but often lost ugly. In one game, the Braves lost 36–2 in a game ended after four innings by Little League's ten-run mercy rule. The high point of the season was a 2–0 loss to the league's best team. "I was very, very proud," Hale said. "They thought they won. They knew they battled the best pitcher and the best team."

A lousy team was part of Hale's plan. Every year, the Owensboro Southern Little League drafts players ages ten, eleven, and twelve. Players stay with the team for as long as three years. Hale picked all ten-year-olds so he could build a superpower in two years. Other managers just laughed. "After the draft, our chances of winning were nothing," he says. "They were giggling, 'Good luck, Rick.'"

Hale got the manager's job for Owensboro because no one else would take the team. But Hale guided the team to the state championship and then the Great Lakes regional championship in Indianapolis. And the all-stars from Owensboro made their second straight appearance in the Little League World Series.

The problem was, Hale cut a Faustian bargain to do it.

———————— • ◆ • ————————

Three of Owensboro's pitchers experienced serious arm problems by the end of the summer. Matthew Johnson hurt his arm so badly toward the end of the regular Little League season that he had a hard time throwing the ball at all. (His teammates made a joke of the underhanded throwing, calling him Finch, after the women's softball star Jenny Finch.) Dalton West, the team's top pitcher, broke down in the team's first game of the series after two and a third innings of work. Nolan Miller also complained about a sore arm, so much that Hale decided to see if Johnson had healed enough to start the team's do-or-die second game against Louisiana.

In his email confessional, Hale told me he contributed to his pitchers' injuries by working them too hard. He emphasized he wasn't alone, that everyone in the Little League World Series "abused" their young pitchers.

"Every Little League coach in the world is using his Number One [pitcher] as often as the rules allow or he risks not advancing in the tournament," Hale said.

Owensboro's ace, Dalton West, pitched three games in the Kentucky state tournament, one with two days of rest and the other with three days of rest. In the Great Lakes regional tournament—which qualifies teams for the World Series—West pitched three times again. After throwing ninety-four pitches in the first game, he threw eighty-nine pitches on two days of rest in game three. Then on two more days of rest, he threw ninety pitches in the semifinal game.

"When we opened up in Williamsport he was but a shell of himself," Hale says. "I knew before the first pitch of that game he would never last the entire game. After two innings, he told me he was starting to tighten. I asked him if he could get me just one more inning and gallantly he told me he would try."

It was a disaster. California won, 7–2. West threw seventy-nine pitches in just two and a third innings. He faced seventeen hitters and gave up seven runs on six hits and three walks. All seven runs came in a third inning without end, in which California hit two home runs, two singles, and got two walks.

"I truly regret sending him out in the third inning, not because of California's outburst, but because he was sore the rest of the tourney," Hale said later. "I only hope it is not a serious injury, but it is the tendon in his elbow. I truly believe it's because of all the games on short rest."

In the next game, with Nolan Miller reporting a sore arm and Luke Daugherty doubtful (more on that in a moment), Hale turned to Matthew Johnson to keep his team alive against Louisiana. Hale had been working with Johnson in the bullpen under Volunteer Stadium, away from the spying eyes of other teams.

"I like the privacy," Hale told me during our first conversation. "I like to do things my way. I don't want anyone looking over my shoulders. It's what works for me. I'm loud and I like to encourage guys: '*All riiiight!*' I think that's what we're looking for—for them to think I think they're the best. I don't want to get self-conscious when I'm working with them."

Hale didn't want anyone to know that he was working with Johnson. Johnson hadn't pitched for two and a half months because of his frayed arm. Every so often, Hale asked him to throw on the side to see if the pain was gone and the pop was back. Johnson tried during the Great Lakes regional tournament, but his arm still hurt too much. But he felt good in Williamsport.

"It was really a gutsy move, because our tournament life was at stake," Hale told me later. "We worked him a couple of times under Volunteer Stadium, let him throw the baseball and it was remarkable how far he had come. He was still favoring his injury—not hurting, but scared to turn the ball loose. He was throwing strikes on the inside and outside parts of plate. The sessions helped release his fears. He relaxed and just *threw*."

When Hale picked Johnson to pitch against Louisiana instead of Luke Daugherty, parents of the players screamed in protest. *How can you have Matthew pitch? He hasn't pitched for months! Luke's a stronger pitcher!*

The question is, why was Daugherty left on the shelf? Hale says it's because the pitcher didn't have the burning desire the team needed for his must-win game. "I always try to push each kid to his limit," he says, adding that the players' different personalities require different approaches. "One kid, you can get all over. Other kids, when you do that, you crush them." Daugherty, Hale said, just didn't have the "look in his eye" he needed to pitch in such an important game.

The Daughertys have a different take. More important than any "look in his eye" was that Hale didn't think Daugherty could win without a curveball—and Daugherty's father wouldn't let him throw a curveball.

"I told Rick at the very beginning that I wouldn't let Luke throw curves, and he accepted it," says Joe Daugherty. "I just want to protect his arm. Even if he gets by at twelve [without an injury] doesn't mean he'll be okay at seventeen. But that meant he wasn't going to be pitching as much [in tournaments]. That bothered him. When he got left out, he would just look at me from across the room."

Even though he wanted to pitch more in big games, Luke Daugherty appreciates his father's caution. "I need to wait until I'm sixteen or so," he says when I ask about throwing a curveball. "It will pay off later. He told me one time and I agreed."

Johnson pitched two and one-third innings, giving up two unearned runs before being replaced by Nolan Miller. Johnson threw thirty-six pitches and reported no soreness after the game.

But a day after the whole Williamsport pageant was over, Hale had regrets. He noted that fully developed major-league pitchers work on four days of rest, while his top Little League pitchers got only two days to recover.

"How in the world can anyone expect not to do damage to these young arms on two days rest again and again? I am as guilty as anyone of abusing my Number One, hoping for the chance to play in the big show, on national television. Well, it got us there, albeit with sore arms...Someone needs to speak out for these young athletes. They are being abused and everyone who has ever coached an all-star team is guilty because the rules allow it."

Joe Daugherty adds a bitter note to the indictment. "This is what breaks my heart about Williamsport," he says. "These kids were exploited for a grown man's personal gain. That's the dark side."

In the weeks before Little League tryouts in 2006, Rick Hale regularly appeared at the doorstep of the Daugherty house, in freezing temperatures, petitioning Luke to play Little League again. Finally, Joe Daugherty told Hale that his son would not be playing Little League again. Luke could have become one of the first players ever to appear in the Little League World Series three times. But the Daughertys decided it was time to move on. "It was like hearing my high school sweetheart was going to the prom with my best friend," Hale told me. "I was sick."

———————— • ◆ • ————————

All over Williamsport, pitchers broke down. The tragedy of the Little League World Series is that the teams who make it there—with a few notable exceptions—are so physically exhausted that they can't count on their best pitchers for strong performances in Williamsport.

At a time when teams should be peaking, they are often starting to fall apart.

In the minds of the coaches and parents—players don't think too much about such matters—getting to the Little League World Series is the most important thing. Advancing to Williamsport means an all-expenses-paid trip to a tournament broadcast on national television. It means daily contact with former big leaguers and TV announcers, collecting boxes and boxes of baseball equipment, parades back home after the series is over, recognition on the streets. For some kids, it means a two- or three-week vacation from school.

Not getting to Williamsport means nothing.

Even when the teams are physically and emotionally wasted, the pressure to win continues. And here's a cruel irony. The weaker the team, the greater the pressure to push one or two stud pitchers to the limit. A team from a place like Davenport, Iowa—which has sent teams to Williamsport four times in the last six years, but lost their last seven games—hangs everything on a big performance by its biggest performers. *If only our big guy can come through, we'll have a chance.*

Steve Keener, Little League's CEO, acknowledges that coaches and parents want to win so much that they often risk the player's health.

"Adults want to win and they lose focus, they lose perspective," Keener told me. "They believe that winning is going to make everybody happy. Sometimes the coaches get a little too important. The key element in all this is that by nature we're all competitive. When we play something we want to win. That's why you compete." The answer, Keener says, is for the coach to set ground rules before the season limiting how much the kids will play. "So now when the parents say, 'Put Luke in!' you tell them, 'Shut up! Remember the meeting when I said I will not compromise safety?'"

But sometimes the coach is the problem, not the victim of overzealous parents. "The league is the most important entity in all this," Keener says. "The league selects the manager and the coaches. Too often, it's the poorly run league that lets a few coaches get out of hand and control everything." Coaches from blue-collar backgrounds often "are undermatched by intellectual or communication skills," Keener says. "You might have a very good technical manager who might be a welder...or guys who can do plumbing or woodwork and stuff." Those coaches need to be taught how to balance the goal of winning with the need to keep the game relaxed and fun for players.

———————— •◆• ————————

The furor over abusing pitchers started on the first day of play. Iowa's Ryan Schumaker threw 132 pitches in a 7–3 loss to Florida. Schumaker was so exhausted and distracted that in the fifth inning he threw two wild pitches in a row and forgot to cover home on one of the errant throws. Florida ran on Schumaker, and he looked like he had been mugged in an alley.

Overextended

Nine pitchers threw more than 100 pitches in a single game during the thirty-one games of the Little League World Series:

Opponent	Pitcher	Number of Pitches
Japan	Martin Cornieles (Venezuela)	137
Florida	Ryan Schumaker (Iowa)	132
Japan	Christopher Garia (Curaçao)	116
Japan	Jurickson Profar (Curaçao)	108
Iowa	Dante Bichette Jr. (Florida)	106
Florida	Kalen Pimentel (California)	103
Curaçao	Richard Alvarez Jr. (Venezuela)	102
Japan	Chris Fischer (Canada)	101
Guam	Jeff Degano (Canada)	101

Jeff Mallonee, the Iowa coach, took responsibility for Schumaker's high pitch count but seemed more concerned about Schumaker's giving up a three-run homer to Florida's Dante Bichette Jr. "It was a bad coaching decision to keep throwing him," he said afterward. "In fact, the batter before, I decided to take him out if we walked the guy before Dante. But we changed our minds and left him in."

When I talked with other coaches after the World Series—not just Little League coaches, but travel-team coaches as well—they all remembered the Iowa team pushing its ace too far. "I was as angry as anybody when that kid threw 130-some pitches," Mike Bono, a travel-team coach in Florida, told me. "It was sick. You just got to *get him off the mound*. You cannot allow him to stand out there and throw that many pitches. It was awful."

For the rest of the series, Little League's reporters and other coaches pointed to Schumaker's long appearance as a prime example of abuse. But he was not the only pitcher to throw too much. In fact, another pitcher—Martin Cornelius of Venezuela—threw 137 pitches in a game against Japan. In the thirty-one games of the tournament, nine pitchers threw more than 100 pitches in a game. In those thirty-one games, thirty-five pitchers threw more than seventy-five pitches.

And it showed. Most teams dragged after their first game or two. Only one team—the all-stars from Ewa Beach, Hawaii—looked stronger at the end of the series than they did at the beginning.

———— •◆• ————

To understand the dangers of pitching on young arms, a good place to start is the American Sports Medicine Institute in Birmingham, Alabama. Created twenty years ago by Dr. James Andrews, the ASMI studies the "biomechanics" of all kinds of sports motions—pitching, hitting, golfing, gymnastics. The ASMI's primary goal is to reduce injuries. A secondary goal is to improve performance. In the last decade, a long parade of major league teams—the Mets, Red Sox, Indians, Orioles, Athletics—has sent top pitching prospects to Birmingham.

Andrews reports that he performed four times as many elbow surgeries on collegiate players in 2000–04 than he did in 1995–99. He performed six times as many surgeries for high school pitchers in 2000–04 than 1995–99.

The crux of the problem is that when pitchers pitch too much—or when they throw dangerous pitches—they put their arms under repeated stresses. Pitch after pitch, the ends of a player's bones grind away at each other—or they pull away from each other. If the stresses happen long enough, a player's shoulder and elbow could be deformed forever, requiring surgery. Repetitive stress injuries have become the cause of more hospital visits than auto accidents.

Pitching too much presents an even more serious problem for boys below ages fourteen or fifteen. The ends of the bones usually remain undeveloped until a child is fourteen years old. Because the bones have not fully developed, pitching too much can grind the ends of the bones down, preventing their full growth. The problem can be serious enough to cause deformities and require surgery. In some cases, even surgery cannot fix the problem, and the boy grows into a man with arms lacking ordinary reach and range of motion.

When I called Glenn Fleisig, ASMI's research director, he told me to look at two major studies of young pitchers, published in *The American Journal of Sports Medicine* in 2002 and 2006. Researchers at ASMI, including Fleisig and ASMI founder Jim Andrews, coauthored both papers.

The data in those papers confirm what experts have been saying, with greater and greater urgency, for years.

The 2006 article, "Risk Factors for Shoulder and Elbow Injuries in Adolescent Baseball Pitchers," compares two groups of 140 ten- to thirteen-year-old pitchers. Ninety-five of them have significant histories of arm problems, while another forty-five have no signs of arm problems. Not surprisingly, the injured group pitched more—more months in the year, more games, and more total innings. They also threw more pitches in games and more warm-ups before games than the healthy group.

The study crunched some scary statistics. Players who pitched eight months a year were five times as likely to suffer an injury as players in a baseline group who pitched five and a half months a year. Throwing more than eighty pitches in a game made an arm injury almost four times as likely as throwing fewer than eighty pitches a game. Pitching with fatigue made an arm injury thirty-six times as likely.

Players with iced arms were a common sight at the LLWS. Hawaii's Vonn Fe'ao took steps to protect his arm after the championship game.

The most telling finding might concern the players' perceptions about their coaches. Half of all the survey's participants said their coach was "more concerned about winning the game and of having a successful season than the pitcher's long-term success."

The 2002 study, "Effect of Pitch Type, Pitch Count, and Pitching Mechanics on Risk of Elbow and Shoulder Pain in Youth Baseball

Pitchers," tracked 476 pitchers, from nine to fourteen years of age, on 146 teams throughout Alabama. The researchers interviewed the players and coaches regularly over the course of the season.

That study also produced scary stats. To develop a point of comparison, the researchers figured out how much a pitcher would complain after throwing between one and fourteen pitches. Then they compared how much more (or less) a pitcher was likely to experience elbow or shoulder pain after throwing more than that baseline number of times. Throwing twenty-five to fifty pitches increased elbow and shoulder pain only slightly (3 and 15 percent). But the results turned alarming when the pitcher threw fifty to seventy-four pitches (21 and 23 percent), and seventy-five to ninety-nine pitches (35 and 52 percent).

The researchers also wanted to see the effects of throwing all season long. The point of comparison here was throwing a total of one to 200 pitches. Elbow and shoulder pain increased dramatically for pitchers throwing 201 to 400 pitches (63 and 65 percent), 401 to 600 pitches (181 and 134 percent), and 601 to 800 pitches (234 percent and 190 percent).

These kinds of statistics are dramatic, but don't often have much effect on coaches, pitchers, and their families. It's a little like the Surgeon General's pronouncements about smoking or obesity. The warnings are so abstract. The odds of long-term problems don't usually motivate people to change their behavior right away.

Only one team's pitchers threw less than the research shows is safe and advisable. In its three games, Russia's pitchers made eight appearances in the series, throwing fifty-five, forty-three, fifteen, thirty-eight, forty-six, twenty, thirty-four, and thirty-three pitches. Not a single pitcher ever came close to the danger zone of seventy-five or eighty pitches.

———•◆•———

The pressure to use an ace pitcher just once more—*one* more batter, *one* more inning, *one* more game—increases as the team advances closer to Williamsport. Using an ace, even when he's tired from a summer of throwing, can determine whether the team has a chance to make it all the way. The baseball cliché about playing "one game at a time"—which these guys *believe*, and which *works*—often leads coaches to sacrifice everything for the immediate challenge.

I met Mike Schweighoffer, the pitching coach for the all-stars from Farmington, Connecticut, during one of the state's district tournaments.

Farmington was widely considered the best team in the New England regional tournament. A star at Trinity College in nearby Hartford, Schweighoffer pitched in the Los Angeles Dodgers' chain from 1985 to 1988. As a minor leaguer, his teachers included Hall of Famer Sandy Koufax.

Farmington's ace pitcher, David Weigard, beat Maine, 5–0, in the tournament's opener. Schweighoffer wanted to take Weigard out early since the win was so easy and the team might need to use his arm a couple more times in the tournament. But manager Bill Spracklin said no.

"Look at the scoreboard," Spracklin told Schweighoffer. "He's pitching a no-hitter." Weigard gave up two hits, but achieved another milestone—getting all eighteen outs on strikeouts. He threw eighty-two pitches, not an excessive pitch count. But what if the game was 1–0, and what if the Mainers worked deeper into the count? Schweighoffer didn't say whether he would have let the young pitcher stay in and throw 100 or more pitches.

The team from Connecticut—which dominated pool play with four straight wins—lost to Maine in the semifinals. Months later, parents criticized the coaches for not using Weigard in that game.

"We've been reminded many times that we could have done things differently," Schweighoffer laughs. "More now than at the time, parents and others say, 'Why didn't you use David?' But we just aren't going to do that, because of his arm. We monitor his pitch count, and he threw something like 155 pitches in two games. We made a decision that we weren't going to jeopardize his career. There was a 99 percent chance that he would have been fine, but that other 1 percent chance is what I worry about."

A practical concern played a part in the decision to hold Weigard back. If he pitched in the semifinals, he would not have been available for the championship game two days later. "We use a decision tree to figure out what to do at different stages," says Schweighoffer, an executive with a bank.

Connecticut allowed a pitcher to throw a lot of pitches for the sake of a landmark game—a no-hitter or an eighteen-K game. The team from Maine lost its top pitcher because of its desperation to quell a rally.

Maine's Westbrook Little League all-stars started the regional tournament 0–3 but then won the next three games to take the New England championship from Connecticut and Rhode Island. In the semifinal game between Maine and Connecticut, manager Rich Knight turned to his top pitcher, Zach Gardiner, with the bases loaded and one out.

"That was the season for us," Knight says. "On the second pitch, I said, 'Whoa, he's really bringing it.' There were 6,500 fans there, all from Connecticut, all cheering for them. That pumped him up. The guy from Nutmeg TV [the local cable network] told me he was throwing seventy [miles an hour]. I said I don't think so. That's five miles an hour faster than he's ever thrown before."

In the excitement of the moment, Gardiner's adrenaline carried him beyond his capacity—baseball people call it "reaching back for something extra"—and he blew his arm out in the process. After the game, Gardiner told Knight he was finished pitching for the year. Gardiner played in Williamsport, but he stayed off the mound. The injury affected his hitting and fielding. Originally, Knight thought Gardiner suffered from tendonitis or a strained muscle. But when the team returned home, a specialist said it was a problem with his growth plate. He prescribed rest.

———————— •◆• ————————

Throwing too many pitches not only tires the pitcher and causes pain, but also distorts his pitching motion. And by the time his coach notices anything wrong with this mechanics, it might be too late.

A pitcher needs exquisite control of a long sequence of movements—maintaining balance, kicking the leg, rearing back, rotating the trunk and torso forward, whipping the ball forward, landing on the mound—and any disturbance can throw the whole sequence off kilter.

When any part of the "kinetic chain" falters, the pitcher eventually puts too much strain on his shoulder and elbow.

"I would keep an eye on the pitcher and look to see when his elbow drops," Mike Ludwikowski, the Little League trainer whose day job is outreach coordinator for athletic training services at the Susquehanna Health System Sports Medicine Center, told me. "That's when he's going to put a lot of strain on his arm, and his elbow especially. It's not always easy to see, especially when you have your eye on the result, getting the batter out. But if that's your priority, you can do it."

But that's not always possible. Michelangelo Celestina, one of the Curaçao coaches, told me he was surprised when he watched videos of the games afterwards. In one game, the team's second-best pitcher struggled to get the ball over the plate. Celestina was puzzled when he watched Sorick Liberia from the dugout, missing, missing, missing. Liberia had superb control all summer long. And his motion looked okay from the bench. But when Celestina started looking at videos, he noticed *serious* flaws.

When the game is going on, when you're depending on a pitcher to come through for you, when you don't have a lot of pitchers who can take over when one pitcher falters—and when you see the game from the odd angles of the bench—you're going to miss a lot.

The impact of throwing too much, and using the wrong kinds of pitches, accumulates over time. Every pitch produces what the researchers call a "microtrauma." And those traumas accumulate. At some point—no one knows quite when—the microtraumas become a macrotrauma.

People debate these points, but some experts advise avoiding pitching *altogether* until a boy fully develops his bone structure in adolescence. Rick Peterson, the pitching coach of the New York Mets, says he will not allow his son to pitch at all until he turns fourteen or fifteen.

Whatever approach teams take, doctors agree that joint pain is a clear sign to stop pitching. *Shut it down.* Muscle soreness is a normal, even healthy, part of physical development. As long as the athlete gets enough time to heal the small tears in his muscles, he will get stronger when he feels muscle pain from exertion.

But joints are another matter. Any pain in the shoulder or elbow—as opposed to simple tiredness—is probably a sign of an overuse injury.

———— •◆• ————

It's not just the number of pitches, but also the *kinds* of pitches that threaten young pitchers' development and future prospects. Throwing a curveball risks ruining any young pitcher's arm.

To throw a curveball, the pitcher brings his arm around like a fastball, but changes his motion when he releases the ball. Instead of letting the ball fall out of the hand with a bottom-to-top spin, with his hand in front of his body, the pitcher snaps his wrist to get a top-to-bottom spin. The pitcher twists his wrist and elbow. The ball falls out of his hand between the index finger and thumb.

Experts agree that pitchers shouldn't throw the curveball until they reach puberty. The rule of thumb is that they should throw just fastballs and changeups until they can shave, a sign of physical maturation.

Most coaches say they cannot *not* let their pitchers throw breaking balls. The curve has become the essential pitch for success in Little League and other youth tournaments.

The research on curveballs is as dramatic as the research on pitch counts. ASMI's 2006 paper found that throwing curves increased the chance of elbow and shoulder pain (14 and 52 percent), as did throwing sliders (86 and 77 percent). Throwing a changeup actually reduces the chance of elbow and shoulder pain (12 and 29 percent).

Only one manager at the Little League World Series—Alexey Erofeev of Russia—said he would not allow his pitchers to throw a curveball.

"We throw only the fastball. Sometimes we use a changeup," he told me through an interpreter. "But the danger to the elbow, why would we have them throw a curveball? We fear about the health, we want them to have a long life in baseball. It's important to play safe and grow, grow, grow. By fourteen, we can teach the curveball, but not before."

In the Little League World Series, just saying no to the curveball is tantamount to unilateral disarmament.

For years, coaches have taught the "Little League Curve" as a way to have the best of both worlds—a breaking pitch that doesn't cause too much strain. Also known as the twelve-to-six curveball because the pitcher throws the ball over the top, the Little League Curve is released like a football spiral. The hope is to get the pitcher to let the ball tumble out of his hand, rather than putting too much stress on his arm with a snap.

"If you're going to throw a curveball—and I know that some coaches and players are going to do it, no matter what you tell them—there's a way to do it with less strain," says Mike Ludwikowski, the Little League World Series trainer. "Throw the ball over the top, without twisting your whole arm and putting your elbow out front. Throw it over the top, like a football. Get a good spiral on it."

Little League coaches say they need a pitcher with a curveball to win national or even regional tournaments. Without the curveball, hitters will learn how to time fastballs. That could do even more damage to pitchers' arms, since they will throw too many pitches, get frustrated, and try to be too fine with the location of pitches.

"Every kid I teach the curveball to, I keep away from that twisting and yanking and jerking," says Rick Hale, the manager of the team from Owensboro, Kentucky. "We don't have to get as many rotations as long as you get the perfect rotations. I try to teach my kids to throw the twelve-to-six and gravity helps you there." But the pressure to win subtly changes the calculus. "As we go further, and we have a kid who can do that, I might tell him you can get a little more of this on it—dropping the hammer, giving it everything you got. I'd be a liar if I didn't try to get them to put a little snap on it."

The problem with the football spiral, says Marty Miller, is that it tends to be a "lollipop curveball." The ball rides a parabola to the plate. It doesn't really break sharply. You might as well just throw the ball more softly.

Every year, more and more pitchers want to throw a hard, biting curve. To do that, you have to twist the shoulders and elbows and wrists to make the ball come out of the hand like a finger snap.

———•◆•———

Rick Hale squirmed when I asked about whether throwing too many pitches, or using the curveball, might deprive a pitcher of his potential for a college or pro career.

Of course, you can't bet on anyone in Williamsport having a shot at a career in baseball. So maybe it's not so bad to let them play their hardest when they have a chance at glory as a kid. If a player advances as far as a state, regional, or national tournament, letting a pitcher throw 100 pitches or snap off a curveball gives him a chance to win it all. The joy of that moment will live forever.

"My little brother David was a prime example," Hale says. "He was not going to be a major-league pitcher. What's he going to play? High school, at best. He had more fun playing Little League baseball and striking out fifteen Southern Owensboro players than anything he did in his whole life. A guy has to be realistic about a kid's future."

In the end, pitchers resort to the curveball to win a big game. Teams that eschew the curveball cut themselves out of the action.

"I don't think they can do anything about a curveball," Hale says. "You're forced to use the curveball, just like you're forced to use your ace as much as possible. But then we don't advance, and it's over and we go home. Nobody got [to Williamsport] that didn't advance, and there's a lot of pressure to keep the thing going. I feel a little guilt over that because there is a balance between winning and doing what's best for the kids. If you want to advance, you have to do what you don't want to do."

"It's almost like in *The Godfather*," says Hale. It's probably not the literary allusion Little League wants to hear. "If they're going to [sell] drugs, we might as well have a piece of the action. If kids are going to throw the curve, we may as well get involved and try to teach them the right way."

Most managers in Williamsport say they aim to limit their pitchers to five or six curveballs a game. But those five or six curveballs have a way of expanding to ten or twelve, or even a couple dozen. The curveball has become the ultimate "out" pitch in Little League and other major tournaments.

And because all the other teams know it's an out pitch, you have to fool 'em. That means using it *before* you need an out pitch, to *set up* an out pitch. Before you know it, the curveball gets sprinkled into every pitch sequence against every batter.

———————•◆•———————

In the midst of the World Series, Steve Keener, Little League's CEO, announced a new study of possible rules changes to protect pitchers' arms. The most viable reform would be to restrict the total number of pitches a pitcher could make in a game and in a week. Little League's study will assess the impact of different pitch counts in fifty different affiliated leagues in 2006.

Then, in December 2005, Little League announced a new set of *optional* rules that all member leagues could use. The rules would set a limit of eighty-five pitches in a day for eleven- and twelve-year old players. The rule also prescribes rest between pitching appearances— four full days for pitchers throwing more than sixty pitches, three days for forty to sixty pitches, two days for twenty to forty pitches, and one day of rest after throwing anything less than twenty pitches. Little League officials say they would consider making the rules mandatory after the 2006 season.

By the time teams started practices for the 2006 season, 400 Little League organizations adopted the pitch-count rule. Over the course of the year, they agreed to report regularly to researchers to determine the effect of the rule. Keener said the rule's greatest impact would be educational.

"What we hope it does is serve notice, tell Mom and Dad that there's a reason for this, and one of the reasons is that if you happen to have this very gifted youngster, if you want this young person to pitch when he's seventeen or eighteen years old, you might want to think about how often he's pitching at a younger age."

Still, Keener acknowledges, the rule cannot limit a Little Leaguer's pitching on travel teams. In fact, Little League's pitch counts might actually make it easier to push a player harder on travel teams. But Keener is hoping that an explicit rule will send a powerful message to protect young arms. Using a pitcher for the maximum number of pitches in Little League and then using him on a travel team, Keener says, "almost borders on child abuse." He adds, "That's where we need to make people aware." Education, he says, is the answer.

But it might be the best tool Little League—or any youth baseball organization—has to protect young arms.

———————•◆•———————

Too many pitches might have cost the team from Vista, California, a chance at the Little League World Series championship. And they knew it before they ever got to Williamsport.

They knew it because of an awful popping sound in Nathan Lewis's left elbow in the fourth inning of the team's West regional championship game against Tracy, California. At the time, Tracy was winning, 2–0. California's manager, Marty Miller, wanted to keep his ace southpaw in the game, and Lewis had no intention of leaving—no matter how awful his arm hurt. So he stayed in, Vista tied the game with two runs in the bottom of the fourth, and won it with five runs in the fifth.

Lewis went all the way. He was the guy who got mobbed on the mound when it was all over.

But on the car trip home, he was crying in agony.

All summer long, through the Vista's 20–0 run to Williamsport, Nathan Lewis was the team's clutch pitcher. Kalen Pimentel got most of the media attention with his record-setting hitting and pitching. He hit home runs until they stopped counting and on more than one occasion he struck out batters for all of his outs.

But Lewis was the pitcher who won all the championship games. The logic of Little League tournaments is that playing in the championship game is more important than winning it—because if you don't get there, you can't win. So R.B.V. used the overpowering Pimentel in the semi-final and Lewis in the final. And Lewis always won—in the district, state, sectional, and regional tournaments.

No one thought to get an MRI. The team had to get on a plane right away to travel from California to Pennsylvania.

Nate's father Jim remembers his son's pain after the game.

"I just thought he was getting tired," Jim Lewis told me later. "But when he gets tired, he's pretty crafty and moves the ball around. When he takes something off, he gets more movement on the ball. He felt something pop in the fourth inning but he didn't want to give the ball up to somebody else, and he battled through it. He was in excruciating pain. He couldn't move his arm. He never said that before. But he was gone in a day so I lost touch. The first game I saw, against Kentucky, he was only underhanding the ball from first base. It's one of those things.

How do you know?"

Nate Lewis has no second thoughts about pitching as much as he did in the summer of 2005. "I wanted to win that game," he told me. "I wanted to finish it. It didn't really hurt, but my velocity went way down, five or ten miles an hour." When I told him his dad said he was in awful pain in the car after the game, he said, "Well, I don't know."

When the team got to Williamsport, Marty Miller brought Lewis to see Ludwikowski. The Little League trainer decided that Lewis needed to strengthen his arm. So he had Lewis lift light weights. After a few days, Lewis reported that his arm wasn't getting any better. Marty Miller called his daughter Kerri, a master's student in sports training at Utah State University. "She told me to have him lay off the weights," he says. "She said it would be a disaster. He needed rest. So that's what we did."

Lewis pitched California's final game. Lewis looked good for the first three innings, holding Hawaii hitless. But he got tired and his motion started to wobble. Hawaii took advantage of errors and walks. Lewis left the game without retiring a batter in the fourth inning. He was charged with giving up two runs, one earned.

Royce Copeland was another California pitcher to experience arm problems after the World Series.

When Lewis got home, his arm still hurt, so he got an MRI at Tri-City Orthopedics. Dr. James Esch found a fracture and dislocation of the growth plate. Esch immobilized the shoulder and told Lewis to avoid all physical activity for three or four months.

"If I knew he had a broken shoulder, I might have had him in a soft spot [position], but not pitcher or catcher," Marty Miller told me later.

I asked Nate Lewis if he had any regrets. "I just wish I wasn't hurt in the U.S. championship game," he said. "I wanted to show what I could do. I didn't show who I was."

Nate and Jim Lewis are both optimistic about the future. "He's throwing *gas* right now, just playing catch," says Jim. "He'll throw twenty or thirty pitches at a time. He's stronger than ever."

California's number three pitcher, Royce Copeland, also visited the doctor when he returned to California. His MRI found a light fracture in his elbow, forcing him to not pitch for a couple of months.

"Royce pitched like crap but he wouldn't tell me anything," Miller grumbled.

Copeland says he knew something was wrong with his arm in Williamsport. He went to the trainer regularly for treatment, but his arm hurt, off and on, the whole tournament. "It was a bummer my arm was hurt," he told me. "It hurt every other day. I went to the trainer and had it frozen. He was fun to be with. He would joke around."

Marty Miller acknowledges that managers often feel pressure to use pitchers with sore arms, but he thinks the problem lies in the sheer number of games some teams need to play to get to the World Series. Somehow, he says, the playing schedule needs to be reduced and all the teams in Williamsport need to play the same number of games.

"Hawaii played fourteen games to get where they were, and we played twenty. Take six games off the schedule and you have a bunch of guys who are a lot more rested. Take six games away and that's two less games for the pitchers. Maybe Nate Lewis doesn't hurt his shoulder. And it's even worse with some of the other teams there. To me it's not fair that Curaçao only had to play seven games to get there. Kalen Pimentel pitched more complete games than Curaçao played all the way. You do get burned out and tired."

For the record, Hawaii's Layton Aliviado dismisses that argument. "We play ball all year, like they do," he says. "That's not it. We just have more guys who can pitch. Almost everyone on my team can pitch. That's the difference."

For what it's worth, Aliviado uses more pitchers in games than other teams. He starts his ace, Alaka'i Aglipay, as often as possible, but he often removes him after an inning. "The first inning is the most important," Aliviado says. "Sometimes I just want Alaka'i to get us off to a good start." Kind of like a closer in reverse.

Alaka'i Aglipay and Sorick Liberia (above) provided star power for Hawaii and Curaçao. The Japanese team was built on strong pitching, defense, and baserunning.

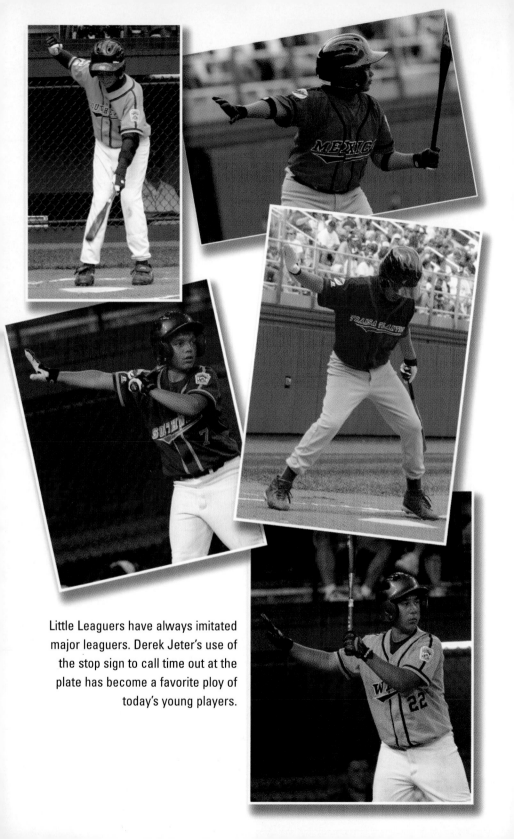

Little Leaguers have always imitated major leaguers. Derek Jeter's use of the stop sign to call time out at the plate has become a favorite ploy of today's young players.

The also-rans in the Little League World Series—including teams from Iowa (top) and Mexico and Guam (below)—still enjoy moments of glory in Williamsport.

The families of the two teams in the 2005 Little League World Series championship game—Ewa Beach, Hawaii, and Willemstad, Curaçao—traveled from their island homes to watch their boys play.

Opponent/Date	Pitcher	Number of Pitches
Pennsylvania/Aug. 19	Alaka'i Aglipay	12
	Quentin Guevara	50
	Vonn Fe'ao	19
	Kini Enos	12
Iowa/Aug. 21	Alaka'i Aglipay	11
	Kini Enos	83
	Vonn Fe'ao	4
Florida/Aug. 22	Alaka'i Aglipay	69
Louisiana/Aug. 25	Kini Enos	64
	Quentin Guevara	14
California/Aug. 27	Alaka'i Aglipay	88
	Vonn Fe'ao	6
	Quinten Guevara	14
Curaçao/Aug. 28	Quinten Guevara	60
	Kini Enos	23
	Vonn Fe'ao	34

———•◆•———

The wrecking of young arms is a morality tale that needs villains. Little League's villains are the travel teams that have come to dominate youth baseball in America. The travel teams point the finger right back at Little League.

Maybe they're both right.

Maybe the problem is the professionalization of childhood, the development of leagues and tournaments that turn sports into a full-time job before a kid grows any facial hair and hears his voice change. Little League officials regularly attack travel teams for creating the problem of sore arms.

Little League baseball "is the only organization that recognizes the risks of said injuries and proactively addresses this concern through its rules and regulations regarding the number of innings a player may pitch in a week," says Chris Downs, one of Little League's PR men.

Outside Little League, he says, "there is a dangerous and reckless dis-regard shown by so-called 'elite' or 'travel ball' teams toward the health of its [sic] players. These programs are to blame for the increase of such injuries due to the fact that there are few, if any, regulations governing the number of games per week a player may play or how many innings a pitcher may pitch."

But supporters of the travel teams make an intriguing case that their approach to baseball might protect arms better than any rules and reg-ulations promulgated by the potentates who are in charge of Little League. Their *laissez-faire* approach says that when people are allowed to pursue their self-interest, without archaic or unnecessary rules, they will protect themselves.

It's Little League, with its elaborate tangle of regulations, that causes the most problems.

The argument has two parts.

First, Little League's catchment area of 20,000 people is too small to harvest enough pitchers needed for competitive games. Travel teams—and some other community leagues, like Cal Ripken Baseball—allow teams to recruit players from broader geographic areas. If you're forming an AAU team in Florida, you can draw from the whole state for players. So you're going to find lots of good strong arms, and you're not going to depend on one or two arms in must-win games and tournaments.

Second, the small footprint of the Little League field creates a power contest between pitchers intent on strikeouts and batters intent on close-your-eyes-and-swing home runs. Especially at critical stages in big games, pitchers reach back for something extra. They put too much of their bodies on the line to get the big out.

Because the outfield dimensions are short—200 or 205 feet to all fields—hitters swing for the fences. Other leagues have broader outfield expanses. The Cal Ripken World Series, for example, takes place on a field that extends 260 feet to center field. And the left-field wall reaches to a height of sixteen feet, so balls that reach the wall often stay in play. The bigger the field, the more pitchers are willing to let the hitters put their bat on the ball. Pitchers don't always try to blow the ball past hit-ters. That means fewer arm-straining fastballs and fewer curveballs, too.

Les Abato, the manager of the PONY League's powerhouse Mililani team in Hawaii, says the bigger field dimensions completely transform the game. "It affects all kinds of things about the game—the outfielder's speed, his arm, his positioning—and baserunning, too. There's just a lot more that happens with the bigger field. It's not just strikeouts and home runs, but the complete game—real baseball."

If Little League is looking for an effective rule change, it might consider increasing the distance between its bases from sixty to seventy feet and moving the fences back twenty or forty feet. (The outfield fences will go back twenty feet in the 2006 World Series, but not for any other tournaments or league play.)

For Little League, the answer seems to be one part regulation (pitch counts) and one part jawboning (attacking travel teams). Will that make a difference?

Most of the coaches and players I talked with like the idea of pitch counts. The possibility always exists for manipulation of the rule. If the umpires don't call a big strike zone, batters will do everything they can to go deep into the count and drive ace pitchers out of games early.

But if umpires do call a generous strike zone, pitchers will be less obsessed with strikeouts and batters will swing away and put the ball into play. And most teams will work to develop deeper staffs. "With pitch counts, teams are going to have to go to their third, fourth, and even fifth pitcher," says Don Copeland, father of a California pitcher. "That's what we thought our advantage was—we were four or five deep. But even we got tired by the end."

Jawboning, though, won't work. Lyle Gabriel is the coach of the San Diego Stars, one of the nation's best travel team organizations. He says that travel teams' broader geographic reach means they can bring more good pitchers onto a team. Most good travel teams, he says, have eight or more players who can pitch, so no one pitcher throws too much. Just as important, he says, is that coaches for travel teams know how to teach their kids. And he resents the charge that travel teams are the only culprits.

"There are too many stupid coaches wrecking kids' arms," he says. "That's the real problem."

Wanna trade?

Outside of baseball, one of the major diversions at the Little League World Series is pin trading.

CHAPTER 8

———•◆•———

Hustling

*N*O MATTER WHAT ATHLETES WEAR OR USE THESE DAYS, chances are it's stamped with the logo of a corporation. Every hat, helmet, uniform, wristband, and undergarment, every pair of socks and shoes, every pair of sunglasses, every bat, ball, and glove—everything is branded with a corporate logo.

And everywhere the players and coaches went during the Little League World Series—even when they ventured outside Little League's village—they were approached by corporate hucksters looking to give away their products. And get them on TV.

It's called "product placement." Advertisers for just about every consumer product in the U.S. today—computers, beer and soda, cereals, clothing, shoes—try to place their product in movies, TV shows, sporting events, festivals, and any place consumers' eyeballs can be found. PQ Media, a research company on media issues, estimates that product placement generated $3.45 billion in advertising revenues in 2004.

When Clint Tirpak took his family to McDonald's, a representative from Easton Sporting Goods approached his son Ty, a player on the Hawaii team. "They're not really supposed to do that. You're at McDonalds and they're coming up to you," Ty says. The older Tirpak told the corporate pusher to take a hike.

"The Easton people were everywhere, giving us bats, asking us to use bats in games," says Joe Daugherty, the father of a Kentucky player. "If we got a dent in the bat, they'd take it back and give us a new one right away. As long as we used the bats in games, that's all they wanted."

Near the batting cages, where all the teams went for refuge and for swings, the Easton representatives came bearing aluminum as well. Easton's drones approached Kaeo Aliviado as he waited for his turn with his Hawaii teammates. "No thanks," he sniffed. "That's not the bat we like. We use the DeMarini."

(Ah, Wilson's DeMarini, everyone's favorite bat in Williamsport. At BP, Guam's manager Shon Muna caught Sean Manley, the team's big hitter, trying to sneak the team's sacred DeMarini F-2, a weapon reserved for official games, into the batting cages. "What makes you think you can use that bat now?" he asked. "I asked and you didn't say anything," Manley answers, lamely. Muna paused for Socratic effect. "If I had $1,000 and you asked and I didn't say anything, would you think you could take it?" Muna asked. "No," Manley said. "Me either," Muna said. Busted.)

All over the Little League complex, players wore colorful long-sleeve undershirts from Reebok called UnderArmor. These synthetic shirts accent the thinness of even the strongest players' arms, but, somehow, they look cool. And feel cool, too, even in the hottest sun. The body moves like a woman's leg in hose. So the Little Leaguers wore color-coordinated shirts under their jerseys for all the world to see.

The Wilson people, meanwhile, pushed a line of glove prototypes. Wilson hauled a rainbow of leather to Williamsport, hoping to get one or two on TV. They got to Dalton West, a player for the all-stars from Owensboro, Kentucky. He agreed to give it a try. Before the games started he approached the supervisor of umpires to ask if it was okay for him to use a blue Wilson prototype in a game. The ump looked it over as if he were asked to throw a slab of spoiled meat on the grill. He wrinkled his nose, looked straight forward, and said no, pushing the glove away.

Don't blame Wilson for trying. Two years before, getting kids to wear Wilson helmets instantly transformed that market. Batting helmets have always been the least glamorous part of hardball haberdashery. Helmets represent fear, protectiveness, and constraint. Little League helmets, traditionally, are grotesque. One size does not fit all, the colors are awful, and the foam inside gets rancid and crumbles with the accumulated sweat of a season. Then, in the 2003 Little League World Series, Wilson gave players prototypes of a new helmet with an ergonomically modern design, with curves and air vents. The helmet was adjustable, so one size did fit all. And most important, stylistically anyway, the helmet's metallic colors—scarlet, royal, silver, forest green, navy, yellow, cardinal, and gold—almost looked custom made for any team's colors.

Every summer the "ice cream guys" travel from California to work the Little League World Series.

Fifteen of the sixteen teams in Williamsport wore the helmets on TV, and ABC and ESPN used the helmets as the transitional "bumpers" between commercials and the game. When one player happily skipped to first base after getting plunked in the head, broadcasters Brent Musberger and Harold Reynolds gushed about the lids. Wilson's phone lines lit up with requests. Wilson originally hoped to sell 20,000 helmets; before the end of the year, sales exceeded 100,000.

Not only did Wilson grab a bigger than expected share of an existing market, but the helmets created a whole new market. Time was when only teams bought helmets, about four or five at a time. Now, with the sleek looks and manageable price (about $20), every kid playing ball is a potential customer. Ka-ching.

◆

Corporations do not just try to get players to use their products. They do everything they can to ride Little League's Norman Rockwell image.

In the 2005 World Series, Little League had sixteen corporate sponsors. Ostensibly, these sponsors selflessly lend their support to the kids living the dream. Every product makes a tenuous "contribution" to the Little League ideal. New Era caps, Russell Athletic, and Wilson Sporting

Goods? All the smart-looking gear you need to play the game. Sunkist? Nutritious snacks. Ace Hardware? Tools for fixing up the local Little League field. CapriSun? "Hydrates kids better than water." Choice Hotels? Great for that endless summer of tournaments. Bank of America? Bryant Cooling Systems? Re/Max Real Estate? Snickers candy bars? Hmmm. The rationale *does* get a little strained.

The corporate presence at the Little League World Series was strong. Companies like Ace Hardware set up games to promote their name.

From its very first year of operation, Little League has depended on partnerships with business to help pay its expenses. Local companies sponsored Little League's first three teams in 1939. In 1947, Little League's founder, Carl Stotz, traveled by train to New York to request financial assistance from executives of Pepsi-Cola and U.S. Rubber. Stotz struck out with Pepsi, but succeeded with U.S. Rubber. After meetings involving a whole roster of vice presidents—including one who once helped Stotz settle a misunderstanding about his Aunt Maggie's pension checks—the company agreed to give Little League $5,000 toward the national tournament. Stotz also convinced the company to create a new shoe with rubber cleats suitable for boys baseball.

Before Michael Jordan revolutionized the sports shoe, Carl Stotz did the same.

Over the years, Little League has brokered deals with manufacturers who make products exclusively for Little League, which markets to its millions of players. Strengthened by its special congressional charter, Little League has parlayed its powerful brand name into a tool for raising money and raising its profile as the premier youth sports league in America.

———————•◆•———————

The newest Little League sponsor in 2006 was Subway, a fast-food chain. Steve Keener, Little League's CEO, called a press conference on the field of Howard Lamade Stadium to make the big announcement. On hand were the all-star teams of Montour and Mill Creek, Pennsylvania, executives from Subway, some PR people, and a few media stragglers.

And Jared Fogel, the man with The Pants.

The conceit for the Subway "partnership" is that Subway and Little League, together, can address the growing concern among public health professionals about childhood obesity. "Eat Smart, Play Hard" is the slogan for the three-year agreement.

Since 2001, when an advertising guy named Hal Riney heard about his astonishing success in weight reduction, Jared Fogel has become the face of Subway.

Riney worked for the Richard Cole Creative Agency in Chicago when he read an article in the *Indianapolis Star* about a college student who lost 245 pounds in less than a year by eating every meal at a Subway shop near Indiana University in Bloomington. Using Fogel in TV commercials, Riney thought, would set Subway apart from McDonald's and Burger King in the increasingly competitive fast-food business.

Fogel's story is every dieter's fantasy: eat fast food and lose hundreds of pounds at the same time.

For years, Jared Fogel got more and more depressed as he got fatter and fatter. He ate all day long—10,000 calories a day, lots of fat and sugar—and isolated himself from other students at IU. Finally, after his weight passed 400 pounds, he decided he needed to do something. He had tried to diet before, but always failed.

One day, eating at the Subway in the first floor of his apartment building, Fogel decided to try an experiment—only eat Subway's healthy line of sandwiches. He ate twice a day—lunch and dinner. He allowed himself a bag of baked potato chips and Diet Cokes. But the main course was always a sub—turkey and tomato in the afternoon, veggie in the evening, always hold the mayo. During the diet, he ate 1,400 or 1,500 calories a day.

From March 1998 to the following February, Fogel says he went from 425 to 180 pounds. His pants size went from a sixty to a fifty-eight to a fifty-six ... all the way down to a size thirty-four.

When he lost all that weight, a friend wrote about Fogel for IU's student paper. The Indianapolis paper picked up the story and the wires rewrote the story. That's when Hal Riney decided to give our fast-food nation a new face.

After test commercials aired in 2000 in Chicago, Subway decided to build its advertising campaign around Jared Fogel. In the spots, Fogel looks into the camera, holds up his size sixty jeans, and talks about how great he feels after losing all those pounds. He has also made appearances on *Today, Oprah,* and other TV shows.

Sales in Subway franchise increased from $3.8 billion to $4.5 billion from 2000 to 2001.

Fogel is a pleasant looking man, now thirty-four years old. Six feet, two inches, he now weights between 190 and 195 pounds, up from his post-diet low of 180. At the press event for the Little League partnership, he wore khakis and a Subway golf shirt. He approaches strangers with a midwesterner's modesty and ease. Given his past, he feels no need to get into perfect shape anytime soon. He jiggles a little when he moves. "It's very difficult to have a routine while traveling," he says. "Maybe down the road I'll get into real shape, once this dies down some."

Since becoming Subway's spokesman, he has spent 200 days a year on the road. He won't reveal his salary, but he says he's now comfortable for life. He's planning an "inspirational" book about his journey. He and his wife just bought a house in a suburb of Indianapolis, where he plans to settle when his run as spokesman ends.

"Activities like Little League can help get them out of the house and watching less TV and playing less video games," he says genially as he poses with his old pants and cameras click.

After all of the presentations—highlighted by Fogel hiding behind his old pants—it was time for the photo op. Fogel gathered the Little Leaguers for some exercise. "Let's start with some stretching exercises, just to show how easy it is," he told his young charges. The kids did ten toe-touches—toe reaches, really. Then it was fifteen jumping jacks. "Now what do we do?" he asked.

"Hey, can we run around the field?" a kid yelled.

"Yeah! Can we run around the field?" another cried.

Claudia Quintero, the PR woman, looked startled. Quickly, she corralled the boys. "Hey, you guys have worked up an appetite!" she said. "Time for sandwiches!" She brought a box to the right field line and got the kids to pose holding sandwiches forward. Then she shooed them off the field.

ABC and ESPN broadcast twenty-nine games of the Little League World Series. Broadcasters Bob Ryan and Harold Reynolds provide pre-game analysis before a game between California and Florida.

Any time Curaçao played on TV, the ESPN and ABC announcers talked about all the loot they got for winning the Little League World Series in 2004. All of the teams in Williamsport got free bats, hats, helmets, gloves, shirts, video games, candy, and more. The complex is like a rich kid's birthday party. But the winners *really* make out. In 2004, each player got, among other things, computers, printers, scanners, digital cameras, watches, rings, KFC for a year, McDonald's for a year, fifty-two six-packs of Pepsi, haircuts, and a savings account with the equivalent of $600.

This year's teams, vying for the championship, know about these prizes and are eager to find out what they get. "I'm waiting for someone to give us computers," said Layton Aliviado, Hawaii's manager.

Brent Musberger, the ancient broadcaster working the games for ABC, says that the gifts could jeopardize the players' amateur status. "Heh heh heh," he chortles. "Just kidding, folks."

———————•◆•———————

Little League has ended one form of hustling. The organization successfully squelched online gambling on the World Series in 2005. Nevada state law forbids betting on the Little League World Series. The Nevada Gambling Commission's Regulation 22.120 (a) bans betting on "any amateur non-collegiate sporting or athletic event." But the rise of the Internet has multiplied the opportunities for betting beyond legal gambling establishments in Las Vegas and Atlantic City and illegal bookies. Surveys have found 1,800 gambling websites in operation.

In 2003, some offshore websites accepted bets on the Little League World Series. "One might be interested (and one might be bothered) to know Japan was a four and a half-run favorite to beat Mexico on Thursday in a Little League World Series game," USA Today's Jeff Zillgitt reported. "The over/under [a measure of odds] was nine. Must have been some big sticks in those lineups. Massachusetts was a two-run favorite to beat Texas. The over/under was five and a half. Must have been two great pitchers on the mound."

Little League officials protested. CEO Steve Keener said he'd ask law-enforcement agencies—beginning with the Justice Department—to shut down the kiddie gaming shops. One of the websites that took bets on the LLWS, pinnaclesports.com, decided against taking wagers in 2005.

But other websites say betting is perfectly okay, as long as it's dressed up to look like trading in the futures market.

Intrade.com, a web firm based in Dublin, offers a brokering service for people who want to trade "contracts" on outcomes of all kinds of events—in politics, business, entertainment, weather, and even Little League World Series games. Mike Knesevitch, a partner at Intrade, says it's like trading futures on the New York Stock Exchange. Since it started in 2001, Intrade has brokered close to $1 billion in "trades."

Someone trading on the Little League World Series might learn, for example, that other traders, collectively, have estimated that Curaçao has a 62 percent chance of beating Japan. If you "buy" the "contract" for Curaçao, you stand to make 38 cents for every dollar's worth of contract you buy. That 38 cents represents the 100-percent chance that Curaçao has established by winning and the cost of the contract that you bought. Minus, of course, Intrade's fees.

Intrade accepts trades of contracts as games progress. "Say it's the bottom of the fifth inning and you have a runner on with no outs. There's a probability of scoring .9 runs," Knesevitch says. "But if you get him to second base, the probability goes to 1.24 runs. People buy and sell contracts as the event is going on."

Intrade didn't take any "trades" for the Little League World Series in 2005. But the site takes "trades" for all kinds of amateur sporting events. And there's no reason why the company would avoid Little League "trading" in the future. If demand calls, supply will respond.

—————————•◆•—————————

The Little League brand doesn't have the cache of the New York Yankees or Manchester United. But it's the ultimate symbol of youth sports in America. Like Coca-Cola and Band-Aids, Little League has become a generic term as well as a brand name. Little League officials know the importance of their brand, and they do everything to promote and protect it. To excess.

Getting press credentials took some effort. When I first called asking for access to the press area, I was told to deal with the marketing people. But I'm just a writer, I said. Well, there might be some fees associated with any book I might want to write. After all, Little League is a federally chartered organization with its right to protect its trademark. But I didn't want to use Little League's logo or trademark. I just wanted to cover the event as a journalist.

Little League gives out 600 to 700 credentials a year. Most of the reporters cover hometown teams. A few, like the *New York Times*, do broader pieces about the whole experience. All I wanted, I said, was the same credentials as *Times* or *Williamsport Sun-Gazette* reporters. Nothing more, nothing less.

I got it, but grew increasingly intrigued by the secretive approach that Little League took about its events. Getting even basic information out of the organization proved difficult. You'd think I was asking the Yankees for their scouting reports.

A reporter from the *San Diego Union-Tribune* named Kevin Gemmell asked Little League officials for a copy of the rulebook. He was told, no, you can't have that. He pressed for three days. Finally, he published a note in the paper about Little League's withholding behavior, which quoted a flak's explanation: "Because you could distribute them. Then everyone would know the rules." He finally got what he wanted, and the information contained no top-secret information. Was that so hard?

A few months after the World Series, I emailed Lance Van Auken, Little League's communications czar, a question about how leagues conduct player drafts. The draft shapes the league's approach to all-star tournaments. In most leagues serious about the Little League World Series, teams draft players just once and then keep their players for as long as they're eligible. In many leagues, the core of the all-star team plays together on the same team. The league champion's manager usually manages the all-star teams, too.

But Van Auken wouldn't answer my question. "The draft options (which cover several pages of a copyrighted publication) have no bearing on the Little League Baseball World Series, or the teams that play in it," he wrote in an email.

Then Van Auken warned me about using Little League's trademark: "Keep in mind as well, that any use of the federally-registered trademarks 'Little League,' 'Little League World Series,' 'Little League Baseball World Series,' etc., as the subject for a book, television program, movie, etc., require the written approval of Little League International."

Here we go again. This is what the self-help books call "controlling behavior."

Later, I wanted to talk to the people who play Dugout, Little League's official mascot. Dugout is a brown rodent designed by the Disney Company in 1980. Over the course of the World Series, Dugout dances with players and fans, poses for pictures, hurls T-shirts and other giveaways into the stands, and wanders around the complex. Dugout wears a series of costumes for between-innings antics—there's Dugout as a cowboy, as Elvis, as a disco dancer, as Uncle Sam, and, of course, as a Little Leaguer.

I wanted to talk with the bodies inside the costume to see what they could tell me about the kids' experience of the World Series. But when I left a phone message with one of the people inside the rodent, a Little League official called to tell me the mascot was off-limits. After answering a few basic questions, he told me that "we're not comfortable" with any other questions. Goodness. What's going on between Dugout and the fans that is such a secret?

From their first moments in Williamsport, PR officials stage-manage the teams, arranging photo shoots, uniform fittings, parade buses, eating schedules. They screen emails that come into Little League headquarters and pass along the acceptable messages to managers. And they lecture the teams about the dangers of talking to media. "There will be occasions when members of the media ask for interviews. All interviews should be cleared with the manager, coaches, and/or the parents," says Chris Downs.

Fair enough. Kids need to be protected against pushy reporters. Most coaches and parents were thrilled to have their kids talk to reporters. It was part of the "big league" environment of the event. And no reporter I saw was trying to tar a kid with scandal.

The media people who *were* intrusive came from the Disney Company, which pays Little League $1.25 million a year. ABC and ESPN cameras were often one or two feet from the players' faces—before, during, and after the games. During one difficult loss, the kids from Curaçao sat on the edge of the dugout. (That, by the way was illegal; they're supposed to be inside the dugout. Where's my walkie-talkie?) The kids were crying, fearing they might not have a chance to repeat as champions. About a foot away was a TV camera, following the tracks of their tears.

———————•◆•———————

"Wanna trade?"

The hustling spirit surfaces earlier than you might think.

A six-year-old girl marched up to a teenaged boy and initiated a transaction. The boy responded as if they were peers.

"Yeah, okay, what do you want? What do you have?"

"I'm looking for cartoon characters. You can have anything in my book except the Snickers. I'm looking for a set of the Snickers jerseys."

At the farthest section of the plaza near Howard J. Lamade Stadium stood a white tent with eighteen picnic tables, lined up in six rows of three. At any given time, from 100 to 400 people shuffled around looking for market opportunities. Many of them carried large floppy notebooks specially produced for the occasion; the pages in the books are cloth and enable users to attach the pins easily.

Kids aged seven to fifteen years dominated the tent. But the rulers of the tent were older men and women, anywhere from thirty to fifty years of age. While the kids moved around from table to table, the adults sat at their stations and waited for traders to come to them.

Pin trading is the most enduring tradition of the Little League World Series. The only rule governing tent transactions is that no money may exchange hands. Most teams coming to Williamsport create small lapel pins—usually about the size of a quarter, sometimes as wide as a golf ball or even bigger—to commemorate their teams and districts. Players arrive in town with floppy books, fat with the pins they got during the summer's tournaments. Pin trading offers an outlet for players to interact with each other, with other kids on hand for the tournament, and with adults. Some adults travel across the country to trade in the pin tent.

Pin trading started at the Olympic Games and has carried over to Little League and other youth tournaments. But it's probably bigger in Williamsport than anywhere else. The languorous pace of the tournament provides lots of opportunities to mill around the complex, wander over to the pin tent, and make some trades.

Harold Ewers, a forty-four-year-old man with a bushy red beard and balding head, travels from his home in Stockton, California, as many years as possible to trade pins in Williamsport. A yard foreman at Bambacigno Steel Company for the last eleven years, Ewers looks more like a gentle motorcycle gang member than a baseball fan. He's married with kids, used to coach Little League, and considers pin trading the ultimate

Pin trading has become a passion that brings people to Williamsport year after year.

way of meeting new people.

"I love to trade pins but I love to BS with people more," he says. "I like to be with the volunteers. I like cars, trucks, planes, characters, and certain district pins. A lot of people want every pin out there."

Ewers wore a red Dodge Motor Sports T-shirt, a black cap with an eight on it, and jeans. He pushed his round body into the restricted seat space of the picnic table and waited for business. He started trading pins since 1980 and has amassed a collection of 9,000 to 10,000 pins. He goes to the West Region tournament in San Bernardino, California, every year to trade pins. He went to the Little League World Series in 2001 but could not get back until 2005.

"I came a week early, went to Gettysburg and Washington, D.C., and then Atlantic City. I'm going to make a nice trip out of it," Ewers says. "I know a whole lot of people who are here, sixty or seventy at least. Once a year I'll get ahold of them and see what's going on. I like to go hunting—deer—and I'm missing opening weekend of archery season to be here. We hunt every spare moment we have. It gives you a chance to be alone with nature and collect your thoughts. But this is where I want to be now."

Every year, Ewers makes his own pins. He sketches out a rough design and sends it to a pin company. The company's graphics people send back a design based on his illustration, he tells him what he wants changed, and the two sides go back and forth until he's happy. Over the years, he's made twenty-five different pins. In recent years, he has made pins in sets. "If you buy 150, it's hard to trade them, but if people like the set they want all of them and then it becomes valuable."

Sets usually correspond with the teams in the World Series. Snickers, the candy bar company, makes sets of sixteen pins, one for each of the teams in the tournament. One of the sets displays the teams' names on jerseys; another uses images of baseball spikes.

In the days before games started, pin trading seemed more important for some players than the games themselves. Mitch Burns, a mop-headed kid on Canada's team, raced around the dorms with his floppy book of pins. Every time a new team arrived, he'd gather a couple of his teammates and race over to get the team's pins. He brought his book to the high cast-iron fence around the dorms and bargained with people outside. On the practice fields and around the complex, he chattered endlessly about pins.

Kids' innate abilities as merchants emerge instantly under the pin tent.

"A lot of these youngsters get savvy in a couple hours," Ewers told me. "Kids end up with better pins than most of the adults. It's the drive they have. Kids are sometimes very hard to deal with. They want the biggest, best thing you have every time. They're competitive. It's like a ball game to them. Winning is getting the best pin."

Pin trading also offers opportunities to flirt.

Miranda Alkire and Heather Higgins, both thirteen-year-olds from Rochester, New York, set up shop under the tent the first day it was open. Alkire's grandmother lives just outside Williamsport. She and her family visit every summer. She has been trading since she was five years old. This year she invited her friend to join her in Pennsylvania.

The girls are both attractive, outgoing blondes. They attend middle school and have started to date—and each met boys on Little League teams to spend time with. "We met in the tent," Alkire says. "One of them's really hot." She looks to her friend. "Both of them, actually." The romances were destined to be short-lived, but the girls didn't care. They were focused on the moment, with pins as just another means of starting conversations.

"Everyone in my family does it, and we make our own pins," Alkire said. "I like geckos, monkeys. My aunt makes Pennsylvania District Five pins. I have 400 pins."

At different times, the girls' romantic interests showed up at the picnic tables. Ryan Bergeron from Louisiana and Cody Webster from Kentucky slid into the seats near the girls. They didn't want to talk, though. They waited until the conversation ended and then led the girls off.

Pin trading also teaches basic lessons about marketing.

My photographer, Isabel Chenoweth, brought her two children, Walker, then ten years old, and Leila, seven years old, to Williamsport. To give them a diversion outside the games, we made our own pins before going to Williamsport. We used Isabel's Mac to make a crude design of a character we call Star Guy—a five-pointed cartoon character wearing a baseball uniform. Crude is the operative word here.

When we got to Williamsport, we realized that most pins are more sophisticated. They have slick cartoon characters, sometimes with textured surfaces on the metal or plastic face of the pin. But our pin was good enough to trade. Or so we thought.

With bags of 400 pins, the kids got busy proposing trades. But few people wanted to trade. Traders would look at Star Guy's rough form, wrinkle their noses, and say, uh, no thanks. A couple of older men traded with us, just to be nice. The kids got discouraged and gave up trading for a few days.

Then we had an idea. Why not just give the pins away to strangers? Leila and I walked along The Hill. I called out like a concessionaire at a ballpark: "Who needs the Star Guy pin? *Get* your Star Guy pin here!" Leila was embarrassed but the approach worked. Most people were so pleased to get a gift that they reached into their collections to give the kids something in return. That's how Walker and Leila got the most sought-after souvenirs in the tournament, the pins from Hawaii and Saudi Arabia. There's no way we could have gotten those pins any other way.

Giving away pins created demand beyond our hillside hawking. When

Isabel was photographing games, kids started approaching her. "Hey, you got one of those star pins?" She kept a big supply of pins in her camera bag to accommodate the growing demand.

Marketing 101.

———————•◆•———————

All one old guy wanted to hustle was a ticket to one of the final games. The last three games of the Series—the U.S. and international championship games, and the World Series title game—require tickets. But Little League gets enough requests that it takes a raffle to pass out the 10,000 ducats (minus tickets for VIPs and team families) fairly.

But Phil Gowdy, a seventy-seven-year-old retired construction worker, didn't send in an application. And now he's here to plead his case in person. He's waiting at a picnic bench like Dorothy outside Oz.

Gowdy has lived his whole life in Williamsport. His pink face looks out from a straw hat. He's missing most of his teeth. His lumpy body fills a gray T-shirt, loose pants, and orthopedic shoes. He holds a cane. He's been going to World Series games since they took place at the Classic Little League field across the river. You'd think they'd give the guy a lifetime pass.

While he waited for his meeting, he watched coaches and players and parents move back and forth between the dorms and the top of the hill overlooking Lamade Stadium. "Hey, where you from?" he asks. "You gonna hit a home run?" He spots someone else: "Hey, you play shortstop? Yeah? Good luck."

Between greetings—he wants to strike up a conversation, but no one wants more than perfunctory contact—he talked about how the Little League World Series has changed. "The locals don't come anymore," he says. "It's all outsiders. There are maybe 1,000 [locals who come to the tournament] and you can pick 'em out. It's because they moved it."

Gowdy's a supporter of Carl Stotz in the long-ago civil war that set purists against expansionists. "The big shots trampled all over him. They wanted to go international."

He chuckled and shook his head as he watched the Saudi players climb the steps. "How many steps are there?" he wondered aloud. One player ran down to count and came back with the answer: fifty-nine. "That's a lot of exercise," the old man said. The players noded and moved forward.

Three hours later, Gowdy walked out of the Little League administration building. He got his tickets. Now he was a happy old guy.

———— •◆• ————

Johnny Dee, whose father Donnie Dee
coordinates college chapters of the
Fellowship of Christian Athletes in
California, was at the center of Rancho
Buena Vista's faith community.

———— •◆• ————

CHAPTER 9

—•◆•—

Faith and Survival

*T*HROUGHOUT THE LITTLE LEAGUE WORLD SERIES, you couldn't help hearing earnest professions of faith. Wherever you looked—in the dugouts, on the field, in their dorm rooms, in tents pitched on the edge of International Grove—you saw players and coaches praying and praising the Lord for this great opportunity to honor His name by playing baseball.

Sid Cash, the bank executive who manages the all-stars from Maitland, Florida, talked about the "miracle" of his presence in Williamsport. "I had kidney stones and found a spot on my liver this summer and it's a miracle I'm here," he told me as his players took cuts in the batting cages. "After all we've been through, it's not my time...yet. I had to have a chance to see it through." After one win, he thanked "the good Lord, our savior Jesus Christ."

After he hit a home run, Vonn Fe'ao of Hawaii's Ewa Beach all-stars looked to the sky and made a sign of the cross as he approached home plate and pointed toward the heavens. That gesture has become common-place in sports, and Fe'ao was following the example of pros like Sammy Sosa. But he was also making a connection to two of the most important people in his life—an uncle who died a month before he was born, and another uncle who died just the year before.

Fe'ao's teammates and their families grew closer and more committed to prayer as the long summer of baseball drew to a close. The Hawaiians believed they were destined to win.

"I felt like nobody could stop them," Denise Baniaga, the mother of infielder Sheyne Baniaga, told me. "It was a spiritual something. We all go to church. Even though we're different religions, we still say the prayers every night and before every game. We knew that He was going to take care of everything. Prayer is so natural for them. It calms them down. They would be less nervous, they know that God is with them. Whatever happens, happens. The adults were more excited. We all cried. My auntie from California cried like somebody passed away. She made this bawling sound. She cried and cried and cried, and she's still crying."

The Hawaiians crossed a line that no other team dared to admit crossing. Here's how one father told me the team prayed: "Lord, we ask for a victory because you always told us, if you want it, you have to ask for it."

The Russian all-stars—the team from the former Soviet Union, which embraced atheism as a state religion—also prayed. On their day off, they went to Holy Cross Orthodox Church in nearby Loyalsock Township. When they walked into the church, the kids took off their hats, crossed themselves, and hushed. Take that, Karl.

And then there were the Californians. Led by a player whose father does missionary work on college campuses for the Fellowship of Christian Athletes, the Rancho Buena Vista all-stars made faith a central part of their personal training. They huddled on the field, stooped down on the mound before the first pitch of a game, and invited in a preacher to hold services before the American championship game.

———————— ◆ ————————

What's the connection between faith and sports?

I have always been a little cynical about that question. Most of the vocal Christian athletes are the ones who have to develop a paint-by-numbers morality to recover from drug rehab (think Darryl Strawberry) or privileged players who use religion to give their impossibly wealthy lives structure and meaning (think Curt Schilling).

Some of the jocks' ideas about God and Christ are laughable. Norm Evans of the Miami Dolphins wrote in his book, *On God's Squad*: "I guarantee you Christ would be the toughest guy who ever played the game. If He were alive today, I would picture a six-foot, six-inch, 280-pound defensive tackle who would always make the big plays and would be hard to keep out of the backfield for offensive linemen like myself. The game is 90 percent desire, and His desire was perhaps His greatest attribute." Jesus as goon.

Religion on the ball fields is nothing new. The nineteenth-century idea of "Muscular Christianity" promoted the belief that physical exertion on playing fields could be part of a higher calling. Corinthians 6:20 says: "Glorify and bear God in your body." By using your body well, you paid homage to the one who gave you that body. As the world became urbanized, young men had fewer opportunities to prove themselves physically—and no one around home to guide them. The factories pulled families off farms and men away from their homes. Sports became an arena for training in manhood and the display of manhood.

Muscular Christianity originated with a British reformer named Charles Kingsley who disdained what he considered to be the effeminate ways of the Catholic Church. The Catholics were so intent on salvation that they did not revel in their physical being. But God gave us bodies, which could express the capacity for joy every bit as much as the loveliest hymn, the most profound sermon, and the most selfless service.

At the turn of the century, the YMCA provided a place for young people to participate in a wide range of sports under an explicitly Christian value system. Leaders like Theodore Roosevelt argued that the physical tests of sports helped to build character, which was essential to promote American interests in the world. Roosevelt captured the spiritual essence of sports when he went to the Dakota Territory to live the vigorous life of a cowboy—his way of recovering from his young wife's death.

For many people of faith, sports is an ideal activity to transform the spirit. Religion has always been a central tenet of youth organizations like Boy Scouts and Little League. The Little League pledge, recited before games, begins with the words: "I trust in God."

Over the years, Jews and Muslims, atheists and agnostics, have complained about the Christian content of Boy Scouts and other organizations. These organizations make official statements expressing openness to all faiths and backgrounds, but the Christian content of their rhetoric remains.

But something *is* new. Religion once provided a moral prod for striving classes. Religious leaders embraced sports as a place to teach discipline, sacrifice, acceptance of pain, and learning how to win and lose. But in the last generation, religion has also been a way to fill the empty spaces of modern life. And nowhere are these problems more evident than sports.

The privileges and riches that sports offer have created a degraded world apart—a world of drug and alcohol abuse and sexual aggression, physical and emotional abuse, raunchiness and prejudice, excuses and blaming.

The culture of professional sports ripples down to the privileged and unaccountable lives of big-time college sports, down to the high schools and youth leagues. Everywhere, the ability to do something with the body confers special status. Exploiters lurk everywhere. Living in the bubble of youth sports can be disorienting as well as corrupting. Faith can provide an essential moral check.

Parents and preachers also feel a need to create a place apart to protect their children from the degradations of modern life found on the Internet, shock-jock radio, popular music, films, and video games.

Religion can teach athletes to control their egos and understand that their athletic gifts are just that—*gifts*—and not evidence of superiority.

———————— •◆• ————————

At the center of the R.B.V. faith community is Donnie Dee, the father of outfielder Johnny Dee and a former National Football League player. Dee gave his life over to Christ while he was a freshman at the University of Tulsa. He has devoted his life to bringing faith to athletes ever since.

Dee is the regional director for the Fellowship of Christian Athletes in southern California. The FCA is one of a handful of organizations created in the last half-century to use the glamour and visibility of sports to spread the gospel. Since athletes have become some of the best-known figures in American life, role models for people of all ages, they can become potent missionaries for the Lord.

Not only do athletes have the ability to reach broad audiences, but they are looking for some kind of meaning in their own lives.

Dee grew up in a sports-crazy household. His father Don played a season for the Indiana Pacers of the old American Basketball Association. He was part of the 1968 U.S. Olympic team—along with future NBA stars Spencer Haywood and Jo Jo White—that won a gold medal in Mexico City. The Dee household was full of enthusiasm for sports—and constant pressure to do well on the field.

Soon after arriving at Tulsa, the freshman players were subject to ritualistic hazing—eating gross food, drinking too much, taking mean dares. When Dee was approached by some upperclass players, who asked him to embrace Christianity, he thought it was part of the initiation rituals—getting sucked into sweet talk about Jesus, only to be exposed as a sissy before a horde of tough jocks.

But he decided that maybe Christianity offered something he was missing.

"For these guys, football was not the biggest thing in their lives, and that was new to me," Dee says. "I didn't have a clue what it meant to be a Christian, but I knew that they had something that I didn't have. So I said a little prayer, asked Christ to come into my life.

"There was a peace about them, about the way they held themselves. There was one guy who was going through some personal adversity and yet his whole world was not falling down around him. Ninety percent of the team was treating me like a rookie and abusing me in freshman initiation. I thought it was a setup, acting like they cared because they were getting ready to pull the rug out from under me, a big joke. But that never happened. That was new to me—their openness and generosity and willingness to walk with me."

The older players prayed together every day and taught him scripture. They answered his questions and helped him to see the connection between faith and the physical aggression he would need on the grid.

After graduating, Dee married his college sweetheart and played for the Indianapolis Colts and Seattle Seahawks. After leaving the NFL, he started working for the Fellowship of Christian Athletes. Dee's campaign has increased the number of college campuses with FCA chapters from twenty to over 200.

And when Jackie and Donnie had kids, they taught them the Christian values they learned through their study groups. And when Johnny became part of the Rancho Buena Vista all-stars, the youngster brought prayer to the playing field—an easy sell, since five of the team's twelve players already attended the same church, the North Coast Church in Vista.

A prototypical megachurch, North Church attracts 6,300 parishioners with a choice of service styles. Sermons get piped into different rooms to accommodate overflow crowds and different tastes—one room with electric guitars, another with Starbucks coffee in a café atmosphere, a third with country music, a fourth with an old-fashioned chapel setting and traditional hymns. But besides catering to the congregation's consumer tastes, the service also provides programming for kids of all ages.

"The church is very accepting of all people, and there's a real commitment to serving God," Travis Sybert, a youth minister, told me. "Once you're here, hopefully we're modeling good behavior, so you say, 'Dang,

I want to know more about who He is.' ... Living for Jesus Christ can be a lot of fun. We can do a lot of sports and still be serving God. Especially with the guys, through physical sports."

Sybert leads 300 junior high students in a variety of activities. He says two R.B.V. players, Johnny Dee and Royce Copeland, have established themselves as leaders.

"The R.B.V. team was outspoken," Sybert says. "It helps when you're not alone. It gave them more confidence, the sense that they also have support. They feel like they know other Christians at school, and we're supporting them. That's all they need, a little bit of confidence. They're drawn by who's cool. They can stand up to pressures. It was a team effort in that realm too.

"Johnny and Royce fit our connected kids. Spiritually they are totally seeking and growing, they are challenging themselves and asking questions. And you can see with their demeanor [that] they are accepting of others. They have more of a gentle spirit, and are less likely to judge others."

———————— • ◆ • ————————

R.B.V.'s overt embrace of faith—praying before games, praying on the field, thanking God for this and that after wins—started in the District 28 tournament. The manager and coaches walked to the plate for a pregame meeting with their counterparts and the umpires—leaving the players on the bench to wait. The team's star pitchers, Kalen Pimentel and Nathan Lewis, turned to Johnny Dee.

"Would you mind praying for us?" Pimentel asked. Dee said a simple prayer, thanking God for the opportunity to play and wishing that no one get hurt in the game.

The players on the team had talked about faith before.

When one of their former teammates was stricken with a brain tumor, the parents rallied to raise money to send him to specialists out of state. Seeing their friend unable to play brought home the message that they were lucky just to play. During their long run to Williamsport, that former player, Ian Kane, was one of the team's top supporters. As the other kids continued to develop physically, Ian's growth was stunted by two rounds of surgery and treatment. When the team started traveling away from home, Kane couldn't watch anymore because he cannot travel long distances in a car. But he saw the games on TV, followed the team's exploits on the Internet, and sent his friends emails and letters. He was also the keeper of the team's scrapbook.

California's manager, Marty Miller, comforts Reeds Reznicek after a difficult outing on the mound.

———————•◆•———————

The California team had other struggles along the way, and the R.B.V. faith community helped to carry the whole team forward.

One of the team's players, Danny Vivier, battled Tourette's Syndrome as the team advanced to Williamsport. The ailment was seriously disrupting his life a year before. Whenever Vivier experiences extreme emotions—positive or negative—he goes through bouts of constant ticking, murmuring, and hiccuping and suffers from intense headaches. His parents took Danny to a number of specialists before getting the diagnosis. Medications have helped to control the problem.

Tourette's creates a divided self. "Any disease introduces a doubleness into life—an 'it,' with its own needs, demands, limitations," writes the medical essayist Oliver Sachs. "With Tourette's, the 'it' takes the form of...a multitude of explicit impulses and compulsions: one is driven to do this, do that, against one's own will, or in deference to the alien will of the 'it.'"

Being part of an intense activity with a larger community of support can help to limit the damaging effects of Tourette's. Tourette's sufferers often perform well at actions requiring extreme concentration like sports. With an activity that concentrates the mind, Tourette's sufferers can strengthen the self in its battle with the alien "it."

Faith has been a critical part of the Viviers' coping with Tourette's. "Our learning and development during this thing comes out of our faith," says Dave Vivier, Danny's father. "Every parent has to work something like this through. Danny struggles with his faith but it's been a big help to him dealing with Tourette's. It's important for him to have something to believe in." Donnie Dee, the FCA activist, has been a major part of his faith. "Donnie is like a second dad," Dave Vivier says.

———————— • ◆ • ————————

Faith guided the father of another player during a life-and-death struggle just as the R.B.V. all-stars began practices.

Don Copeland was diagnosed with colon cancer when his son Royce was selected for the R.B.V. all-stars. After spending five days in the hospital, Copeland went straight to the team's practice field. And all summer long, he gave himself the assignment of scouting other teams that R.B.V. might play in tournaments leading to Williamsport. He'd get in a car and drive around southern California—down near San Diego, up toward Los Angeles, out in Orange County—and keep himself busy. Copeland says he never really feared for his life, but the team gave him something constructive to do as he went through rounds of chemotherapy.

And the families on the team prayed for him every day. Other parents volunteered to take Royce to practice and back. They made him meals twice a week to take some of the burden off his wife Lorelei. And they followed his lead, taking an upbeat attitude toward a disease that could have frightened his two kids.

In fact, Copeland didn't tell his kids he had cancer. He told them he was having problems with his stomach and doctors had the matter under control. Royce Copeland didn't learn his father had cancer until he was watching an ESPN broadcast during the regional tournament in San Bernardino.

Through it all, other families on the team helped out by not only dropping four-course dinners off at his house, but also by calling to see if he wanted a visitor or needed someone to run an errand. "They're always taking care of you," he says. "It's a big support group. 'Hey, Don, you want us to bring Royce to practice?' and 'We're going to have a prayer group for you.' They're always there, thank God."

———————— • ◆ • ————————

A longhaired kid from Hawaii named Vonn Fe'ao became one of the most memorable sights in Williamsport. As he approached home plate after a home run, Fe'ao pointed to the sky and made the sign of the cross. Sometimes he looked close to tears as he crossed the plate.

Yes, Fe'ao was imitating the brash big leaguers with the gesture. It's show biz. But Fe'ao also had a look of shyness and vulnerability on his face when he approached the plate and looked skyward.

"He really believes that his uncles up there are helping him out," his mother, Heather Fe'ao, says.

Over the summer, Fe'ao made a journey from anger and fear to acceptance and confidence. Part of that journey was about leaving his mother behind in the islands.

During the Little League tournaments back in Hawaii—the district, sectional, and state competitions—Fe'ao struggled as his mother Heather shouted encouragements from the sidelines. Fe'ao tightened up when he heard her. Heather stayed behind when the Hawaii team went to San Bernardino for the Northwest regional tournament. She had seven other kids to look after, and school was starting. With her out of earshot, he relaxed and hit the ball hard every day. And he kept hitting and pitching hard in Williamsport.

Fans of the team from Rancho Buena Vista Little League showed their support by face-painting handlebar mustaches like that of Marty Miller.

Every day, he talked with his mom on the phone and cried. It was the first time he had ever spent so much time away from her.

At twelve years, Vonn Fe'ao is still just a boy, but he's not so fragile and innocent anymore. He has some of the toughness and inner drive—and anger—of a grown man. View Vonn Fe'ao from some angles and he looks delicate and vulnerable. View him from other angles and he looks ferocious.

In the last year, he put on twenty pounds, mostly muscle. Fe'ao now stands five feet, seven inches and weighs 160 pounds. In the Northwest regional tournament, he was nicknamed Danny Almonte because no one could believe that he was still twelve years old. But the other players in the tournament fell in love with him, and followed him like an idol or an older brother. When Hawaii beat Oregon in the title game, the Oregon players insisted on being photographed with Vonn Fe'ao. There he stands in the middle of the picture, surrounded by eager Oregonians. They're so proud to be with Fe'ao, they could be members of the Red Hat Society posing with Angela Lansbury.

Fe'ao is a power hitter and a power pitcher. Unlike most Little League power hitters, he does not loop a long swing with the hope of connecting. He has the most compact, and most wicked, swing in town. His eyes burn. He's learning how to control his emotions. After some swinging strikes, you can see him refocus, channeling Deepak Chopra. Other times, he gets angry, squeezes the bat, and swings harder, channeling Ron Artest.

What he's trying to do is concentrate on the task at hand—pushing aside any thoughts that would interfere with his performance. Darryl Stevenson, his football coach, says he was struck by Fe'ao's look at the plate when a pitch came close to hitting him. "When the kid threw the ball too close to him, I saw Vonn's eyes. He just focused in and hung in there, and he thought, 'Now, how can I beat this person? What's the *one thing* I can do to beat this person?' I've seen that look a lot of times. It's what some call The Glare. But it's just Vonn trying to figure out how to control himself and do his job."

But the emotion is undeniable.

In the dugout, he barks. It actually sounds like a roar as he paces back and forth. When he does something big on the field, he talks smack to the other side. He uses Hawaiian slang to put down the other side without their knowing it. But he also has his gentle side. When he broke Ryan Hartley's finger with a pitch in Hawaii's game against Pennsylvania, he walked to first base to say he was sorry.

Always in the center of Fe'ao's consciousness is the man he was named for, his father's brother. The older Vonn Fe'ao spent time with a bad crowd in Oakland.

"Vonn Senior played every sport but never had talent," Heather Fe'ao remembers. "He played track, football, baseball."

On one awful night in Oakland, Vonn Senior got in a fight in a bar and was shot to death. Heather gave birth to Vonn a couple months later.

Sese and Heather Fe'ao talk often with Vonn about his dead uncle, who has become a mythical figure—flawed, foolish, inadequate in so many ways, but basically good. Vonn Senior was running with a bad crowd and it cost him his life. The lesson is that bad things can happen to good people. If you don't watch out, you can become part of something ugly and hateful and deadly.

"Vonn's constantly asking about his uncle," Heather says. "He knows that he died when he was just twenty-one. He wants to know what his uncle was like."

Sese Fe'ao, Vonn's father, moved to Hawaii from Tonga when he was fifteen. He played rugby but quit when he broke his ribs. Sese is as blocky and strong as a bank safe. Sese met Heather in California, where she grew up. But after the older Vonn's murder, they decided to leave the mainland. "We wanted a fresh start," Sese tells me. He's standing nearby, wearing a Che Guevara T-shirt, as Heather and I talk. "I used to work one or two months in Hawaii and go back and forth. But we finally decided to move everyone here."

Raising eight children—now aged from eight to twenty-three—has not been easy on a mechanic's wages. But the Fe'aos survive. When Hawaii advanced to Williamsport, Sese couldn't afford a plane ticket. One of Sese's brothers offered to pay gas and tolls and the two drove his truck from California. They wanted to surprise Vonn, but he suspected they were coming.

Vonn Fe'ao was a sickly baby, so Heather spent more time caring for him than her other seven kids. He still stays close to her, asks her wide-eyed questions that he can't ask of anyone else.

"He was a child that had problems," Heather says. "When he was born he was six pounds, and the other kids were eight pounds. He stayed behind in the hospital. He had an irregular heartbeat. The first year of his life, my life was nothing but catering to him. I had to watch to make sure he didn't get overexcited. So you could say Vonn's a mama's boy."

Just last year he lost another uncle, a man named Sitini Suguturange, who succumbed to a brain tumor. Uncle Sitini rooted for Vonn when he played baseball and football. When Sese and Heather Fe'ao couldn't afford uniforms or equipment, Uncle Sitini paid for them. He was one of the fundraisers for Vonn's teams, and he always told Vonn to keep working.

Fe'ao's teammates—Mike Memea, Ty Tirpak, Alaka'i Aglipay, Kini Enos—all say that he is the most religious player on a team full of believers. "When we pray before going to sleep, he's the last one up off his knees," says Tirpak. "Everyone else has gotten under the covers and he's still there, praying."

Playing in the Little League World Series changed him. He used to get angry at school and get in fights. By his own admission, he was quick to fight when he got into disputes. But he's calmer now. "Now I can just walk away," he says. His celebrity has changed the way his former tormentors treat him. "They're my friends now."

The fame of the Little League World Series offers new opportunities. High school coaches watched Fe'ao on TV and say they want him to play football or baseball for them. The Fe'aos are interested in Vonn going to Saint Louis High or Punahou, golf phenom Michelle Wie's school. But there are no guarantees. His grades have to be better. The clock on new opportunities could tick away before long.

"Of the two of us, I'm the pusher," Heather Fe'ao says. Sese, standing by, smiles broadly and nods. "It's because I see potential. God doesn't give everyone athletic talent. My son was blessed to be given that kind of talent. I want him to take it as far as he can."

———— • ◆ • ————

The fates tested another member of Hawaii's family with cancer right before the team made its long journey to the promised land of Williamsport. Clint Tirpak, the father of Ty and one of the architects of the West Oahu Little League's all-stars, got diagnosed with cancer on December 2, 2004. During lunch that day, he experienced a sharp pain that made it difficult for him to get through the day, so he went to the hospital for tests.

Surgery to remove a testicle was moved up two days when Tirpak collapsed in church. The surgery at the Straub Clinic and Hospital was successful and doctors monitored his blood for four months. Everything looked good until the final test in April 2005, as Little League's regular season got into full swing.

"They said, 'I see something on the CAT scan, we need to do chemo,'" Tirpak said later. Doctors found a tumor on his lower abdomen.

Because Tirpak wanted to be part of the team's run to the Little League World Series, he decided to take the most aggressive chemotherapy schedule and to isolate himself at home to avoid any infection. "The whole immune system was shot," he says. "No one was allowed in the house and I didn't want to go out because my goal was to get back. I kept telling the doctor that I had to get back for the state tournament."

That kind of isolation meant no possibility of participating in family activities—his forty-first birthday, his wedding anniversary, Memorial Day weekend, and other red-letter days.

Chemo took three months. Each intravenous treatment lasted eight hours. Treatments took place for four weeks, five days one week, two the next.

After a long struggle with testicular cancer, Clint Tirpak was able to join the team from the state tournament through the championship celebration.

When he wasn't getting chemo, Tirpak stayed home, sealed off in his bedroom, sleeping and following the progress of the Little Leaguers via telephone and videos. Andy Kam delivered a play-by-play account of games on his cell phone and Jesse Aglipay taped the team's games.

Tirpak's eighty-year-old father-in-law, John Van Valkenburg, stayed with the Tirpaks to help with his windows business and haul pitching machines and other equipment to the baseball fields. He stayed until Tirpak was healthy enough to rejoin the team at the state tournament in Hilo. Zachary Rosete's father Jerry took over his coaching duties. He stepped away when Tirpak was healthy enough to rejoin the team.

Baseball provided a welcome distraction for Ty. Teammates and coaches say the skinny, angular kid was constantly worried by his father's cancer. He couldn't get it off his mind, except for the moments his mind was in the game. Having an outside goal was an essential distraction from his father's ordeal with cancer.

Clint Tirpak felt strong enough to watch the final two games of the district tournament from his truck, parked beyond the outfield fence at the field in Ewa Beach. "It was good to see the game live," he says. "I watched it with binoculars. The kids came by the truck to say hi."

It wasn't until after the district tournament, around the Fourth of July, that Tirpak got the final word from doctors that he was clean. Then he emerged from his isolation and joined the team. Still, he tired easily. After games in Hilo, he went to the hotel to sleep. He lost twenty-five pounds during the ordeal and went bald. Usually a vigorous man, he was gaunt.

Layton Aliviado looked at him and said, "Wow, now you really *are* my whitest friend."

Over the run to Williamsport, Tirpak looked like a Chia Pet growing hair and slowly coming to life. But once he was back with the team, he forgot about his battle with cancer and stoked the team's emotions. While Layton Aliviado told the players what they needed to do—and the consequences if they didn't do it—Tirpak expressed the team's fighting spirit. He shouted in the dugout and on the field, where he coached at first base. He looked for things to use to get the players emotionally involved—another team's nonchalance or arrogance, a player's strength or weakness. If Aliviado was the brains and the organizer of the team, Tirpak was often its emotional soul.

When I talked with Tirpak at his window manufacturing company, he was as jumpy as anyone I've seen. He was wearing one of those yellow wristbands that Lance Armstrong, another testicular cancer survivor, made into a fashion statement. He leapt up from his desk, imitated players, gestured, and leaned in to emphasize a point. A lot of energy got tamped during the chemo. And now it was still spilling over, long after the World Series was over.

Tirpak's explanation for his recovery is simple: "God pulled me through."

When he recovered, he didn't pray as much for his health as for the team to win.

As his friend Andy Kam said over and over, "You have to ask for the win when you pray." Now that his life-and-death battle was over, the team needed a different kind of outside assistance.

———————— • ◆ • ————————

Sometimes, survival is less about faith and more about just learning how to solve petty problems. Even when sights are raised to the mountaintops, life still takes place mostly in the valley.

When you live on the road with a dozen other people—whether you're athletes or musicians or actors or evangelists—you're going to get sick of each other once in a while. You're going to fight. The qualities you once found endearing are going to become irritating. Jokes that were funny during the first week on the road are going to be annoying during the sixth or seventh week.

Just ask Rick Hale.

Months after returning home from Williamsport—where, for the second year in a row, his team lost three games in a row—Hale was trying to understand the pressures that go along with playing a boy's game on an international stage. He reflected on the pressure to win, the need to protect the growing bodies of boys, pressures among peer groups, and how to teach abstract concepts.

And he tried to understand what happens when the same traits that hold a group together begin to pull the group apart.

"I try to tell the kids don't be overwhelmed, and I was overwhelmed," he says. "It's a big stage, and there are a lot of people and a lot of attention, media and phone calls all the time. I'm just a guy from a small town, so I never get used to it. We got there on Monday and didn't have a game till Saturday. I didn't know how I'd fill the time. I'd come up with activities like they were in school. You can't practice them to death, that's for sure. We needed things to fill their time. It's a carnival atmosphere."

Just hours before Hale's Kentucky team played the all-stars from Lafayette, Louisiana—a game Kentucky had to win to have any chance to advance—Hale walked into the dorms and found his best starting pitcher bloodied.

Dalton West crouched in the middle of the room full of bunk beds. The rest of the players tended to him, debating how to fix him up before the game.

What happened?

"The door hit him, coach."

"Yeah, he ran into the door, coach."

Hale looked at West and asked him if that was right.

"Yes, sir."

Hale took West to the infirmary and got his cuts dressed. Later, a coach of the team from Saudi Arabia told him what had really happened. Kentucky shared dorm space with the Saudi team.

One of Kentucky's scrawny players grabbed a towel and rubbed his butt, and hit Dalton West with the towel. Then the two started to fight.

Hale was distracted from his team's growing tensions because "I was getting ready for a game that we have to win. We already lost once and if we lose again we're probably going to be eliminated. All I have on my mind is baseball, baseball, baseball."

The players thought Hale still believed their story when he called them together.

"I had them in a group and I told them, 'I don't care if you guys get into a fight in the shower and stuff happens. I don't like it, but I can't control everything. I just want you guys to stick together.' Their eyes were like silver dollars. They had no idea I knew. I told them, 'I don't condone what you did but I love the way you stick together as a team.'"

Even as they were losing and struggling to control their frayed nerves, they also stood together when two players got into trouble for missing practice. Only after Hale sent someone up to retrieve the boys from the game room did they show up on the field.

After practice, Hale made the boys call their parents to report their misdeed and propose a punishment. They decided that since they got to the practice field fifteen minutes late, their punishment should be fifteen minutes running wind sprints.

The next day, the other players asked what the punishment would be, and Hale told them.

Bryce Morrow had an idea. "Well, if we're a team, and they have to run," he said, "we all have to run as a team."

And they did.

"I was standing there trying to hide from the kids that I had goose-bumps," he said. "I didn't know what to say."

Most teams struggled with pushy parents.

Bill Hartley, the manager of the team from Newtown, Pennsylvania, struggled with a couple parents throughout the summer.

"I had a couple parents constantly complaining about not enough playing time," he says. "They don't understand all the things I'm thinking about when I take one kid out and put another in. In the last game of the series—after we were eliminated—I'm trying to make sure every kid gets a chance for a hit. I got a call on my cell phone from a father letting me know that I embarrassed his kid because I took him off on national TV. How many millions of kids would love to be there? Are these guys crazy or something?"

Rick Hale, the manager of the all-stars from Owensboro, Kentucky, had a different problem with parents.

Parents of two players roomed with each other in hotels all summer long, as the boys advanced through the sectional, state, and regional tournaments. All the time, they were best of friends. They sat together, ate together, joked together, visited with their kids together. "But in Williamsport, they got into a fight and they haven't spoken since," Hale says months later. "Kids get over it in no time, but the parents are still mad at each other."

Losing requires a salve.

When Pennsylvania defeated the all-stars from Davenport, Iowa—a 15–0, four-inning no-hitter—a few Little League officials scrambled for a way to cheer up the kids from the Midwest. Jeff Mallonee, Iowa's man-ager, took the edge off with comic bursts of bravado in the dugout. "We got 'em right where we want 'em!" he said.

After the game, trainer Mike Ludwikowski approached coach Ed Grothus.

"Ever been to Yankee Stadium?" Ludwikowski asked. "Want to get a bus and go?"

Soon a bus was booked. Calls went to Mike Mussina, an all-star pitcher for the Yankees who is also a Williamsport native and member of Little League's board of directors.

Within a day, the Iowa kids were brought to the Bronx for a game. They got Yankee hats and shirts and got to spend time on the field and in the dugout.

One of the enduring traditions of the Little League World Series is sneaking the kids into Lamade Stadium to fill baggies with dirt from the infield.

People who have worked at the series for years—team hosts, trainers, security people, groundskeepers, and gofers—told me that giving players a small sample of the infield dirt from Lamade Stadium makes it easier to get over losing.

"We're not supposed to do it, but I've sneaked the kids in, two or three at a time, so they can go home with some dirt," says Tom Lyons, a deputy fire chief in Clifton, New Jersey, who volunteers every summer to work security at the Little League World Series. "You go when no one else is there and it cheers the kids up."

Taking dirt home has become a sanctioned activity. Groundskeepers now collect dirt in a wheelbarrow and invite whole teams to come and get their samples. They provide zip-lock bags and plastic cups.

"They can tell their friends back home that they made it to the biggest stage in baseball—the World Series," says Mike Ludwikowski, Little League's trainer. "They're bringing home something sacred."

One of the best teams in Williamsport in 2005—and one of the most serious—was the all-star squad from Vista, California.

Kalen Pimentel managed to beat
Florida to advance to the
U.S. championship game, but a small
strike zone made it the hardest game
of the year for both teams.

CHAPTER 10

It's Not Whether You Win or Lose...

EVEN WHEN THEY WERE STILL VERY MUCH ALIVE—in fact, at a moment of great triumph and possibility—the recriminations started for the all-stars of the Rancho Buena Vista Little League.

Marty Miller, the manager of the team from Vista, California, was leaning on a bat as he watched his players take batting practice for the umpteenth time. Later that day, before a national television audience on ABC's *Wide World of Sports*, the Californians would play in the U.S. championship game against the all-stars from Ewa Beach, Hawaii.

But Miller could not get past the events of two days before. That's when his team beat the all-stars from Maitland, Florida. But even though R.B.V. won that game, 6–2, Miller was angry. As he watched his players take cuts in the cage—*clank, clank, clank*—Miller complained about the umpiring and the intimidation tactics of Florida's coaches.

"I'm a big conspiracy theorist," Miller told me, his white handlebar mustache dancing on his red face. "I don't think they wanted us in the final." By "they," Miller means the Walt Disney Company, which owns the ESPN and ABC television networks that broadcast the Little League World Series.

"During that game, 75 percent of the camera time was on the Florida team, and 25 percent was on us. 'Florida this, Florida that. Oh, by the way, California...' There was really one-sided coverage. I just have to sit here and ask why."

Miller then complained about the umpiring in that game against Florida. "I've never seen a strike called that way," Miller says. "Five pitches in a row—ball, ball, ball, ball, ball—right down the middle of the plate." Miller pauses, exhales. "It's okay," he says. "The best team won. The evil team lost."

Miller, fifty-six years old, is a pear-shaped owner of a construction company in Vista. Miller devotes most of his waking hours, outside of his business, to sports. He played men's baseball until he put on too much weight to continue, and then he played in hard-core softball leagues. He has been coaching boys baseball since his son started playing a decade and a half ago.

I asked Miller if he ever gets too much baseball. "Yeah, right now," he says. "You go from January to July, that's half the year, and then all this to get to Williamsport," Miller tells me. "Every day, it's all baseball. When my kid played, we played year round. They played 115 games of travel ball and a full PONY schedule at the same time, so that's 150, plus another fifteen or twenty games of winter ball, so they play a lot of baseball." His daughter was also an athlete in high school. "But she got tired of it, burned out," Miller says.

When California beat Florida in a battle of the teams' aces, I thought Marty Miller and his players would be jubilant. They advanced to the U.S. championship game and had a chance to win the Little League World Series. But everyone's faces looked grim, tight—on the field, in the press conference, and around the complex. During the Florida game, I circulated on the California side of the stands, and it was tense. I walked out to a pavilion where a high-definition TV was showing the game, and Jim Lewis paced around complaining about the umpire's strike zone. And now, at BP, the kids were quiet, like they were doing a job.

Hey, I thought, *you guys are winning! You have a chance to go all the way! What gives?*

Partly, they were upset. But they were also grim by design, as Joe Pimentel told me. No coach works harder with players than Pimentel. He's smart and dedicated, and he wants to teach the kids life lessons as well as hitting lessons.

"There are lots of peaks and valleys," he said. "You might hit the ball hard four times and go 0 for 4. What you're trying to do, not just in baseball, is turn the peaks and valleys closer together. You should not be so high when you homer. As soon as you touch home plate, that at-bat is done, and you need to focus on the next challenge. You can't fly as high as a kite or else you don't get a hit after a home run. Once it's over, you focus on the moment."

That's why the Californians never celebrated like the other teams. The Hawaiians hit a home run, and the guys were jumping up and down. The Mainers rallied and total joy filled their faces. The Japanese just did an infield practice, and they wore open, smiling faces.

The California kids were all business.

———————————— • ◆ • ————————————

Before I went to Williamsport, I talked with a number of experts on youth sports. Most said events like the Little League World Series took the fun out of the game.

Bob Bigelow, a former NBA player and author of *Just Let the Kids Play*, was critical of the impact that TV has as on the tendency for adults to run teams like army sergeants and do anything to win. "The child's need to play is trumped by the adult's need to win," he said. "And they practice too much. I hear about teams on the field for five hours of practice. Come on! If you can keep them interested in practice for an hour and a half, you're doing a hell of a job."

Bigelow didn't play competitive basketball until he was fourteen. But that's the age when kids now strut their stuff at summer tournaments. LeBron James was already a household name in basketball circles at that tender age. "It's just too much," Bigelow says, "and it's happening in all sports."

Jay Coakley, a University of Colorado sociologist whose Little League team almost made it to Williamsport in 1955, worries that parents "use their kids' success for their own purposes" and "look at their kids' games with an investment mentality."

Coakley grew up in a *Peanuts* world. "When I was a kid," Coakley told me, "we played pickup games, with different rules every time we played. We were making decisions outside an authority structure, settling disputes on our own. We were playing outside a pre-fab model of games made by someone else. I don't want to romanticize that, but it's important. I worry about the pressure cooker, where kids don't have any room to do things on their own."

Virginia Tech's Richard Stratton worries that players get so serious that "they're unable to separate their on-field personalities from who they are away from the game." When kids start to believe their press clippings—that they're the best around, that they epitomize all the motherhood-and-apple-pie virtues of hard work and sacrifice—they could lose sight of their limitations as kids. Past participants in the Little League World

Series have gotten miffed when they did not star on other teams when they got home. "The reality will strike when they start to play PONY or American Legion ball," he said.

There's nothing inherently good or bad about sports. What matters—in sports, in school, at camp, and in the neighborhood—is whether kids have the opportunity to explore and play as well as work with discipline toward a goal.

When I arrived at the Little League World Series, I wanted to see which teams looked like they were having fun and which ones took losing—and winning—hard.

———— • ◆ • ————

One of the first people I met in Williamsport was Bill Hartley, the owner of a pizzeria outside Philadelphia and manager of the Council Rock Little League's all-stars. Hartley was bursting with hope—not only for his team, but also for his own ability to keep the game in perspective. He was like an AA member who had just reached another milestone.

Five years before, on a gray and cold January day, Hartley lost four members of his family in a house fire. His sister Dale Connor, her husband Don, their daughter Colleen, and her daughter Kacie, all died in a fire apparently caused by a faulty bathroom light switch. The Bucks County coroner said the four died of smoke inhalation and carbon monoxide poisoning.

Bill Hartley's always been an intense man. In the years of coaching his children in Little League and guiding them through other sports—like wrestling—he's always demanded the greatest physical effort and the greatest mental focus. And when they did not deliver, he sometimes responded with sharp words. In his own words, he was "intense" and "hard-nosed." Everyone in the family played sports for generations, and the purpose of playing was to win. Even more importantly, the purpose was to do the little things right.

But the awful fire changed something in Bill Hartley. His eyes still burned deeply and he still cared about the coaching lessons of his father and his college coach, and he still wanted to win. But he decided that he had to show more love when he coached, react less to what happened whether it was good or bad. He worked hard to corral his emotions, and to teach his youngest son Ryan—a twelve-year-old who plays shortstop for the Newtown team—how to win without the old tensions he used to bring to the field.

"I decided that I had to make baseball more of a game, and less of that intense passion," Hartley says. "Now it's back to being a game. That hard-nosed passion is still there, but with that loving stuff behind it now."

When Newtown made it to the World Series—when the team used its discipline to beat great fields of teams in Pennsylvania and then in the Mid-Atlantic tournament—it looked like Hartley and his kids were writing a story of healing and inspiration, faith and redemption. What they lacked in physical ability, they would compensate with cleverness.

All summer long, the team worked on tricks to gain an advantage in close games. On one play, called the Scoobie Doo, the baserunner at first would pretend to break for second with the bases loaded and the coach would shout out in mock panic: "Hey! Whaddaya think you're doing?" The catcher would then rush a throw to first base, sometimes throwing it away and allowing a run to score. Darren Lewis called that play in a game against Tamaqua in the state tournament, with the score tied and Ryan Hartley on third base. Another fake-out happened when the opposition had a runner on third base. The Newtown pitcher would throw a wild pitch on purpose, causing the runner to run home. But the catcher would quickly grab the ball and throw to the pitcher covering home for an easy out.

Whatever it takes.

Back home, at Parkway Pizza in Levittown, crowds gathered to cheer on the Little Leaguers. Kids from Truman High School, white-collar workers and lunch-bucket types, and mothers with smaller kids all gathered to pass along their best wishes all summer long. And when the Newtown kids made it to Williamsport, the crowds swelled for their games.

But then a superior Hawaii team beat them easily—and, in the process, Ryan Hartley broke his finger waving a bunt at a hard fastball from Hawaii's flamethrower. He cried in agony for all of TV Land to hear.

Against Florida, things got worse before the game even started. Bill Hartley wanted to have his injured son coach first base. Other teams used players as first base coaches, so why not? But Little League officials balked at even letting him in the dugout. He wanted to know why. Rules are rules, was the answer. The rules state that all players on the field have to play an inning in the field and have one plate appearance—and young Hartley could do neither. The Little League gendarmes were willing to let him sit on the bench, but not to coach. They argued in front of the dugout and then under the stadium.

Hartley approached Florida's manager, Sid Cash, and asked if he had any problem with Ryan coaching at first base. Cash was okay with Ryan coaching. When Little League officials said they'd face legal liability if Ryan got hurt, Hartley said he'd sign a waiver. But the Little League officials held their ground.

After the game—after Florida killed Pennsylvania's hopes with a 3–1 victory that probably turned on a missed call at second base—Hartley talked with reporters in the media room under Lamade Stadium.

"Try to be gentle," he said as he took a seat in front of the room.

Then he questioned an umpire's call at second base. Florida snuffed a Pennsylvania rally with a double play, but the shortstop never touched the bag before throwing to first base.

Then he complained about Little League's treatment of Ryan. "This kid worked his rear off to be here," he said. "The kid's a total gentleman. For them to do that to me…"

Then he broke. The old intensity and the new heart melted together. He stood up to walk out. "Guys, I've had enough, I'm done. Sorry."

Bill Hartley was still battling his demons.

A measure of redemption came a couple days later when Pennsylvania beat up the all-stars from Davenport, Iowa, 15–0. Under Little League's mercy rule, the game ends early if a team leads by ten runs after four innings. Not only did Newtown pound thirteen hits and four home runs in three innings, for a .682 batting average, but Keith Terry no-hit the Iowans in the abbreviated game.

On a perfect night—warm, with a gentle breeze, and 10,300 fans dispersed across the stadium and in the hills beyond the outfield fence—the kids from Pennsylvania found some joy on the last night of their Little League careers.

———————— • ◆ • ————————

The team from Westbrook, Maine, was not supposed to be in Williamsport. The best team in the New England regional tournament was the all-star team from Farmington, Connecticut. Maine, in fact, lost its first three games in the regionals. But Maine got hot at the right time and breezed the rest of the way to Williamsport.

Which might explain why Maine's team was both just happy to be in Williamsport and also nervous to the point of sickness as the games approached.

The player who seemed to have the roughest time was Michael

Mowatt, a skinny kid with a mop of brown hair who looked like he was too sick to play a single game.

Rich Knight took Mowatt and other players to the infirmary almost nightly. "At two or three in the morning, I'd get a knock at the door," the Maine manager said. "We were always going to the infirmary with poison ivy, sore arms, and stomachaches. The nurse would say, 'Oh, here's the guys from Westbrook again.'"

Going back to the regional tournament, Mowatt vomited and had stomachaches. "We figured it was something he ate. We didn't think too, too much of it. But it continued. He had one good night and two in a row when he was up. He would knock on my door at night and tell me he was feeling sick again." Nothing settled him.

This wasn't the first time he had had problems. He almost quit the all-star team during the district tournament. "He's not getting enough playing time," his father told Knight, who asked to talk with the boy. "He's already decided. He's in the car now."

Mowatt stayed on the team but didn't do well at the plate or in the field. He was a bench player most of the summer.

Knight is a slender man with dark hair and the familiar New England accent. He talks softly. Knight has never had children, but he started coaching Little League twenty-five years ago as part of his company's efforts to get employees to do volunteer work in the community. "I had to ask what I want to do. Do I want to go to nursing homes with old people?" Knight says. "Sorry, no, I want to do something else. Verizon always gave funding for the league. I liked kids, so I decided to give it a try. That's also why I got into the Big Brothers program."

After several visits to the infirmary, one of the nurses pulled Knight aside and suggested that Mowatt might be homesick. Because his parents were struggling financially, they could not come to Williamsport to watch their son play in the World Series.

Knight asked Mowatt about the nurse's theory. "Do you want to go home?" Knight asked him. Maybe, was the answer. Knight said he would get in a car and drive Mowatt home before Maine's next game in Williamsport.

"It's your choice," Knight told Mowatt. "In the morning, if you want me to drive you back to Maine, your parents can meet us halfway."

In the morning, Mowatt decided to stay and play in the upcoming game against California.

"Knowing he could go home," Knight says, "created a sense that he could breathe again." He became one of the best hitters in the Little League World Series. He finished with a 1.500 slugging percentage, the best in the tournament.

"He kept saying, 'I'm not homesick,'" says his mother Linda Mowatt. "But once Rich told him he could come home, he knew he wasn't trapped and he had an option and it relieved Michael." Linda Mowatt was able to watch her son play when a local Little League supporter paid for a bus.

In their first game against Louisiana, the Mainers swung at the first thirteen pitches. Nick Finocchiaro ripped two fouls before slapping a flat fastball over the right center field fence. Mowatt also hacked away— foul, swinging strike, foul—before lining a hanging curveball fastball over the center field fence.

"I thought I was going to strike out," Mowatt told me later. "I mean, it was 0–2. I was looking for a pitch outside of the zone, and I got one down the middle. It was a little slow curveball. It hung...I just couldn't believe it. I still can't believe it."

Louisiana rallied for the win, but Maine achieved its first goal: avoid embarrassment.

In the next game, down 2–0 to California, Maine took a nanosecond lead when Mowatt hit a 250-foot home run with two runners on base. "I could hardly believe how happy I felt at that time," Knight remembers. California won the game in the next inning with a big rally that included a grand slam from manchild Kalen Pimentel.

Maine finally won, 3–2, against Owensboro, Kentucky, in one of those everybody-chips-in games.

Win or lose, Mowatt and the other Mainers bopped along. No complaints about bad breaks or mean opponents. No ugly words about umpires. After the first game, manager Rich Knight acknowledged the hurt with a classic if-I-stop-laughing-I'll-cry line: "It was Christy Matthewson who said that I learn a little from a victory and a lot from a loss."

———————— • ◆ • ————————

There's losing hard and there's losing gently. The team from Lafayette, Louisiana, did both.

After winning the first two games of pool play—with stirring comebacks against Maine and Kentucky—Louisiana clinched a spot in the next round of play. Louisiana could afford to lose the next game, against the powerful team from Vista, California. But nothing went right in a 9–3 loss. And Mike Conrad, the manager, was tense and angry after the game.

A reporter asked Mike Conrad, Louisiana's manager, what he expected from California.

"Not a 9–3 loss," Conrad says, eyes glaring, lips pursed, voice clipped.

An ugly pause.

"You *can't* hang pitches up in the middle of the strike zone to any of these kids here."

"I am *very* disappointed in the way that we ran the bases tonight."

"The hitting—even though we out-hit them, 11–10, was just *totally* untimely. We left [runners on] second and third a couple times with two outs, we left [runners on] first and second with two outs."

"We basically choked it off at the plate. You can't let a team like this group get any kind of momentum whatsoever."

"It's just a matter of being patient at the plate. We are not being patient...For some reason, I

Jace Conrad made his father Mike Conrad, the manager of the team from Lafayette, Louisiana, proud in pitching a one-hitter against Hawaii.

don't know if it's 10,000 people in the stands, we're not very patient. We're not being smart offensively."

"Whether you're seven or you're twelve [years old], you just hit that spot. I don't care if it's high, if it's low. You can't leave it belt high when you're asking for an outside pitch. And I went out and told Ryan [Bergeron] that. Especially against a West Coast team that plays 365 days a year. These guys are *outstanding* hitters from top to bottom, and they're very well coached. It's like vultures, once they start feeding on you it's going to get ugly quick."

Any other questions?

It was up to Conrad's son, Jace, to change the mood. Louisiana lost its next game, against Hawaii, 2–0. But it's hard to imagine anyone losing any better. Jace Conrad walked one batter and gave up a home run, but otherwise he was as perfect as anyone ever gets in kidball.

No one has ever shut down Hawaii's hitters, but Jace Conrad baffled them as completely as if he had asked them to calculate pi. The foot movement on the rubber didn't seem part of the same motion as the arm whipping forward, and the Hawaii guys got confused and their timing was off. Conrad pitched them inside, where other teams were too scared to throw the ball. For his age, young Conrad looked as clever as Greg Maddux. Even when he gave up the home run, he remained steady. He just got ready for the next batter.

After the game, Mike Conrad was subdued but positive as if he were absorbing a new lesson about losing. "I'm real proud of my son," he said softly. "He had good stuff tonight...He wanted it more. He's a tough kid, he's a competitor, and he felt he had to try to redeem himself tonight. The baseball gods just weren't with us tonight...I have said from the get-go that this was such a special group of kids who work so hard. You hate to see it end like this, but this is a lesson in life, too. Sometimes you don't have enough to finish that job."

Somehow, a moment of grace in losing wiped everything else away.

And so the Cajun kids, once the tournament's masters of comebacks with their first two victories, experienced a comeback of temper.

Then they returned home to see their lives change completely. As the World Series drew to a close, Hurricane Katrina raged toward the Gulf Coast. In days, the city of New Orleans was almost wiped off the map. As the people of that city fled, 50,000 went to Lafayette. A couple months later, I asked Mike Conrad how the Gulf Coast region was holding up. "We're going to get through this," he said. "It makes the other stuff look less important, doesn't it?"

———————— •◆• ————————

As I looked back on the Little League World Series—hard losses and redemptive wins, stoic losers and surprise heroes—I kept coming back to that bitter matchup between California and Florida. Months later, the two sides still argued about what happened in that semifinal game for the American championship.

After it was over, the two sides agreed on only one matter: the better team won. "If we played them ten times, we'd win two at most," said Sid Cash, the rotund bank executive with the thick Southern drawl who has coached Little League for three decades. "They are without question the better team. But that happened to be one of the nights we *might* have won."

Florida came into the game with a 2–1 record. The Maitland all-stars took advantage of their opponents' weaknesses, using trick plays, out-hustling them, and taking advantage of bad umpiring calls. They also rode their budding superhero Dante Bichette Jr., the son of the former major leaguer. Florida beat the all-stars from Davenport, Iowa, 7–3, and Newtown, Pennsylvania, 3–1. Then they lost to Hawaii, 10–0.

California was even better. After going 20–0 in the qualifying tournaments, the Vista all-stars went 3–0 in Williamsport. The star was Kalen Pimentel, who got strike-outs for all eighteen outs in the opener against Owensboro, Kentucky. Pimentel also hit grand slams in California's 7–3 win over Maine and its 9–3 win over Louisiana.

But if California was so good, so dominant, why did the victory over Florida feel so lousy?

Dante Bichette Jr., son of the former major leaguer, was the star for Florida's team all summer .

At the center of the controversy was Dante Bichette Sr., a big—six feet, three inches, 225 pounds—and strong former major league star. In thirteen years playing for five teams, Bichette hit a total of 274 home runs with a lifetime average just eight hits shy of the magic .300 mark. All summer long, Bichette told and retold his heartwarming story of fatherhood—how he quit the Los Angeles Dodgers' training camp in 2002 when he heard that his son Dante Junior hit his first Little League home run. "I was wavering anyway, but that was the final straw. If I was still going strong and still had the passion, I would have probably kept playing." But he decided to come home to Florida and teach his kid how to play baseball.

From the time his kid understood anything about baseball, he wanted to play in the Little League World Series. In 2004, Bichette created a travel team called the Maitland Pride to train the local Little League all-stars for a run at Williamsport. The team played other travel teams in tournaments and exhibitions, winning twenty-four of thirty-one games. Playing tough games against better teams, the Pride came together as a team. Every one of the Little League's all-stars played for the Pride from December 2004 until July 2005—just a couple weeks before the Little League tournaments started.

When he played in the big leagues, Bichette had a strange reputation. Charlie Metro, a longtime coach and scout, summarized it perfectly: "He's got a pixie disposition. He's got a delightful arrogance. He's a hard-nosed type of ballplayer." In short, a playful toughie. Most players liked Bichette, but he didn't completely avoid controversy. In 1998, a *Denver Post* writer found androstenidione, a steroid variant, in his locker. Toward the end of his career, after he lost his starting position in spring training, he was part of a cabal that got Boston Red Sox manager Jimy Williams fired.

The big pixie was one of the happier campers during the Little League World Series. He reveled in the opportunity to proclaim the virtues of the event. Afterward, he told me he learned lessons in Williamsport that he wished he had understood before. "I learned so much more about teamwork as a coach than as a player," he says. "I wish I had my career to do over again now that I've had these kids. I'm going to have Dante coach younger kids, because what you're talking about is teamwork. In pro ball, you miss it. It's more about the individual."

Bichette taught baseball as if his Little Leaguers were high school players. Every practice, every game, he dissected hitting, pitching, fielding, and baserunning.

"We broke everything down to fundamentals—why it's so tough to hit, what you have to do to field or pitch," Bichette says. "The true measure of a master is the absence of wasted motion. So I taught them why you have to have a short swing, because you don't have much time. It really is a simple game. What it comes down to is 'I got to get to the ball quick.' We turned the pitching machine up and we did it and did it and did it. And you have to teach kids different ways. Some are visual, some are audial, some have to just do it to understand. I made them understand why we have to field a ball at shortstop quick, [that] taking one extra step helps the runner have one extra step too."

Like James Mill preparing his son for life as an intellectual or John Huston teaching his daughter Anjelica the art of acting, Dante Senior has made a project out of Dante Junior. He won't say it, but the goal is the major leagues. Bichette built a batting cage in his garage and the

Pride players came over for swings. When the Little League season started, the Pride continued to play, so Bichette never lost control of his charges. In Williamsport, the two Bichettes were seen walking down to the cages together, apart from the others on the team, to take some extra swings in the cages.

Dante is homeschooled by his former fifth-grade teacher, a six-foot-six giant from Boston named Nathan Sweet. The plan is for Dante Junior to work at home for three years before enrolling in high school.

"With most little guys who want to play baseball, the focus isn't on education, so we're going to make sure that happens," Senior says. "Nathan is a huge Boston fan, so they have that in common. He works with Dante three days, full days on Tuesday and Thursday. Wednesdays are kind of a half-day. It's a project-based approach. The way we look at it, instead of teaching a lot of information, we want to teach him how to think, how to figure things out himself. They go golfing together, but Dante respects him. He calls him Mr. Sweet."

While his son pitched well and hit home runs and Florida won games, Dante Senior merrily chatted up the virtues of Little League as the purest example of the joy of sports. "Thirteen is probably the perfect year for something like this—it's right before the world changes, right before puberty and other things get important. It's the last year of innocence. [Next year,] they're no longer on the little field, and they're on the big field. They're teenagers. It's a great way to turn into a teenager and be a little man."

But the gooey teen talk disappears when the topic of the California-Florida game comes up.

———————•◆•———————

California's version of the great controversy goes like this:

Home plate umpire Don Singleton created the worst possible context for the the game. Like all of the other umpires who worked the Little League World Series, Singleton paid his own way to Williamsport from his home in Williamstown, Massachusetts. Once he got to the series, he and other umpires got precious little training on how to work a game. And he called the tightest strike zone in the series. Forget about pitches that cut the corners of the strike zone. Those were always called balls. But Singleton also called balls on pitches over the heart of the plate.

When Singleton squeezed California's starting pitcher, Kalen Pimentel, the result was predictable. Pimentel would get behind in the count and then have to throw the ball over the plate to force the Florida hitters to swing. By throwing to a tiny strike zone, Pimentel put extra stress on his arm at a time of year—the end of the summer, after playing in almost sixty games, with growing pressure in each game—when he could least afford it.

Florida had a legitimate grievance about the umpires blowing a home run call in the third inning. With two men on, Florida's Mike Tomlinson hit a drive that hit the netting near the left-field foul pole, bounced down to the top of the outfield fence and onto the field. The umpires ruled the ball a double off the wall, but replays showed the ball was a home run. Instead of a 3–2 Florida lead, the game was now tied 2–2. Still, that call was just evidence of how badly California's pitcher got squeezed. "They make a big deal out of that call, but that ball was *strike five*," Jim Lewis, a California parent, told me. "Come on! The problem was that the strike zone was impossibly small."

When a pitcher is confused about the strike zone, he often asks the umpire for clarification about different calls. But that didn't work for young Kalen Pimentel in this game. "Our pitcher tried to ask him what the strike zone was, and the guy [Singleton] is just, '*Grrrrr! Grrrrr!*'" Marty Miller told me a day later. "Kalen, if he throws a bad pitch, he doesn't beg for a strike. But Kalen makes motions out there, [so] you know something isn't right. None of our pitchers is out there begging. They're good enough that they don't need to beg for strikes."

But the sandwich-size strike zone was not the worst handicap. The behavior of the Florida team—especially Dante Bichette, a grown man who should know better—was worse.

Bichette played mind games with the Californians.

"He had his son icing the hitter," Joe Pimentel said months later, still bitter. "The hitter gets into the batter's box and he waits and waits and waits. Dante Junior waited very long between pitches, waiting for the hitter to get jittery. Then he'd throw when they [the California hitters] were uncomfortable. I told our hitters to turn around and ask for time, but we weren't granted time."

Marty Miller always tells his players not to play until they're ready.

"Don't let anyone rush you, you don't start till you're ready," Miller says in his clipped drawl. "They can't play the game without you. The first thing we tell the pitcher is to play at your own pace. If the other players aren't ready when you're ready, turn back and relax to go at your speed. Other teams will ask for time as the pitcher goes in to the windup. But these kids know how to take charge of themselves."

Starting in the second or third inning, Dante Senior started to bait the California team. Bench-jockeying is a time-honored practice in the big leagues, but it's supposed to be verboten in Little League. But Bichette barked away, yelling that the California team was stealing signs. Bichette yelled at Nathan Lewis, the California catcher. He barked at Kalen Pimentel, the pitcher. He complained to the umpires, who, impressed with his celebrity status, warned the California bench.

ESPN wires the managers to capture their words of encouragement and instruction to players during the game. Wiring the managers also helps to enforce basic manners on the field. But Bichette was only a coach, so he wasn't wired. He was free to snipe all game long without getting recorded.

And who was Bichette to complain about stealing signals? He spent the whole game trying to steal the signs that Joe Pimentel relayed to Nate Lewis behind the plate. Bichette even admitted stealing signs! Bichette paced up and down the Florida bench, looking for a good angle to see the senior Pimentel's signs. Luckily, Pimentel was able to use a door as a barrier. That just got Bichette angrier. So he sent a couple players outside the dugout to get a better angle—until umpires told them to get back in the dugout where they belonged.

In the sixth inning, Dante Bichette Jr. hit Kalen Pimentel with a pitch. Dante Senior told Miller and Pimentel the pitch was retribution for the sign stealing.

"When Kalen was going to first [after getting hit], Dante Senior was yelling at him," Joe Pimentel says. "After they hit him, Royce [Copeland] came up and he hit the ball off the fence and Kalen scored from first. I yelled out, 'Hey, hit another guy!' When Kalen took the mound, Dante was screaming and yelling at him, and Kalen's laughing at him."

The final insults came after the game. With the TV cameras recording the Rockwellian scene of the two teams lining up on the field to congratulate each other, Dante Senior approached Marty Miller with a smile on his face.

"He smiled and called us names," Miller says. "'Cheaters!' he says. 'Is this the way you got here—cheating and stealing signs?' I don't know if he called us a son of a bitch or what, but he did it with a nice smile on his face."

———————◆·———————

That's California's version of the tale. Here's Florida's:

Home plate umpire Don Singleton called a tight strike zone, all right. But that tight zone affected both pitchers—not just Kalen Pimentel. Dante Junior also had lots of strikes called balls. So both sides played with a disadvantage.

"That's Little League umpires," says Sid Cash. "If you don't pay professional umpires, you're going to get something like that. He didn't call some strikes for us and for them…Normally Little League umpires call a bigger zone. But this was a big game—Florida and against California, on national TV—and [the umpire] tightened up some."

But, really, that tight zone didn't affect much. Sure, Kalen Pimentel threw more pitches than usual. But that was because the Florida hitters showed discipline at the plate. Pimentel overwhelmed Kentucky, but so what! Kentucky lost all six of its games in Williamsport in 2004 and 2005! The Florida hitters—schooled for a year by Dante Bichette Sr.—made Pimentel work deep into the count. Take Florida's first batter, Max Moroff. He forced Pimentel to throw ten pitches before popping up to shortstop.

"If you look at the tapes of the game, there were only five pitches that were over the plate and got called balls," Cash says. "Again, somebody wants to talk about five strikes for them, but that doesn't equal a run."

The *real* problem was that California's hitters stole signs—blatantly, throughout the World Series. Florida's manager and coaches decided they weren't going to let the Californians cheat against them. Not when they had a chance to advance to the American championship game.

"Their kids looked back at home plate to get the [catcher's] signs," Cash said. "They taught their kids to raise their hand—like they were asking for time out—so they could see the position of the catcher's glove. That tells you what pitch is coming. An inside pitch was not going to be a curveball, got that? They cheated [in an earlier game against Maine]. From the get-go, we were not going to let it happen to us."

What's a Little League team going to do when the other side steals signs?

One recourse is for the catcher to fool the hitter after he steals his sign. Big-league catchers do it all the time. Set up in one place, let the hitter look back, then shift when the pitcher rocks into his motion. "That's one too many demands to make," says Cash. "Our kid was eleven years old!"

"In pro ball, you take care of it then and there," says Dante Bichette Sr., "and the runner at second base has to answer too."

Cash is more direct. "In the big leagues, [if] you look back at the catcher, you get pitches near the head," Cash says. "You can't do that in Little League."

Since the beanball was out, Florida's response was to ride California's players—yell at them, rattle them, and intimidate them. Bichette makes no apologies for yelling at Kalen Pimentel and Nathan Lewis. He says they were looking back at signs so blatantly that someone needed to call them on it. If he could shake up the youngsters, so much the better.

"This was Little League, so you can't drill the kid," says Bichette. "So I yelled at them."

———————— • ◆ • ————————

The underlying explanation for the ongoing signs-stealing controversy might go back to the creation of Little League by Carl Stotz in 1939.

From the beginning, Stotz's idea was to provide kids with a small-scale imitation of the big leagues. By giving players uniforms, groomed fields, scoreboards, umpires, scoresheets, statistics, and writeups in local newspapers, Stotz encouraged boys to imitate their heroes in the major leagues.

Everywhere Little League is played, kids mimic the star players. Curaçao players imitate native Andruw Jones's method of catching the ball by the side of their bodies. Other players, like Saudi Arabia's Alexander Robinett, imitate Gary Sheffield's extreme bat wagging while waiting for the pitcher to deliver the ball. A couple of players—like Raysheldon Carolina of Curaçao—imitate Ichiro Suzuki's hop-step in the batter's box as the pitcher delivers the ball. Japan's pitchers imitate Hideo Nomo's hesitation kick and powerful thrust forward to the plate.

It has always been thus. The comic Billy Crystal remembers mimicking Mickey Mantle's labored limp to the plate.

"Jetering" is the most common mimic in all of youth baseball today.

The New York Yankees' shortstop, Derek Jeter, has made a habit of holding his right hand in the umpire's face when he digs into the batter's box. Ostensibly, he's asking for time. More importantly, he's taking symbolic control of the plate.

One possibility is that the California hitters were just Jetering. They held up their arms to take control of the game's tempo, just like the Yankees' captain does. But Dante Bichette doesn't buy it.

"They didn't peek back, they *looked* back," he says. "It was blatant. There's a difference between Jetering and looking back, staring blatantly at the signals."

Bichette acknowledges most of the coaches in the World Series stole signs. "Hawaii had our signals till the second inning and then we noticed and changed them. We had Hawaii's signals the whole game, but they were so good it didn't matter."

So what's wrong if California's players were stealing signals, too? It's part of the game. Everybody does it.

Bichette says it's okay for the coaches to steal signals, but not the players.

"Baseball's facing cheating right now in a big way," he says, referring to the steroids scandal that shadows stars like Barry Bonds, Sammy Sosa, and Rafael Palmiero. "If coaches steal signals, that's one thing, but you shouldn't get the kids stealing signals. It's teaching them the wrong thing."

When the emotions swirl, ethical arguments can get mixed up. The coaches and parents claimed a certain right to steal signals, argue with each other, argue with umpires, and taunt the other side.

The players themselves claimed no such rights. Only the adults.

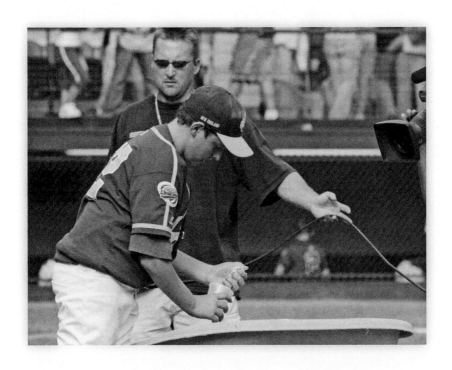

After getting eliminated, many teams
pad down to the stadiums to gather
samples of dirt for souvenirs.

The best players in amateur baseball
compete on travel teams in tournaments
across the country—but the allure
of television causes many travel-ball
players to also compete
for the Little League World Series.

CHAPTER 11

————— • ◆ • —————

The Future Is Here

T HE WARMTH OF UPSTATE NEW YORK'S SUMMER along the Otsego Lake snapped cold when the sun went down. The parents and brothers and sisters of the players scurried to their SUVs and campers parked along the edge of the eighteen-acre baseball complex to retrieve sweatshirts and blankets. The players themselves didn't bother. They played all week in shirtsleeves, and they wore a cake of dirt and sweat to keep themselves warm.

A couple days later, Ryne Sandberg and Wade Boggs would be inducted into the National Baseball Hall of Fame in Cooperstown Village. The area around the historic town would be overwhelmed with baseball fans wearing Cubs and Red Sox jerseys and hats. Throngs would gather for the induction ceremonies, tearing up as the brand new immortals thanked the people who made their glorious careers possible. Baseball's greatest players would relive their past glories and decry the modern corruption of money and steroids.

But at the Cooperstown Dreams Park, four miles away from the Hall of Fame, baseball remains a present-tense game played by twelve-year-old kids.

————— • ◆ • —————

All the experts on youth baseball told me that I'd find the best baseball in the country at one of the Cooperstown Dreams Park tournaments.

Allen Simpson probably knows as much about youth baseball as anyone. A former executive with the legendary Alaska Goldpanners and the Montreal Expos, Simpson is the founder and publisher of a trade publication called *Baseball America*. In an era when major leaguers make an average of $2.5 million a year, baseball people at all levels need reliable information about the game's up-and-coming players. Simpson's publication, a baseball version of *Variety* or *Billboard*, uses a thick network of writers and stringers, scouts and coaches, to cover baseball's vast landscape.

"Every one of the best players in the country, at some time, goes through Cooperstown," Simpson said. "It's where you'll see every great player in the country."

Over eleven weeks every summer, about 10,000 twelve-year-old boys participate in tournaments at Dreams Park. Each week's tournament involves eighty teams, each with twelve or thirteen players. They play from early in the morning until late at night. The tournaments begin on Sunday mornings and end Thursday nights. The championship game starts around 9:30 p.m. A few thousand people fill the stands to watch the game, which lasts until around midnight.

After ten weeks of these tournaments, each week's winners are invited to participate in a tournament of champions that concludes just before Labor Day Weekend.

———————— ◆ ————————

To get to the sprawling baseball encampment, you travel about eleven miles north along a twisting, turning State Highway 28, which juts off Interstate 88 about sixty miles west of Albany. You pass farms and office parks and malls before getting to Lake Otsego on the edge of the timeless little village of Cooperstown.

Once, the name of Cooperstown could be taken literally. It was a town of skilled carpenters, as well as a farming community. That past gets gentle nods from the Fenimore Art Museum and the Farmer's Museum. But for more than a half century, Cooperstown has been synonymous with baseball. Cooperstown is where, according to the long-disproved myth, Abner Doubleday invented baseball. Over the years, baseball has overwhelmed other activities in the village. The old brick and wood-framed buildings along Main Street are mostly the same. But in place of old hardware stores and coffee shops, insurance and law offices, now stand baseball-themed restaurants and memorabilia stores and hat and T-shirt stores. Baseball's mythology is Cooperstown's biggest business.

The game of baseball—as opposed to the memory and mythology of baseball—takes place at the address of 4550 State Highway 28, four miles up the road in Milford, New York. Beyond a cast-iron archway announcing the complex, kids frolic in T-shirts and shorts and uniforms.

They throw baseballs, endlessly, in twos and threes, usually from long distances. The arcs of balls frame the lawn sloping down to the complex's main baseball field. That field is a simple diamond, enclosed inside a wooden green outfield fence and aluminum stands along the first and third base lines. At a distance, it looks like the old Huntington Avenue Grounds in Boston, original home of the Red Sox.

Cooperstown Dreams Park is on the leading edge of a nationwide transformation of youth baseball.

Not long ago, youth baseball was a community affair. When you played organized baseball, you signed up for a local league. If it wasn't Little League, it was PONY or Babe Ruth or Dixie Baseball. Fathers coached teams and neighbors umpired games. Most teams played a dozen games or so through June, when the all-star teams were picked. Virtually everyone was finished playing ball by early July, then took the rest of the summer off for family vacations.

But in the last decade or so, youth baseball has become a serious business. Community leagues are not the only option. Upwards of 35,000 travel teams have sprung up across the country. Kids can not only play all summer long, but all *year* long. Some of the best players play in Little League, but it's more of a sidelight than their main focus.

Organizations like Cooperstown Dreams Park, the Amateur Athletic Union (AAU), the United States Specialty Sports Association (USSSA), and the Continental American Baseball League have created hundreds of opportunities for elite travel teams to play in tournaments all year long.

The AAU and USSSA rank teams throughout the year, as if they're Division 1 college basketball or football teams. And every year, *Baseball America* publishes a national all-star team for players in age brackets starting twelve-and-under. The 2005 "Baseball for the Ages" team included two players from the Little League World Series—Michael Memea of Hawaii and Kalen Pimentel of California. The other players on the list devoted themselves exclusively to travel teams. The Southern California Redwings, based in Claremont, often listed as the top travel team in the nation, placed three players on *Baseball America*'s exclusive list—Josh Anderson, Erick Cruz, and Christian Lopes.

Travel teams operate outside the confines of leagues. Teams often hire professional coaches, conduct tryouts for kids from broad geographic areas, and play a schedule of 100 or more games over the summer. The top tournaments include Cooperstown Dreams Park and the Elite 24 World Series at Disney World in Orlando.

"Of all the teams in the Little League World Series, maybe one or two would be competitive in Cooperstown Dreams or AAU," says Allen Simpson. "One of the differences is in the depth of the teams, which you need to play all these games. The best teams in the Cooperstown Dreams Park tournaments have seven or eight elite pitchers, and they're all usually better than the one or two pitchers on the best teams in the Little League World Series."

Rather than playing with neighborhood kids over their whole childhood, players on travel teams have started to act like major-league free agents. Some tournaments let teams recruit ringers. On an Internet chat group, someone offered this mock classified ad to make the point:

WANTED—ANY TALENTED BASEBALL PLAYER
WHOSE TEAM DID NOT QUALIFY FOR DISNEY,
FOR ADDITION TO ROSTER OF QUALIFYING TEAM.
MUST BE ABLE TO (1) ENDURE SCOWLS OF PARENTS WHOSE CHILDREN YOU
WILL REPLACE, (2) DEFLECT ANY RIDICULE TOWARD TEAM MANAGER, (3) WEAR
FASHIONABLE UNIFORMS OF VARYING SIZE, COLOR, AND NAME, (4) DEFEND
THE HONOR AND SANCTITY OF THE ELITE 24 TOURNAMENT.
PLEASE CALL 1-800-RINGERS FOR AN IMMEDIATE EVALUATION.

Travel teams have metastasized so fast that the top coaches, like Lyle Gabriel of the San Diego Stars, are grumbling about a decline in the quality of play. "There are so many teams, I think it's defeating the purpose," Gabriel told one newspaper. "It's just so diluted. Most of these travel teams now are not much better than a Little League all-star team."

Players on travel teams live in a total baseball environment twelve months a year. When they're not playing in tournaments, they're working out in gyms and taking hacks in batting cages.

Families of players on traveling teams spend thousands of dollars a year to play on a team—money needed to hire coaches, buy uniforms and equipment, and travel all over the country. It costs about $1,000 a week to send kids to tournaments. It's not unusual for families to spend $10,000 to keep their kids busy in travel ball. Some families pay as much as $20,000 a year.

Travel baseball is part of a nationwide trend in all sports to specialize. Once upon a time in America, the best athletes played three sports—football in the fall, basketball in the winter, and baseball in the spring and summer. But many coaches tell kids to pick a sport when they are as young as ten or eleven years old. "This is an age of specialization," says Simpson. "The parents' mindset is that there is so much money in baseball now, there are so many opportunities for college baseball and scholarships, that the only opportunity I have for getting my kid a chance is to focus on one sport only."

The specter of college scholarships drives many parents to "invest" these thousands of dollars in travel teams and tournaments. The chances of getting that scholarship or pro contract are remote. Of the nation's 455,000 high school players, about 25,000 will play some college ball. That means about 7,300 freshman roster positions open every year. So about one out of seven high schoolers can expect to find a position on a college team—but only a small fraction of those players get a scholarship. The picture is bleaker for going pro. Only about 600 college ballplayers get drafted. Overall, about one-half of 1 percent of all high school ballplayers play some pro ball.

But even a remote chance to win the great sports lottery is enough for countless families. And so, for the love of the game and the ambition to strike it rich, thousands of the best young players go to Cooperstown.

———————•◆•———————

Lyle Gabriel, the coach of the perennial powerhouse San Diego Stars, also considers the competition at Cooperstown Dreams Park to be the best in the nation—tied, maybe, with the Disney World tournament in Orlando, Florida, that showcases twenty-four teams in early August.

Gabriel expresses fondness for Little League. He admires the environment of Williamsport and the marketing prowess that puts dozens of games in the Little League World Series on national television. But he hastens to add that some of the weaker traveling teams could easily win the Little League World Series on a bad day.

"There's no comparison. The Little League World Series does not showcase much talent," he told me. "Pitchers have nowhere near the same quality. A Little League team might have one six-foot kid pitching. My team will have four of them."

Traveling teams that compete in Cooperstown possess three advantages over Little League.

First, they can recruit whatever players they want from a broad geographic area. The players on Little League all-star teams come from a geographic area of no more than 20,000 people. "My team draws from an area of two million people," says Gabriel. Some traveling teams draw from a region that encompasses five states.

Second, the traveling teams benefit from professional coaches. Those coaches have often played professional baseball and worked with some of the game's best teachers. They learn their trade—understanding baseball mechanics like scientists, and then teaching what they know to kids—with as much intense dedication as a med student. And they take advantage of all the new technologies, like videos and computer imaging, in modern workout facilities.

Coaches on travel teams usually know how to run a practice. When the Stars work out, they have ten coaches on the field working in groups of four to eight players. Each kid is working hard to master a specific technique. No one is standing around.

Third, there is the schedule. Most Little League teams play only about a dozen games in the regular season, which ends in late June or early July. Then, all-star teams compete in tournaments until they're eliminated. All but a handful of Little League players see their season end with two months left in the summer. Most travel teams play eighty or ninety games. Some play as many as 100, 110, 120, or even 140 games.

"These kids want to play a lot of games over spring, summer, and fall," says Simpson. "For Little League, if you get beat in the tournaments, baseball is over in the first week of July. That's discouraging for a kid who wants to play baseball and get better. That's why the travel teams have sprung up. They have a physically demanding schedule. But for kids to get better, they have to play a lot of baseball. You don't get better by playing twelve or thirteen games over the summer. You have to be competitive over a long period—and you can't play other sports—to become the best."

* ◆ *

The awesome quality of travel ball is underscored by some of the state fair-style contests staged at the best tournaments. One contest at Cooperstown Dreams Park times players streaking around the bases. Another contest times how quickly players can throw the ball around the field.

Delino DeShields Jr., the son of a major leaguer and the star for Alabama's Boys of Baseball National Travel Team, ran the bases in 12.39

seconds, the best time in 2005. (That's about the time it takes to read the previous sentence aloud.)

The Corona Dodgers, a California travel team, had the best time for the "Around the Horn Plus" event—21.85 seconds—in which players make twelve throws around the field. The game of blitzball starts with the pitcher throwing to the catcher when the clock starts. Then the ball travels from the catcher to the third baseman, the second baseman, the first baseman, the catcher (again), the shortstop, the right fielder, the second baseman (again), the center fielder, the third baseman (again), the left fielder, and finally back to the catcher (again). (Corona performed the feat in the time it takes to read the previous two sentences aloud.) Oh, yes. Every player has to touch the nearest base or a designated spot in the outfield.

If Little League's only challenge came from travel teams, that would be bad enough. Little League would still have the corner on the community baseball niche. So what if the Little League World Series isn't the best baseball? That's not the point.

But in fact, Little League faces a tough challenge from other community-based leagues. Cal Ripken Baseball, affiliated with the Babe Ruth League, now involves 600,000 kids in the twelve-and-under division and stages a World Series with all the fanfare of the Little League World Series. Dixie Youth Baseball, once a segregationist alternative to Little League in the old Confederacy, now has 400,000 players. The PONY League, long an alternative for more serious baseball because it has a bigger field, involves almost 300,000 kids and also ends in a World Series.

Cal Ripken is the only community-based program that's growing every year. Within a few years, Ripken Baseball hopes to have one million players.

More important than the numbers, Ripken has a mission.

In every possible way, Cal Ripken Jr. is leveraging the value of his name—priceless because of his stunning 2,632 consecutive games streak and the baseball family values embodied in his father Cal Senior and mother Val. His book *Play Baseball the Ripken Way* has become the standard operating manual for many coaches. Ripken has also produced instructional videos. The Ripken complex is home to summer baseball camps and tournaments—all of which will grow as the complex fills out in the coming years. Ripken heads a consulting firm that offers guidance on stadium design and marketing strategy.

He also endorses a number of products and hosts a weekly talk show on XM Satellite Radio.

Ripken leagues offer a comfortable middle ground between Little League and travel ball. In many parts of the country, Ripken leagues play three seasons a year. Ripken teams are drawn from broader areas, allowing teams to have better athletes and especially more pitchers—a major plus at a time when arm injuries have become the most pressing challenge facing youth ball.

Ripken's complex will match anything that Little League has to offer. Ripken inaugurated Cal Senior's Yard in 2005 to rave reviews. The Yard's dimensions—210 feet to the left-field wall, 260 feet to center field, and 205 feet to right field—produce a more athletic brand of baseball than Little League's 205-feet all around. With more room for fielders to roam, pitchers don't gun for strikeouts. Their goal is to get grounders and fly balls, which puts greater demands on both fielders and baserunners. (Little League announced that it would set back the fences twenty feet starting with the 2006 Little League World Series.)

Cal Senior's Yard, modeled after Oriole Park at Camden Yards in Baltimore, is just one of four classic stadiums planned for the Ripken Baseball Center. Other stadium designs mimic Fenway Park, Wrigley Field, and Memorial Stadium (the Orioles' park before moving to Camden Yards in 1991). The Ripken complex—planned to rise on a 110-acre site—will also include practice fields, training facilities, a baseball museum, and hotel, office, and shopping areas. Nearby, the Aberdeen IronBirds of the Class A New York-Penn League play at Ripken Stadium, one of the most celebrated minor-league parks in America.

In 2006, Ripken Baseball opened a new front in the war for dominance in youth baseball. At a $24-million baseball complex in Myrtle Beach, Ripken Baseball holds tournaments close to golf courses and the beach. The idea is that while a family's young baseball players play tournament games all week, the parents and siblings can have their own structured vacations. The South Carolina facility began operations with nine playing fields and a "training island" with cages, mounds, bunting fields, and practice infields—and plans to expand in coming years.

With his growing portfolio of fields and facilities, Ripken is following the model of golfers like Jack Nicklaus, who has shaped the game long after his prime playing days by designing facilities all across the nation.

———————— • ◆ • ————————

When I visited Cooperstown in the summer of 2005, the tournament's top two seeds in Week Six—the South Oakland A's and the North Tampa Yankees—were getting ready to play for the championship.

At the time, the A's were ranked first of all twelve-and-under teams across the United States. Going into the title game, the A's had a season record of ninety-four wins and three losses. The A's already had won eleven of the thirteen tournaments they entered in 2005. Like all the best teams, the A's were deep in pitching—they had three pitchers capable of throwing the equivalent of ninety-five-miles-an-hour fastballs and mixing the heat with well-placed junk pitches—and they were strong in the game's fundamentals. And they could hit. They won the first six games in Cooperstown with an earned-run average just over one.

The manager of the A's, based in Madison Heights, Michigan, is Buster Sunde. A top pitcher at Western Michigan University, where he made the Mid-American Conference all-star team in 1982, Sunde was a promising prospect in the Chicago White Sox organization. He had a 10–2 record in Class A ball before a torn rotator cuff ended his career. He has been coaching boys baseball for more than a decade.

———————— • ◆ • ————————

Before the championship game, Cooperstown Dreams Park's founder, Louis Presutti III, inducted new members into its American Youth Baseball Hall of Fame. All 937 of them. It took forever. But it was a shrewd part of Presutti's master plan to make Cooperstown Dreams Park the center of the youth baseball world.

Teams lined up just outside the field while their coaches lined up on the third-base line. Each coach took a cordless microphone for about two minutes and read a list of his players. The players trotted through a gaudy arch decorated with images from the Cooperstown Dreams Park tournaments, usually tipping their caps, and then ran on to the field to get a handshake and a ring from Presutti. As each coach completed his list, one of Presutti's employees read the coach's name into the list of immortals.

Before they play the championship game every week, the players and spectators are treated to a fireworks display over the lake. A booming sound system plays patriotic songs—"God Bless America" (Kate Smith version), "Stars and Stripes Forever," "I'm Glad to Be an American"—and then standards from the disco era. Then the players for the championship game are announced, and they line up along the bases like major leaguers do before all-star games. The six umpires are introduced. Then a dignitary throws the first pitch.

This happens week after week. But it works. Just as the Little League World Series taps into the mythology of the American small town, Cooperstown Dreams Park taps into the ethos of American power and patriotic sentimentality. When I visited, some parents were close to tears in the pregame ceremonies. Staff members linked arms and swayed back and forth for "America the Beautiful." On the sidelines, as the PA system blares, an umpire sings "I'm Proud to Be an American" out loud.

Finally, after the week's 385 games and countless ceremonies, the championship game began.

———————— •◆• ————————

Lou Presutti started planning Cooperstown Dreams Park in 1975, when he visited Cooperstown with his father and grandfather. The three Presuttis had been going to the Hall of Fame since 1947—coincidentally, the year of the first Little League World Series. Year after year, grandfather Lou, father Lou Junior, and Lou III came to look at the plaques of Babe Ruth and Ty Cobb and baseball's other immortals.

In 1975, caught in the emotional undertow of the moment, Lou I made a pronouncement and and a request. The pronouncement: Every kid in America should see this place. The request: Do something to make it happen.

When Lou III grew up, he became a demographer. His life revolved around the numbers that paint portraits of different population groups. He got to know the buying habits, recreational patterns, and attitudes of every age group from every ZIP code. In his spare time, he coached youth baseball. Eventually, he analyzed the potential for a new baseball park and tournament, where the love of the game would intersect profitably with the disposable income of middle-class American families.

"Everything pointed to the twelve-and-under age group," he told me. Something about that age group—the impressionability of the group, the influence over family decisions, the desirability for marketers—makes it a natural target for recreational programs.

The twelve-and-under age group happens to be the same group that plays in the Little League World Series in Williamsport. Presutti started to gather investors for what he calls "the total baseball experience." That experience includes the historic allure of Cooperstown, the pageantry of a Fourth of July celebration, and baseball, baseball, baseball.

I asked Presutti what he thinks of Little League and he looked like he just ate a lemon. I mean, he looked *really* pained. I might as well have asked him whether Cooperstown Dreams Park might start a hopscotch tournament some day. I pushed a little and he wouldn't answer. "Look, we have the best baseball anywhere," he says. "Little League isn't even close. What's the point?"

Cooperstown Dreams Park is in the midst of expanding exponentially. The number of teams playing at the park will increase from eighty to ninety-six starting in 2006. Close to 1,000 different teams come to Cooperstown every summer, but the waiting list is much longer than that. So Presutti plans to open two more parks in the U.S. in the next five years. He won't say where the parks will be located, since he's in negotiations with local governments over zoning, infrastructure, and taxes. He expects one of the new parks to open in 2007 or 2008 and both of the new ones to be in business by 2010.

By the time he's finished, Presutti's tournaments will host as many as 15,000 elite baseball games a summer. He will be the king of all of youth baseball. And then he's going to tell the story of how he made it happen. Hollywood producers and directors have contacted him about doing a movie, but he's not interested just yet. He wants the movie to be the definitive story, and the tale is only beginning.

———————— • ◆ • ————————

The South Oakland A's took the field to battle for the Week Six championship at Cooperstown Dreams Park. The A's sent a tall redheaded lad named Alex Maodus to the mound. He throws the ball in the seventies, which means the ball gets to the plate at an equivalent major-league speed in the upper eighties. He also tosses the ball softly once in a while.

At the fuzzy-faced age of twelve years, good players understand the elements of pitching. If you have a hard fastball, that's great, but hitters are going to hit it hard if you don't mix in some soft stuff and move the ball around the strike zone. The catcher's ability to receive the ball is the most important aspect of youth baseball. If the catcher can catch anything, the pitcher can throw anything. And the best way to get hitters out is to throw stuff out of reach—down in the dirt, up near the eyes, or away from the plate. Set 'em up with strikes and near-strikes, and then get 'em out with junk.

But North Tampa had a line on Alex Maodus, the A's pitcher. After two innings, the Yankees led 5–0. The Yankees scored one run in the first inning on two hits, three walks, a balk, and a wild pitch. It could have been worse. One Yankee got caught stealing third base, and the team left the bases full. A solo home run, three singles, and a walk scored four more runs in the second.

Manager Buster Sunde replaced Maodus with one out in the second, but the change didn't help much right away. But after allowing three runs—one of Maodus's, two of his own—John Keith shut down North Tampa for the rest of the game. Keith throws hard, in the upper seventies (close to 100 when calibrated to major-league distances). He rocks into a full motion and drives his body home like Roger Clemens or Curt Schilling. His overhanded delivery is hard for hitters to pick up.

I watched the game on the A's bench. The players were excited and energetic, but tired. They bounced around like a kid rubbing his eyes while insisting that he doesn't need to go to bed. The fatigue had an effect. By the time the game was over, the two teams combined for five errors, two wild pitches, five passed balls, one balk, and one hit batsman. Remember, this is the best twelve-year-old baseball in the country.

Despite the errors, the players usually looked good in the field. With a baserunner at second base, the shortstop and second baseman took turns covering the bag for pickoff throws. Infielders took bounding grounders and shots in the hole and made strong pegs to first base with perfect timing—the throws are quick and deliberate, but not rushed.

And the catchers! Like hockey goalies, the catchers took every kind of abuse behind the plate—foul tips, balls in the dirt—and usually kept the ball in front.

The players do not imitate major-league players the way some Little League players do. No one holds his hand back toward the umpire like Derek Jeter. No one uses the exaggerated bat wagging like Gary Sheffield. "We teach them proper technique, period," says Larry Lobur, one of the A's coaches. "There's no time for anything else."

There *was* one showboater on the field, a short second baseman named Opie Brodbeck. Between innings, as he takes his position, Opie does one, two, three, four flips—the way Hall of Famer Ozzie Smith used to do for the St. Louis Cardinals.

———————— • ◆ • ————————

During the game, Lou Presutti sat for a while in the A's dugout. He talked with a couple boys about the game. Introduced only minutes before, Presutti was already teaching them the fine points of baseball.

"Watch where that ball is coming out of his hand," he tells the boys, sons of an executive for Disney World, which hosts another elite baseball tournament for twelve-and-under players. The pitch burned up and inside.

"Where's he going to throw it now? I think he's going to throw some outside junk now. He had him set up for outside junk. Junk is an important part of pitching. Fastballs are great, but junk's what makes it work."

But the pitcher threw another fastball on the inside part of the plate. "Okay, he fooled me, too," Presutti says.

He watched intently for another thirty seconds. The boys followed his example, scanning the field, examining the pitcher and then the hitter. Presutti had another nugget for the boys. "Look at the way he holds the bat. Look at his palms—the way he's holding them opposite to each other."

The pitch-by-pitch tutorial continued for two batters, and then Presutti moved on. The boys stayed behind, watching the game like medical students sitting in on surgery performed by a seasoned doctor.

Their education in baseball continued, even after the doctor left the operating room.

———————————— • ◆ • ————————————

The game had its share of harsh moments. The families and other fans of the two teams took turns with their "Let's Go" chants, sometimes screaming louder to drown out the other side. Close calls—force plays, ball and strike calls—prompted groans and boos. The fans jeered loudly when the A's Mitch Kozlowski got tagged in a rundown play in the first inning. "Aw, *come on*, ump!" shouts one A's dad after a close strike call. On a couple of occasions, the managers protested calls.

In the top of the first inning, the North Tampa team had runners on second and third when South Oakland pitcher Alex Maodus made a quick throw to third base to get Opie Brodbeck running to third base. Brodbeck got caught in a rundown play and got tagged out after three throws. It was the third out, the end of the inning. The South Oakland fielders left the field. The North Tampa players took their positions on the diamond.

But North Tampa manager John DiSanto could not believe it. He ran out to talk with the home plate umpire. The discussion went on for a minute or two. Then the umpire convened the other umpires for a discussion. DiSanto made his case to the blue crew and then backed off while they talked. Soon the South Oakland manager, Buster Sunde, came out to ask what was happening. More discussion.

Finally, the umpires signaled for the teams to trade places on the field. They were persuaded that the pitcher balked. Brodbeck was called safe at third, and Kevin Gomes was allowed to score on the play. Then there came more arguments. Finally, play resumed.

In the bottom of the sixth inning, the home plate umpire made a foul call on a sacrifice bunt attempt along the third-base line. Sunde argued vociferously. After hearing Sunde's cries for a half-minute, the umpire ripped off his mask and shouted back: "The ball landed there," he said, moving halfway up the line. "It was foul! I had it all the way! Foul!" End of discussion.

———————— •◆• ————————

The A's and Yankees went into the bottom of the sixth inning—the end of regulation play—tied 5–5.

In the sixth, the A's Ryan Horvath started a rally when he reached first on a walk and took second on a groundout. One out later, Mitch Kozlowski hit a fly ball to the 200-foot wall in right field. The Yankees' Cody Mizolle got handcuffed on the ball—he couldn't decide whether to come in or back up on the play—and let it drop. The A's Horvath, running on the hit, had no trouble coming all the way around to give the A's the winning run. As they had in eleven other tournaments that summer, the A's flocked to the plate to mob each other in celebration.

At the very moment that Horvath crossed the plate, Presutti grabbed a pair of trophies and moved toward the field for yet another championship celebration. North Tampa took its runner-up award and then South Oakland reveled in its victory.

It was after midnight when the brief celebrations took place on the field before a dwindling crowd.

And then it was time to get ready to go to the Albany Airport. The team was on its way to Disney World's Elite World Series, where twenty-four teams were getting ready to compete for yet another championship.

If it's August, this must be Orlando.

Most experts on youth baseball consider the best travel teams to be far superior to the teams playing in the Little League World Series.

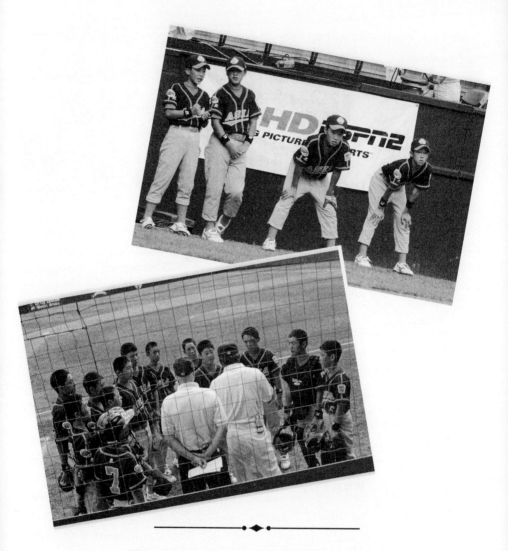

The team from Chiba City, Japan, combines rigorous discipline and fundaments with open expression of the joy of play.

CHAPTER 12

•◆•

How They Play the Game

O N THEIR FIRST MORNING OF WORKOUTS in Williamsport, I was watching the team from Davenport, Iowa, take cuts in the batting cages when the all-stars from Chiba City, Japan, briskly walked down the long hill from International Grove. I knew they had arrived at one in the morning—after spending a full day traveling from Tokyo to California, and then on to Philadelphia—and it was now just 9:30 a.m.

But they looked better—more organized, more energetic—than the Iowans hacking away in the cages.

Wearing practice uniforms and carrying bags of bats and balls and helmets, the Japanese players approached the batting cages.

"Good morning!" the Japanese kids said with an energy not usually found in global travelers working on six hours of sleep. "Good morning!" "Good morning!"

The players from Davenport looked puzzled as the Japanese players glided by. A few imitated their greetings—"Good morning!"—before a coach told them to respond politely and not mockingly. But the Japanese were gone before the Iowans had a chance to think up greetings of their own.

—————— •◆• ——————

Within minutes, the Japanese stood on the farthest of the five practice fields in the complex. They spread out on the field, stretched, ran, and did calisthenics.

With every movement, they shouted out: "*Ui!*" (It's pronounced "Way!") That chant can be loosely translated as "Let's go!" The chant is part grunt, part chirp, depending on the player's stage of physical development.

And go is what they did. After limbering up in the rhythms of the chant, they took the field for a fast-paced set of drills to quicken their reaction times and sharpen their brains.

A morning fog shrouded the mountains in the distance, creating an ethereal effect. The scene looked like a Japanese watercolor.

One exercise had the mesmerizing quality of Riverdance. Groups of three or four players clustered around the bases and home plate. Their manager shouted out game situations. And then the players whipped the ball from base to base, without a pause. If the situation was a steal attempt, the catcher made a hard throw from the plate to second base—answering the manager's order—and then the fielders threw the ball around the diamond faster and faster. After making a catch and a throw, one player stepped back and a second one moved in for the next throw; after he got the ball and whipped it across the diamond, the third player stepped in for his catch and throw.

Yusuke Taira and other pitchers from Chiba City emulate the motion that Hideo Nomo used to become one of the first Japanese stars to play in the American major leagues.

A quick look at a wristwatch showed that the players made about thirty-five throws every minute—more than a throw every two seconds. As the ball zipped back and forth across the diamond, the kids tittered in anticipation of which player would miss the ball first. When it happened—when one of the players stationed near third base let the ball tip off the top of his glove—everyone laughed. He ran after the ball, ran back, the manager shouted the next game situation, and the game of lightning catch began anew.

At one point, a ball got away from another player around third base and hit a teammate on the right wrist. He went down, crying. The manager and coaches gathered. The manager's wife walked over from the third-base bench. One of the team's "uncles"—the volunteers who look after the teams' everyday needs—made a walkie-talkie call to Little League's trainer. Minutes later, Mike Ludwikowski arrived on the scene. He found no broken bones, only a bruise. He guided the player toward a golf cart and took him away for ice treatment. The rest of the Japanese players then resumed the lightning drill.

In another exercise, the players did a fast-paced hitting/fielding drill. One player threw the ball to the other, who hit it back on the ground. The throws—short-distance pitches—were almost all accurate, and the hitters hit the balls directly back at the fielders. The manager and coaches walked around, shouting encouragement and instructions. Every once in a while a ball got away. But the players threw and hit the ball with near-perfect control.

———————— • ◆ • ————————

Discipline was high for the Japanese players. The team's manager, Hirofumi Oda, seemed an interested bystander for much of the team's practices. He walked around, wearing a white golf shirt and long white pants—the ice cream man's outfit that he wore for the whole tournament—while the players disciplined themselves. The team's catcher and captain, Kisho Watanabe, shouted out instructions to his teammates. But even he did not need to do anything to rally his teammates. They all knew what to do, how, and when.

It's *wa*, the Japanese word for group effort.

Wherever they go on the field, the players run. They run in and out of the dugout for bats, catching gear, everything. They run from a position on the diamond to the batter's box. The Japan team was all about movement. There was urgency in everything these players did.

At first glance, the Japanese team seemed to reinforce all the cultural stereotypes of seriousness and formality. The Japanese worked through drills constantly, burning into the players' muscles and minds automatic responses to different game situations.

But the Japanese players burst out laughing every five or ten minutes. And then they got back to work. Work, work, work, laugh; work, work, work, laugh. Enthusiasm ran high on this team.

After the practice, Oda asked Japan's team hosts—through the volunteer translators who would shadow the team during the tournament—whether they needed to groom the field before they left. At first, the hosts could not believe they heard the question right. Translator Bill Lundy—grandson of one of the three original sponsors of Little League, back in 1939—then told Oda not to worry.

Before they departed, the players lined up along the third base line, took off their hats, turned toward the diamond, and bowed—a silent closing gesture of respect for the field.

———————— •◆• ————————

Baseball first came to Japan sometime in the Meiji era, which promoted westernization and modernization, in the latter half of the nineteenth century. Because it was seen as a variation of martial arts—with this high-speed duel between pitcher and hitter—*besuboru* quickly captured the imagination of the Japanese.

At the turn of the century, the Japanese formed their first professional league. In the 1930s, Americans led by Babe Ruth and Lou Gehrig barnstormed Japan, creating a frenzy of interest. In the 1960s and 1970s, the home-run prowess of Sadaharu Oh gave Japan its great mythic figure. In the 1990s and 2000s, the migration of Hideo Nomo, Ichiro Suzuki, Hideki Matsui, and others to the U.S. showed a growing parity in the quality of players on both sides of the Pacific. In 2006, Japan triumphed in the first World Baseball Classic.

Baseball in Japan has always been embedded in school sports, rather than community leagues. For years, when Japan and Taiwan dominated the Little League World Series, detractors complained that the Japanese had an unfair advantage because they drew teams from broad geographic areas and taught the game in schools like a basic subject. Youth baseball reaches its peak every spring when a million fans attend the national high school baseball tournament. To understand the atmosphere of those games, think of a college bowl game or the NCAA's March Madness.

The cliché about Japan is that it's a rigid, conformist society. There's no room for innovation or joy. The individual gets lost in the system. Maybe there's some truth to that. But at the same time, the game is open to innovation. Ichiro challenged the way hitters approach the game. Bobby Valentine, a two-time major league manager, brought a looser, player-friendly attitude to running a team. Not long ago, Japanese teams did not give players time off for family occasions like having a baby. Valentine's attitude, once scorned but now accepted, is: Why not?

The Chiba City Little League showed that even if discipline remains the defining characteristic of Japanese baseball, there's still plenty of space for exuberance.

One Japanese grandfather told me that his grandson was so shy that

The Japanese team paid its respects to the crowd after every game in the Little League World Series.

he doubted that the boy would last long in a team sport. His place was home and in the classroom. But baseball has transformed him. He's learned some discipline, but he had plenty of that already. "He's more playful because of playing on this team," he said. "I like to see him smile, not be so serious. I like to see that my grandson is always helping the others—picking up balls or bats. I didn't realize he is such a generous or helpful boy."

Teams throughout Japan work out endlessly, using repetitive drills to hone skills and make every conceivable action a reflex. One pro player set a record by fielding 900 straight ground balls over a period of almost three hours—before dropping from exhaustion. When he played for the Hiroshima Carp, one of the most relentless organizations in Japan, Alfonso Soriano swung bats until his hands were bloody. I once asked Soriano what he thinks about the Japanese approach. "I hated it," he said. "But it made me a better player. I improved my bat speed like you wouldn't believe. I'm glad I played there, but I'm glad I got out."

The *sensei*—the master or, in this case, the coach—demands and gets the absolute devotion of his players. When the coach calls the players together for words of encouragement, the players take off their hats and form a semicircle around him. They're there to listen, not be distracted.

But it's not just mannerisms. It's also the play on the field. The Japanese players play crisply. Every action has a snap to it—swinging the bat, scooping up grounders in the infield, throwing the ball, and getting into position for a cutoff throw.

Intense practices—professional teams work intensely into the night during spring training, while their American counterparts often work just a few hours before heading off to play golf—are designed as much to train the mind as the body. "These drills are primarily mental," one Japanese journalist wrote. "Yes, they do wear a player out, but that is necessary in order to develop his spirit. Athletics are essentially an act of will. You can always do more than you think you are capable of. It is our philosophy that only by pushing a player to his limits can he discover and develop the power to surpass them, and that is what these drills accomplish."

———————— •◆• ————————

The best place to see Japan's discipline is on the mound.

It doesn't matter who's pitching. It could be Takuya Sakamoto, the starter who allowed just two hits in a 3–0 win against Saudi Arabia in the first game of pool play. It could be Yusuke Taira, who allowed Curaçao just three hits in Japan's 9–0 victory in the next game. It could be Shuhei Iwata or Yuki Mizuma, who pitched less effectively but still won, 7–4, over the powerful team from Valencia, Venezuela. Or try Tomokazu Kaise, who pitched a hitless inning to close out Sakamoto's one-hit 11–0 victory over Canada in the first game after pool play.

No matter who took the mound for Japan, it was Hideo Nomo who was really pitching.

Nomo was the Japanese pioneer in the major leagues when he joined the Los Angeles Dodgers in 1995. In eleven seasons, Nomo won 123 games, including a no-hitter with the Boston Red Sox.

Little Leaguers all over Japan imitate Nomo's distinctive motion, which produces the sharpest curveballs in Williamsport and keeps the hitters off balance.

Sakamoto—or Taira or Iwata or Mizuma or Kaise—begins with a soft step toward the pitching runner. Carefully bending his back leg, he kicks out his front foot as if he was gently kicking a can, and then turns his foot up and away from the plate. As he draws his right arm back, he hesitates before bringing his whole body forward. There's a moment when his body actually stops, in the middle of his motion. In practices, some pitching coaches have their pitchers stop at that point to make sure they maintain their balance. But the Japanese pitchers freeze themselves mid-motion every pitch. After the momentary pause, they whip the pitching arm forward from a three-quarters motion.

The motion helps to produce some of the best fastballs anywhere in the World Series—and the most wicked curveballs of all.

Other pitchers throw the curveball with some wariness. Most curveballs in Little League are really slower fastballs coming at a different speed with a different spin. Coaches teach their kids the "Little League curve," a twelve-to-six-o'clock delivery that produces some spin but mostly slows the ball down. It's a lollipop curve, a rainbow curve.

But the Japanese curve is a sharp snap. Move around the stands among the other coaches and baseball lifers, and the snap of the Japanese deuce produces gasps. *Did he really do that?* Yes, and it's the kind of pitching that allows an average of just one earned run every game.

————————— •◆• —————————

Baseball is different for Curaçao. The old saying about Caribbean baseball is that you can't walk off the island. Young players are eager to show some muscle when they get up to the plate, do something flashy that catches the eye of coaches and (some day) scouts.

The Caribbean game begins with the players' sinewy strength. These elastic bodies stretch into motion, rearing back to pitch or leaning back to swing the bat. Even the fielders have an elastic quality, as they range into the hole for a ground ball or extend their glove hand to throw a ball across the diamond.

The Caribbean game grows out of the ground. The rock-strewn infields and the grassy outfields (occasionally populated by goats on lunch break) make fielding a random activity. The randomness of the bouncing ball gives Caribbean players unmatchable reflexes on grounders. The unevenness of the ground everywhere—the infield *and* the outfield—provides the feet extra sensitivity to what lies beneath. The feet are the most sensitive part of the body, but affluent Westerners lose the feel for the ground because the ground is usually so smooth and their shoes are equipped with high-tech shock absorbers. But when you have to lope over thick and thin grass and pebbles, the field a random pattern of soft and hard spots, you develop an ability to *read* wherever you run.

But as important as these topographic conditions, Curaçao's Little League programs are built on the dictatorial discipline of the managers. Figures like Frank Curiel and Vernon Isabella demand, and get, strict obedience.

European school traditions affect everything in Curaçao, from career tracks to sports. The Dutch schools are hierarchical. The teacher demands, and gets, absolute obedience. Kids wear uniforms to schools everywhere. No T-shirts and jeans. And they're subject to rigorous curriculum and tough tests. Kids take oral exams, administered off the school site to prevent favoritism.

That strictness gets carried over to the ballfields. When Vernon Isabella manages his team—whether it's the Refineria Isla or the Pabou League all-stars—he demands total control. He tells the kids that their only job is to win. And when their attention wanders, he scolds them. If they crumble a little, that's too bad. They need to learn how to be tough.

Randy Wiel, a basketball coach who was once one of Curaçao's best athletes, says he was watching the Little League games on ESPN and was intrigued—but not surprised—by what manager Vernon Isabella told his kids on the field. Because ESPN and ABC miked the managers, Wiel heard a lot that non-Papiamentu speakers like me missed. "He was telling his pitcher, 'Are you going to pitch, or should I get someone else in here?'" Wiel says.

Vernon Isabella is no Tommy Lasorda.

I asked Isabella about his determination to win every single game and he smiled and raised his arm. "You play to win," he said through an interpreter. "That's why we're here. The children need to know that."

Curaçao's greatest test in Williamsport came in the international championship game against Japan. As far as Vernon Isabella was concerned, only Jurickson Profar could guarantee that the Caribbean team advance to the final against the winner of the California-Hawaii game.

Sure enough, Profar carried the team. He pitched a complete-game shutout—a two-hitter, in fact—and scored a run in Curaçao's 2–0 win. His only flaw was walking six batters, but that was more a sign of his respect for Japan than of any control problems.

The respect for the Japan team—especially shortstop Yuki Mizuma—was ever visible.

In the first inning, with a runner on third base, Curaçao intentionally walked Mizuma. Vernon Isabella asked the umpire if he could just send the hitter to first base without throwing any pitches, but the answer was no, you gotta throw the ball four times.

"It doesn't matter what inning it is—you still have to make the big decision," Isabella told me later. "The first inning could make the difference for the whole game. You don't like the team to be down. I'd rather put the pressure on the other team. Make them hit the ball. Make them score the run without their best hitter. If you play against strong teams, you can't let them have the advantage. You've got to keep them close."

Curaçao took a 2–0 lead in the first inning on singles by Profar and Liberia.

Play at the plate.

In the third, with a runner on first, Curaçao intentionally walked Mizuma again. Fans filled Lamade Stadium with boos. *Who does this guy think he is? Imagine! Walking a kid two times in one game! Why can't he just let the kids play?*

"My philosophy is that we're up 2–0, and this guy comes up with a guy at second base; with one swing the guy can tie it up," Isabella said, before noting that he pitched to Mizuma in the fifth inning. "That last time, the bases were empty. If he hits a home run, you're still winning. So you have to face him like a man."

Face him like a man when it's not too dangerous. Otherwise, avoid him.

That's how Isabella manages all his games—whether it's a single-elimination game in Williamsport or a scrimmage on dusty Frank Curiel Field in Willemstad. When I was in Curaçao, I watched one game in which Isabella pulled a pitcher in the second inning with the score 2–1. The game didn't count for anything, and the move backfired—the other team hit the ball harder against the new pitcher. But Isabella was there to win—more important, to teach his players to *play to win*, no matter what.

Isabella's field strategy could be drawn from *On War*, Baron von Clauswitz's classic study of military strategy and tactics:

Use your best against the best. Avoid the battles you cannot afford to lose. Hit the other side at its weakest links. Survive first, then fight the next battle with whatever weapons are left.

———————— • ◆ • ————————

What can someone who grew up in the Soviet Union, a country now on the ash heap of history, teach you about baseball?

A lot, actually—maybe even more than you can learn from someone from the Americas or Japan, where baseball has been suffused into the culture for more than a century.

I first approached Alexey Erofeev, the manager of the Little Leaguers from Moscow, because he seemed such an anomaly. Here's a guy who teaches baseball in a place where the ground is frozen like stone from October to May—and where Cold War rhetoric once marginalized the game as a bourgeois, individualist, and exploitive opiate.

Erofeev is a thin man with thinning silver hair. When you think of Russians on the world stage, think Putin, not Yeltsin. He discusses baseball with the discipline of a KGB agent in a spy thriller. But he's a lot nicer.

When Erofeev thinks about how to teach baseball to Russian kids, he thinks of lapta. In lapta, one of the games Erofeev played as a child, a striker stands at one base and hits a ball tossed by a teammate. When the striker hits the ball, he runs toward the other base (called the kon) and back. Fielders chase down the ball. Fielders get the runner out by hitting him with the ball, which is softer than a baseball.

Leon Trotsky, the Russian revolutionary, claimed that baseball evolved out of lapta when Russian émigrés moved to the American west in the mid-1700s. Whatever the value of Trotsky's thesis, the larger truth is that history is full of games with bats and balls—cricket, rounders, *pesäpallo*, stool-ball. "People have always played these games," John Gilmore, an American businessman who has made it a mission to promote baseball in Russia, told me. "Look at the hieroglyphics and you see the caveman with sticks and rocks." Baseball emerged from a primordial soup of stick games. Sorry, Abner Doubleday fans.

Baseball as we know it in Russia came when the Olympics approved baseball on a trial basis in 1984. Soon, countries with no tradition of baseball put together instructional programs so they could field a team. The Soviet Baseball Federation came into being in 1986 and, with the help of their Cuban comrades, quickly established a presence at two of the country's thirty-eight sports academies. By 1990, the Russians competed in the Goodwill Games, and in 1992 Olympic baseball began.

Little League chartered its first program in Russia in 1991. By 2005, seven Little League teams involving 105 players competed in Little League and Junior League, the programs for players aged eleven to fourteen.

When I talked with Erofeev, he volunteered right away that he didn't think his Little League team had much of a chance in Williamsport. But even though he would love to win a game, that's not what mattered to him. What mattered was taking home lessons on how the real stars play baseball.

Sure enough, Russia went 0–3 in the tournament. Guam beat Russia 6–2. Then Mexico beat Russia, 7–0. And then Canada beat Russia, 2–1.

But the Moscow kids didn't look bad. The pitchers threw well, usually keeping the team in the game. The infielders performed well, too, showing they could turn a double play. Sometimes, nervousness led to some errors—but not often. The hitters struggled, but they had some good at-bats against intimidating pitchers.

Even though baseball remains a minor sport in Russia, Vikto Elkin and his teammates from Moscow's Brateevo Little League showed good fundamental skills in Williamsport.

Moscow's biggest problem in Williamsport was the curveball—the fact that they don't throw it *and* the fact that they can't hit it.

Erofeev does not let his pitchers even *tinker* with the curveball because he believes the medical research that warns against it. Other managers in Williamsport acknowledged the dangers of the curve…but just as quickly added that the need to win trumped those concerns. But Erofeev is an absolutist.

Not letting his pitchers throw the curveball can make them better pitchers, Erofeev insisted. "We can get hitters out with fastballs and changeups if we do it right," he told me. "So we just have to do better. Sometimes, when you're not allowed to do something, you learn how to do the other things better."

Erofeev thinks he can teach his pitchers to throw three fastballs instead of one, and two good changeups. That should be enough. They'll be smarter pitchers *and* enjoy the bonus of not wrecking their arms.

At the same time, Erofeev accepts the reality that other teams use the curve. "We need to learn how to hit curveballs," he says. "We can hit fast-balls, and we have the patience to hit changeups. But the curveball is new to us."

Hitting a curveball is really no different than any other athletic feat, he says.

"It's all about quick thinking leading to quick actions," he said. "The mental aspect is more important than the physical right now. A good player thinks anywhere, on the field, in the dugout, at bat. If you think, you win. We need to get so that the players automatically move, they have instincts for everything that happens in a game."

Even hitting the deuce. If you understand it, if you see it in your mind's eye, you can learn how to hit any curveball. Can it be any harder than hitting a blistering-fast hockey puck while flying on the ice before a goon body-checks you while skating at top speed? No, Erofeev says.

Erofeev took up baseball when knee injuries forced him off the hockey rink. His command of a hockey stick instantly carried over to command of a baseball bat. He played outfield and shortstop for the Moscow Red Devils, one of the ten teams created immediately after the decision to bring baseball to the Olympics. The Red Devils won the championship eight times.

Sports are sports, Erofeev told me. Athletes thrive when they apply the skills and mental training from one sport to another.

"Hockey and baseball are team sports," he said. "In both games, it's very important to have good, quick thinking. To develop physical condition, I bring from hockey different running exercises. To make quick movements and good reactions, and concentration, it's very important to have different exercises. When they grow, kids are interested in different exercises. They run races. There is no hard and stupid work. Only games, games, games. Both hockey and baseball use stick and balls. Two teams in a small diamond and one team with four players. Like passing the puck in 'Ducks.'"

It's a challenge teaching baseball in a place with no real baseball tradition and only about three or four months of real baseball weather. Baseball in Russia is played under primitive conditions. There are only a couple baseball diamonds in Moscow. Most games and practices take place at soccer fields, with a short left field and a deep right field—"just like your Fenway Park," Erofeev says. But the fields are about as well-groomed as Willie Nelson. And the Russians have little equipment. The players share gloves; helmets and catching gear are scarce, and coaches use their own money to buy balls. One of the benefits of winning a trip to Williamsport is getting free bats and other supplies to bring home.

But to Erofeev, limitations also offer potential advantages. Over the winter, Moscow's Little Leaguers play sports requiring quick reactions and good hand-eye coordination.

"We play other games for physical reaction time and endurance. Different sports help to develop all the qualities needed for baseball. When we started, we had awful physical condition. Now, there's no need to develop condition. Now, it's very much a problem to teach them how to stay strong and get quick, quick, quick."

Darren Van Tassell, the technical commissioner of the International Baseball Association, was one of the first Americans to travel to the Soviet Union to teach baseball. He agrees with Erofeev's approach.

Building skills, one by one, is an approach often lost on coaches and players in countries with baseball traditions—like the U.S. When you're watching baseball on cable TV all the time, the tendency is to want to *act* like a major leaguer rather than learn the game's fundamentals.

"There's nothing natural about being an athlete," Van Tassell told me. "It requires lots of work and repetition. The saying is that 'practice makes perfect,' but that's not right. It's 'perfect practice that makes perfect' or 'practice makes permanent.' If you teach the wrong way, you can make a player bad for a long time....To get good production, there are physical things you do with the body—hands out fielding ground balls, waiting for a pitch, moving to the right and to the left. The way you hit the ball hard—that comes from good mechanics, and that's what practice is all about."

That's the plan, Erofeev says—do all the little things right, and avoid dangerous temptations like the curveball.

"We care about the long term," he says. "We want to make players for your major leagues. That means we have to do little things right now. Being here is not about winning. It's about learning."

———————— • ◆ • ————————

Foreigners appreciate American baseball for its verve and power. But they're often puzzled about why the Americans don't have a more disciplined approach.

When I asked Vernon Isabella who the best teams were in the Little League World Series, he mentioned Curaçao, Japan, Venezuela, and Guam. I asked him about Hawaii and California, but he waved me away. "Yeah, they're good," he says. "But not as good as they should be."

When I asked Curaçao's players the same question, they named most of the same teams as Isabella. They never mentioned the American teams. When I asked why, they said the Americans didn't work on their skills enough. They won on strength alone.

"They cheated," Rudmichaell Brandao said when I ask him about Hawaii. "They had older guys on the team. They *had* to be older. They were so big. They were monsters."

I told him that, as far as I knew, the Hawaiian players were all under the Little League's age limit (players cannot turn thirteen before the cutoff date of July 31; starting in 2006, that cutoff date is April 30). He didn't believe me. He shook his head. "But they're so *big*," he said again.

———————•◆•———————

The American game is like the rest of American society—committed to the exercise of power, and creative in devising new approaches to the game, but often deficient in fundamentals and discipline.

If only they worked harder, foreigners often say with a sigh, they would be so much better. But look at the way they conduct themselves on the field. They goof off. They ignore their coaches. They stubbornly cling to their idiosyncratic batting styles and pitching motions. They swing for home runs. They try to strike out every batter. They hot-dog it in the field. They're big enough so they can win, sure, but they *really should work harder.*

Robert Whiting explored the contrasting styles of baseball in the U.S. and Japan for his book *You Gotta Have Wa.* Whiting lived in Tokyo and interviewed players and coaches from both sides of the Pacific who played in the Japanese leagues. "They really admire the power and dynamism and creativity of it all," Whiting says. "But they note all the little things they don't do, like advancing the runner, hitting to the opposite field, and defensive positioning. If they *applied* themselves, they'd be so much better."

The American game begins with power—and that game is especially suited to the Little League World Series. Throw hard, hit hard, and slide hard. Games are won and lost with strikeouts and home runs. Running into walls and diving into the stands doesn't make much sense.

The teams from Hawaii and California offered perfect representations of the American game's raw power.

Kalen Pimentel, California's goateed pitcher/shortstop/catcher, started the series for the Rancho Buena Vista Little Leaguers by striking out eighteen batters in the opening day win over Owensboro, Kentucky. California won 7–2 when Nathan Lewis and Aaron Kim hit home runs.

In California's next two games—against Westbrook, Maine, and Lafayette, Louisiana—Pimentel showed his power at the plate. He hit grand slams in both games to lead R.B.V. to 7–2 and 9–3 victories. Reed Reznicek also homered for R.B.V.

In the American semifinal game against Florida, Pimentel struck out nine batters and beat another marquee pitcher, Dante Bichette Jr., 6–2. But Pimentel's strength took the form of perseverance in this game. Confronting a small strike zone, which pushed his pitch count to 103, Pimentel had to fight for every out.

Hawaii hit thirteen home runs in the World Series, more than any other team in Williamsport and two short of the record. It seemed like everyone hit those homers—Alaka'i Aglipay and Bubbles Baniaga, Kini Enos and Michael Memea, Vonn Fe'ao and Quentin Guevara. Even when the Hawaiians got fooled—like the time Louisiana's Jace Conrad baffled them with his odd motion—they won with a big home run.

Home runs accounted for twenty of Hawaii's thirty-two runs in the first five games of the World Series. How very American. All or nothing.

And the physical domination continued on the mound. Pitchers like Alaka'i Aglipay and Vonn Fe'ao were completely dominating. Fe'ao probably threw the ball as hard as anyone in the ten-day tournament.

* * *

Hawaii's Michael Memea is exactly the kind of player that makes foreigners critical of the American game. Lots of power, not enough quickness or skill.

When I visited Curaçao a few months after the Series, I talked with Isabella about a wide range of players from both American and international teams. When I got to Memea's name, he was especially emphatic.

"I would not take him on my team," Isabella said. "He's not a guy who makes a lot of contact. If I could use someone like him only to catch, and not have to use him batting, then I would take someone like him on my team."

Michael Memea's bat scorched Curaçao in the championship game, but Isabella was not impressed. Typical American—big and strong, but undisciplined, rough, and unreliable.

Isabella's missed something important in his assessment. Yes, Mike Memea is big and clunky. Catcher, first base, and third base are probably the only positions he can play in a competitive league. He doesn't have the quickness that other positions demand. You could say he's a one-dimensional player—strong enough to pound the ball when he connects, but not terribly helpful otherwise.

But that misses how American baseball works. American baseball is a game not only of power—which Memea can supply—but also role-players. The international teams often boasted that their players could play almost all positions. They're all-around players. Which is great. But the Americans put together teams not of interchangeable parts, but of specific parts designed for specific purposes.

Michael Memea would be a disaster, probably, at shortstop. He's no Jurickson Profar. But what he does works, at least in Little League.

Michael Memea's background, the way he is driven, is also classically American. He's an immigrant's kid. His father didn't have much growing up, but he made a steady career in the navy that enabled his youngsters to play sports. And since Michael has those opportunities his parents didn't have, he's pushed hard to make good.

Michael's father Mack, a career navy logistics officer who retired at the end of the year with twenty years service, came to Hawaii at the age of thirteen from Samoa. He played some high school sports with middling success, and then got a job. His name is appropriate—he's about as square and solid and intimidating as a Mack truck. He has short black hair and a round and inviting face. But he sets strict standards and pushes his kids to meet them. The kids have found that the only way past their father's will is to have an even more intense will of their own.

Michael Memea is the second great athlete in the Memea household. His older sister Desiree is a world champion wrestler who hopes to make the U.S. Olympic team in 2008.

"I tried to put Desiree into softball," Mack Memea told me as we drank coffee at a McDonald's before meeting Michael for basketball practice. "She had the right physique and all the potential but she couldn't put it together. The ball hit her in the face and that was it, she stopped. Then I tried to put her in basketball and volleyball, and she was uncoordinated, and it was so frustrating to me. She finally molded herself to play basketball and volleyball, but now she's in wrestling."

In fact, Desiree won the national championship in the 175-pound division in Fargo, North Dakota. At five feet, eight inches, 158 pounds, she has a lot of room to develop physically. At first, Mack opposed her wrestling. He told her she didn't have the toughness or the "mentality" to succeed in such a rough sport—in such a boy's sport. But he's happy to be proven wrong. When he was stationed in Bahrain, he had videos of her matches emailed to him.

Mack also pushes Michael. He takes him to batting cages and gyms for workouts. He goes to baseball and basketball practices. And he lectures him about everything—how to be around girls, how to follow a coach's instructions, how to talk with strangers, dating (when he's sixteen, he can start group dating but nothing more), and whether to stick with catching despite his strong desire to play center field.

Mack's overbearing ways can be a burden, but he succeeds in provoking his children: *You got a better way? Then tell me—and prove it!* Teammates say Michael is one of the most stubborn members of the team. Mack says, with some pride, that he's a "kiss-my-butt kind of kid."

Memea's body-type is perfect for a catcher—big and bulky, slow moving but sturdy—but Memea openly resents playing the position. He played the position for the Hawaii all-stars because he respected his manager, Layton Aliviado, and wanted to be part of a team that went all the way. Mack Memea once intervened on the catcher issue. He asked Aliviado to play Vonn Fe'ao behind the plate, but Aliviado said no, since Fe'ao was a critical late-innings pitcher, and catching would put too much strain on his arm.

I spent a few hours with the two Memeas, and Mike would not let go of his desire to quit catching. He talked about how he wanted to be like Bernie Williams. I told him that the Yankees were going to get another center fielder. He was crestfallen. Then I told him that catching is the quickest route to the major leagues. "*See!*" Mack Memea almost shouted with glee. "Listen to him! Maybe that's what you should think about, Mike!"

Mike wouldn't budge. "I want to play center, like Bernie," he said.

Mike Memea has not yet grown into his body or his place in the world. He shuffles around, seeming to occupy his own time zone. He swings the bat slowly—but powerfully. He swings and misses at pitch after pitch, trying to get his timing and rhythm. When he connects, the sheer power of his body and swing can send the ball far. He bats in the middle of Hawaii's order because he connects enough. Other teams don't see him enough to pitch to his weaknesses.

But like powerful American athletes everywhere, he's not embarrassed by his failures. He checks his swing on an inside pitch. Strike! He reaches for an outside pitch. Strike! He swings past a high fastball so late you wonder if he's just getting an early start on the next pitch. Strike! He uppercuts and misses. Strike! And when he's not swinging around pitches, he's hitting them late, fouling the ball the other way or just nicking it back to the backstop.

I got DVDs of all of Hawaii's games from the regional tournament's final game through the World Series finale. I decided to look carefully at Memea's at-bats to see how fair Isabella was being. At times, Memea looked awful. He brought his bat around in a big, slow arc, sometimes long after the ball popped into the catcher's glove. But there was something steady about him too. He's smart enough to learn during an at-bat. And he's confident enough to forget about an awful swing and come back and hit the ball hard. Who cares about the ugly swing on the curveball? There's always another pitch.

He takes those deep breaths, wags the bat behind his head, makes his head still, and gets ready.

And then he connects. After a couple bad swings, he puts the fat part of the bat on the ball. If he just lays the bat on the ball, he's so strong that the ball whistles on a line to the outfield.

"He has that ugly swing," says his manager, Layton Aliviado. "But then, you know what? He could still hit it hard."

At the age of twelve, Memea's already something of a journeyman, constantly on the search for the right fit. His first Little League coach was a nightmare, screaming and yelling and not doing too much teaching. Then he tried the PONY League, but the schedule didn't work out. He played in Little League again when he found out Aliviado was building a team to take a run at Williamsport.

If all this sounds like it's too serious for a kid, it is. Sometimes, Mike Memea seems like he'd rather play in the days before Little League. What kind of sandlot baseball did they once play in Ewa Beach? For Mike Memea, it would be enough to play all day without the trappings of uniforms and interviews and championships.

But in the modern age, baseball has become another project for American kids. If he's going to keep up, as Mack wants him to and as Desiree challenges him to, he's got to work hard at the pieces of his game. He does it with baseball and basketball, too.

Memea has been playing baseball practically since he was crawling.

"When he was nine months old, he threw a plastic ball across the living room and it was hard and fast," Mack Memea remembers. "When he was three, a neighbor had a pitching thing that pitched the ball and he hit it over the house. From then on, that's when we knew he had a fit in baseball. Till he was ten, I worked with him, throwing plastic golf balls at close range. I take him to the batting cage and get him to set the ball fast."

Michael Memea has learned at a young age how to sort through what his strong-willed father and sister push him to do. They've been testing him since he was a baby. He follows his parents' teachings on hard work and good manners. But he's going to find his own way. Everyone—family members, teammates, coaches—agrees about that.

Maybe he knows something other people around him don't know, that he's got to do it his way or it's not worth the trouble. Sure, there's lots to learn. But learning requires not just following orders, but also deciding things for yourself.

How very American.

The team from Willemstad, Curaçao,
celebrated rallies and victories
throughout the Little League
World Series.

Layton Aliviado celebrates
one last victory in the
Little League World Series
with his players.

CHAPTER 13

—•◆•—

The Greatest Little League World Series Ever

FANS START GATHERING BEFORE NINE in the morning—some years they gather as early as six—for a game that's scheduled to begin a little after four in the afternoon.

They bring lawn chairs and blankets and picnics and balls and Frisbees. When the cast-iron gates to the Little League complex open, they come spilling through unevenly, like lumpy gravy, to claim spaces on the two ridges of grass that lie beyond the outfield fence at Howard Lamade Stadium. They spread their blankets until The Hill looks like a giant quilt, with patches of red and blue and green and yellow.

In the Woodstock of youth baseball, kids are free to run around with little supervision from parents. Lemonade stands set up on the edge of The Hill. Kids start hurling their baseballs in long arcs that fly over the picnicking fans. Kids run back and forth between their blankets and the corporate tents—like the Wilson tent where youngsters hit against pitching machines—or the section of the complex where hundreds of people ages five to seventy trade pins.

———————•◆•———————

The finalists in the World Series—the West Oahu Little League of Ewa, Hawaii, and the Pabou Little League of Willemstad, Curaçao—go through their settled routines before the last game of summer.

Vernon Isabella talks sternly to his Curaçao players. He tells them to stay focused, not make stupid mistakes, and win the title again. He speaks in

Papiamentu, with a rapid-fire delivery a bit faster than a machine gun. He stands erect as his players gather in a circle around him. The kids have been told, again and again, that they need to win the game.

Kini Enos's home run in the third inning helped Hawaii's team from Ewa Beach win the Little League World Series against the defending champions from Willemstad, Curaçao.

Layton Aliviado tells his kids to hang loose. He flashes the shaka sign for the 2,359th time of the tournament. The shaka sign—thumb and pinky extended, the three middle fingers closed—is the Hawaiian symbol for "hang loose." Everywhere you go—games, picnics, malls, even highways—Hawaiians flash the shaka sign to say everything's going to be okay.

"You want it, go get it," he says in his staccato voice, a blend of deep baritone and singsong.

A sixty-foot American flag is brought out on field for presentation of colors. Little League's mascot, Dugout, shakes hands with the fathers and sons who recite the Little League pledges. Dugout comically places his paw over his heart during the recitation.

A scratchy tape plays the ethereal national anthem of Curaçao—after a few beats of rock music accidentally blare over the speakers. A local group, the Vocal Jazz Quartet, performs the American anthem. The teams line up and hit each other's fists—this generation's version of the high five—as they line up along the base paths after introductions.

Dugout motions the crowd to do the wave during the blaring of "I Can Move It Like This, I Can Shake Like That." Fans do the wave, which ripples all around the stadium and onto The Hill. The public address announcer calls the Hawaii team "United States" and the Curaçao team "Caribbean," a sly invitation for "U.S.A.! U.S.A!" chants at any international sporting event.

———————— •◆• ————————

The game almost ends in the first inning.

Sorick Liberia—who almost pitched a perfect game earlier in the tournament, giving up one lousy (but clean) double at the last possible moment against Saudi Arabia—struggles to find the strike zone and walks the first three batters.

Long and lean, Liberia shifts his back foot on the rubber. His right leg collapses, like a loose hinge, as he takes the ball out of his glove and kicks his front foot forward. He holds the ball loosely, as if displaying a Faberge egg. He throws the ball directly overhand, at twelve o'clock. His body is a rubber band that snaps a devastating fastball and a hard curve. When he's going well, the release looks the same for all of his pitches. But today, he's off balance. As he throws, his front foot lands off the imaginary line between the mound and plate.

Isabella tells Liberia, again and again, to pitch away from Hawaii's hitters, who have earned a reputation for hacking at any pitch near the strike zone. "Go away, away, away," Isabella says. And that's what Liberia does. He goes to a full count on all three hitters. Hawaii's hitters hack balls foul when the pitches come close to the zone and hold back when the pitches go too far outside.

Later, Liberia tells me he wanted to challenge the hitters but Isabella wouldn't let him.

"I was actually aiming for the outside corner, but I started to go way wide," Liberia says. "I probably would have felt better if I was allowed to throw one over the middle of the plate. Also, the umpire called a strike zone that was too small—smaller than other umpires."

By the second batter, Liberia loses his ability to bring the ball back near the plate. He starts aiming the ball off the plate, and soon he can't find the plate when he wants to. The more he throws the ball outside, the more scared he gets that the Hawaiians would maul anything near the plate.

Midway through the third batter, Isabella starts to panic. As he scans the dugout and the field, he panics even more. Who could replace Liberia? His best pitcher, Jurickson Profar, is ineligible to pitch because he started the international championship game against Japan the day before. Other pitchers have not shown much mettle in the face of adversity.

Hawaii's next hitter is the strong kid with the bubble butt named Sheyne Baniaga. Baniaga is dangerous because he has the meat to power his swing and drive the ball over the wall. In Hawaii's 2–0 win over Louisiana, Baniaga hit the home run that won it. Baniaga is a power athlete. In football, he gets the ball and runs it hard past everyone. He doesn't look agile, but he races so hard and so fast that he's streaking down the edge of the field as the defenders are just arriving on the scene, like ineffectual cops ready to take notes of what got burgled from a house.

When Liberia is even more tentative against Baniaga, Isabella gets an even sicker feeling.

Baniaga is taking it all the way. Liberia's first pitch flies so high that Willie Rifaela has to stand and reach to keep it from sailing to the backstop.

Isabella decides he can't wait any more for Liberia to right himself. He walks to the mound.

"I wanted to stay in the game," Liberia tells me later. "I would have found the plate if I stayed in the game. The umpire called a strike zone that was too small. It was smaller than other umpires. All the umpires had ups and downs, but they usually had wider strike zones."

Naeem Lourens, the new pitcher, is a risky choice. He has pitched to one batter in the entire World Series. He does not throw the ball hard. But that might be an advantage—after all, the Hawaii hitters feast on fastballs.

———————— •◆• ————————

When Isabella gives Lourens the ball, he gives him the same advice he gave Liberia: *Throw the balls away from the plate. The Hawaiians are hackers, and you can't let them catch up to the pitches.*

Lourens ignores his orders. He throws the ball *inside*. He retires the next three hitters easily, with two strikeouts and a weak pop fly.

Isabella prays that Lourens can pitch the rest of the game. By lifting Liberia without an out, the manager has deprived himself of any pitching depth. If Lourens falters, only little Christopher Garia remains.

A couple of others—Sherman La Crus and Alexander Rodrigues—can pitch. But Isabella wants to avoid using them no matter what happens. He winces when asked about his confidence in them. "No, no," he says.

Vernon Isabella has a stern appearance for being such a young man—twenty-three years old, still an active player himself at the island's highest levels of baseball. He never allows himself to get giddy or morose. Every day's a job, win or lose. In that first game against Japan, when Curaçao lost 9–0, Isabella and his players acted as if it was all part of the plan: *Yeah, we lose now, but we're setting up for the game that matters.*

But no matter how controlled this slender young manager is, he cannot hold back his happiness at the great escape.

"When he got us out of that jam, I said it was impossible for us to lose the game," Isabella raves about Lourens' clutch pitching performance.

Months later—back in Willemstad, right before Christmas, deep into planning for the 2006 run at the Little League World Series—a smile breaks out on Isabella's face. It's as if that first-inning escape did in fact clinch the game for Curaçao.

———— • ◆ • ————

Hawaii takes a brief lead in the second. Willowy Quentin Guevara lines a ball off the first baseman's glove—it would be a soft out in PONY ball—and takes second on a passed ball. And then Zachary Rosete hits the ball past third baseman Denjerick Virginie, who plays in front of the infield dirt looking for a bunt. Rosete swings down on the ball and hits it just above his hands.

"The hitter has to stay on top of the ball," Aliviado says. "If you get under the ball, if you hit it in the air, they only have to do one thing—catch the ball. But if you hit a grounder, they have to field the ball and throw the ball and then someone's got to catch it. Hit a line drive or hit it hard on the ground. I keep it all simple."

The left fielder grabs the ball near the line but doesn't have much forward momentum. When he throws home, Virginie cuts off the throw and guns it to second for an inning-ending out.

Catcher Willie Rifaela has his left foot on the plate as he waits for the throw that never arrives. He's upset. He shouts out to his teammates, waving his hands high in exasperation. *What were you doing? Let the throw come home! We had the guy!*

———— • ◆ • ————

Curaçao takes the lead in the third inning when Hawaii disintegrates on a Texas League single.

With two men on base, Jurickson Profar—hero of the 2004 and 2005 Little League World Series—takes an emergency hack on a 2–1 fastball. He swings late, but still gets the fat of the bat on the ball. The ball clanks out to right field.

Then the classic Little League play begins. The ball bounces past Zachary Rosete, to the wall. The first runner scores easily. Rosete retrieves the ball and throws to Sheyne Baniaga in short center field. After hesitating, Baniaga throws home to catcher Michael Memea. But the runner, Rayshelon Carolina, is not going home. He's staying at third base. But Profar also lopes toward third.

Panicked, Profar pedals back toward second base. As soon as he draws a throw, Carolina scoots home.

Quentin Guevara played a crucial role in Hawaii's championship, providing a strong left-handed complement to the team's pitching staff.

Jolted, Kini Enos throws home. Guevara waits for the ball two feet in front of the plate as Carolina dives. Guevara catches the throw with his right (glove) hand and spins around, on his knees, to tag Carolina. Carolina belly-flops around Guevara and slaps the plate with his right hand.

Home plate umpire David Murphy, standing seven feet away, doesn't see the play. Hawaii's Kaeo Aliviado, backing up the play, blocks his view.

Murphy calls Carolina safe. It's 2–1 in favor of Curaçao.

Guevara jumps in disbelief when he hears the safe call. He *felt* his glove hit Carolina's foot. But he knows he's not allowed to argue calls.

Layton Aliviado walks out onto the field but goes nowhere near the umpires. He makes a show of accepting the call, like Nixon accepting Kennedy's 1960 election despite all those votes from Chicago's grave-yards. Aliviado wants to calm his players and show confidence in their ability to come back.

"Hey, no problem," he says, again and again. He stays with Guevara until his pitcher locks eyes with him. He puts out his fist for acknowledgment, and Guevara taps him with his glove. "Let's get this guy."

The manager isn't sure how much energy Guevara has left. He wants to make sure he uses what he has.

"Everything was chaos," he says later. "Things started to go wrong. But my job is to say, 'Let's go. *Focus!*' They know what I'm talking about. To me that [the botched play] is history. We cannot go back and change nothing. I know the umpires will stick together. Instead of fighting them, settle this team down. We are a better team. We had a goal two years ago, we worked hard for this; no problem, focus on the next guy."

Swinging at the next pitch, Sorick Liberia hits a fastball ball up the middle for a single. That scores Profar from third base. That's a second free run. Curaçao now leads, 3–1.

———————— • ◆ • ————————

In the bottom of the third inning, Vernon Isabella tells Lourens to pitch Hawaii's Kini Enos away but Lourens plops the ball over the middle of the plate and Enos whacks it over the left-center field fence. Enos grins wildly as he circles the bases, shyly raising the shaka sign as he runs. Pure joy.

Isabella walks deliberately to the mound. He tells Lourens not to get behind in the count.

Alaka'i Aglipay, Hawaii's batting star, swings too hard at a couple of fastballs. Aglipay reaches down and gets in front of the pitch. He pulls the ball just over the left field fence for a game-tying home run.

Later, Isabella blames both home runs on missed signals.

"The catcher got confused and gave the wrong signal on the first batter," Isabella says. "They were so confused that he didn't use a sign for the second batter. The catcher, and the pitcher, didn't know what we were calling for."

Isabella tries to tell Rifaela what to do, but the catcher doesn't hear. It's Rifaela's fault, Isabella says.

"I was still upset with the call, yelling at the catcher to stay outside," he says. "Rifaela is not the regular catcher. We had another catcher but Profar was throwing so fast he couldn't handle the ball so he didn't make the team. Profar is also a catcher but we couldn't use him there because we needed him at shortstop."

Isabella also blames Lourens, the pitcher, for a lack of zeal.

"If it was Profar [on the mound], he would have stopped to see if the coach was sending the same signal," Isabella says. "You need to double-check. Profar, when he gets the inside pitch call and he knows the hitter is a good inside hitter, will stop and look at the coach and decide if the catcher needs to send another signal."

When the next hitter singles, Isabella brings in his third pitcher. Christopher Garia gets three quick outs and stifles Hawaii's rally.

— • ◆ • —

Vernon Isabella, the micromanager coaching at third base, steals the game back in the fifth inning.

With a runner on first, Sorick Liberia comes to the plate.

Isabella has been studying the relay of signs—from dugout to catcher to pitcher—all day. He thinks he has figured out Hawaii's system. He sees that Hawaii is calling for a fastball inside.

Isabella shouts to Liberia, in Papiamentu: "Fastball! Over the plate! Hit it hard!"

Liberia stands ready for the first pitch with the overactive appetite of a teenager. He swings hard.

Aliviado has been begging Enos to throw inside, on the hands, even if he hits a Curaçao batter or two. But Enos resisted. "They're hugging the plate, coach," he said.

"Then brush them back," Aliviado says. "Don't bean them, but brush them back."

But the lanky Caribbean kids hanging over the plate distract Enos.

The fear of hitting the batters, the distraction, makes Enos miss his spots. It also takes something off his pitches. And Liberia pounces.

It's now Curaçao 5, Hawaii 3, in the fifth inning.

— • ◆ • —

Layton Aliviado now brings in Hawaii's most ferocious player to pitch.

Vonn Fe'ao is Hawaii's X factor. Nobody throws harder, but he can have a difficult time finding the plate. He is the Armando Benitez of Little League—completely intimidating, angry, menacing, blistering fast, but he can lose his focus, get wild, and occasionally get hit hard.

Hawaii has used Fe'ao mostly in late-game situations. He's not a closer per se, but he's someone who can pitch one or two innings and throw the other team off stride.

The first batter, Naeem Lourens, quickly falls behind 0–2. Then Fe'ao starts to play with him, the way the *Far Side* urchin burns ants under microscopes. He throws one fastball low and inside, causing Lourens to dance away. It's a ball, but it sends a message of intimidation. The next pitch carries even more of a message—a fastball up in the eyes. His own confidence neutered, Lourens weakly grounds out to shortstop.

Fe'ao, usually a bundle of angry energy, is loose on the mound.

Hawaii brought a balanced team—with a deep pitching staff and a lineup full of power hitters—to Williamsport.

Next up is Darren Seferina. At four feet, ten inches, and seventy-nine pounds, he's one of the smallest players in Williamsport. Only five players weigh less in the tournament.

With the count 1–0, Fe'ao lays a ball on the outside part of the plate, belt high. The left-handed Seferina extends his arms and lets the ball hit his bat. Fe'ao throws the ball seventy-one m.p.h., the major-league equivalent of ninety-four m.p.h. Seferina hits it perfectly. The ball sails over the right-center field fence for a home run.

As he rounds the bases, Seferina wears the expression of someone doing chores—relaxed, but no smile. When he reaches the plate, he finally breaks out in a grin.

Now, with his team down 6–3, Fe'ao is angry. He takes the throw from the catcher with a snap. He glares. He stomps around the mound.

"I was very mad after the home run. I got lazy. I threw a seventy mile-an-hour pitch and it went right over the plate. I laid it over too much. I thought the guy wasn't going to hit it. I [should] know that size doesn't matter. Kaeo can hit even though he's small."

Teammates, coaches, fans, TV announcers—everyone—notice that Fe'ao becomes a different pitcher after his lazy pitch to Seferina.

When athletes get angry, one of two things happens. They get wild and out of control, losing their focus and their precision. Or they get so locked into focus that they can do no wrong.

"If he's throwing hardest, he sometimes loses control and it gets scary," says teammate Ty Tirpak. "But he just got in his zone."

———— • ◆ • ————

Vonn Fe'ao is not the only one angry. His manager is upset that his fireballing pitcher would let up under any circumstances. And he thinks some of his players are starting to accept defeat.

"I was mad," Layton Aliviado says. "Vonn was thinking he's a small guy and doesn't have to throw hard. I say, 'Vonn, why you lay off? Give it to him. Give him heat.' After he ripped that ball he got mad. I told him, 'You guys are giving the game away. We're down already. If we lose, we want to fight. We can win. Come on you guys.'…Vonn got mad and I was like, 'Hey, man, this is what we want.' It turned around everything."

Aliviado's faith—his belief in the plan that God has for everyone in the world—produces a mixture of determination and acceptance. God both wills what happens in the world and demands that His subjects *make* it happen. Aliviado's job is to push His subjects.

"I have this belief that if we didn't win, it was not meant to be. I believe that the Lord meant it to go our way. But we still have to do our part. We still have to fight. That's what I wanted. Then, if we don't win, fine, it was not meant to be."

The fight is back on the next batter. Fe'ao strikes out Sherman La Crus on three pitches to end the inning.

———— • ◆ • ————

After Michael Memea strikes out in the fifth inning—and looks ugly doing it, waving weakly through three fastballs—a flash of excitement bursts out among Hawaii's fans and on its bench.

"There's a *bachi*!" Ed Javier, the father of Ethan Javier, shouts gleefully to Mack Memea, Michael's dad. "Curaçao's going to lose!"

Bachi is Hawaiian for bad karma. When someone does something unseemly, something arrogant or foolish, it comes back to haunt him with a vengeance. After Memea strikes out, Curaçao's catcher Willie Rifaela flips the ball high in the air rather than demurely rolling it to the mound. Rifaela and Christopher Garia and the rest of the Curaçao players smile broadly as they trot back to their bench.

In the dugout coach Clint Tirpak also sees the flip.

"Are you going to let him insult you guys like that?" Tirpak shouts at the Hawaii players. "See? They think they won the game already! Let's do it!"

Because of television commercials, the players have to stay in the dugout for a extra couple minutes before taking the field again. And Willie Rifaela's flip gives Team Hawaii an excuse to get angry—and to focus on rallying back.

They're down to their last three outs of the game, and the Hawaiian side of the field has never looked more confident. The players take up Tirpak's challenge. All the usual cheerleaders on the bench—Tirpak's son Ty, sparkplug Kaeo Aliviado—take the bait. And the other players start barking too. Vonn Fe'ao *growls*.

Fe'ao is the player to watch for Hawaii. Pitching in the top of the sixth inning, he overwhelms Curaçao. He allows a walk but gets three easy outs on a sacrifice bunt, strikeout, and a grounder to first base.

Layton Aliviado calls for some curveballs and changeups, but Fe'ao just wants to throw heat. "I just decided, okay, let him throw what he wants," Aliviado says.

Fe'ao leads off in the bottom of the inning. To the Hawaii players, Fe'ao's at-bat will determine whether they had a chance to rally.

"I was thinking, 'Vonn, don't try to knock it out of the park,' because he tends to want to do that," says Ty Tirpak. "I was like, 'Just get on, and I'll bring you in.'"

But Fe'ao swings hard. He hacks away, missing on the first pitch. After taking a pitch low and outside for a ball, Fe'ao takes another vicious cut through a fastball outside and high.

Oh, no. Hawaii is doomed. Vonn's swinging for the fences.

Ahead in the count, Garia tries to get Fe'ao to chase a ball for strike three. Fe'ao leans forward on a pitch a foot and a half off the plate, but he resists. The next one is a foot outside and just above the dirt. With the count full, Garia throws one even further outside for ball four.

A sigh of collective relief washes over the Hawaii bench.

He took a walk! We have a chance!

———————•◆•———————

Fans filled The Hill beyond the outfield fence of Lamade Stadium before the championship game between Hawaii and Curaçao.

Curaçao's Christopher Garia is working his fourth inning. He has now thrown forty pitches. But it's not the number of pitches that matters here. Those are forty *straining* pitches. And he has a long afternoon of work ahead of him. For the first time in the game, he is showing signs of wear. He slumps while waiting for the catcher to return the ball. He labors before extending his arms in his motion.

Vernon Isabella has no intention of taking Garia out of the game. He has two players who could take the mound. But he has no intention of using either one.

"The last inning is the one where you need to be more intense. You shouldn't loosen up. I would stay with Garia even if he has to throw his arm out, because it's the last game of the year. They can treat the arm afterwards. Even if Garia told me that he was tired, he was the one who would have to tough it out...The only thing that would make me change my mind is if Garia said his arm was hurting—and even then I'd ask him to throw some more pitches to see if he really was tired."

Still, Isabella worries that Garia will not be tough enough to stand up to the Hawaii hitters.

"If you tell Garia to be more focused, he looks down." Isabella imitates the boy pretending not to notice when someone's talking to him. He closes his eyes, purses his lips, and stares at the dirt. "Profar is different. He puts on a face that says you can't beat him. That's something you can't teach—the fighting spirit. You have to believe that even if you think you can't give more, you have to listen to the coach. If you ask Garia whether he wants to stay in the game, he would say it's up to you. Profar would say, no, I want to stay. Garia didn't say anything."

———————— •◆• ————————

Christopher Garia looks sharp again against the next hitter, Quentin Guevara. Garia gets two quick strikes when Guevara swings late on fast-balls on the outside part of the plate, hip high.

Hawaii hitters always take a step closer to the plate and a step closer to the pitcher when they have two strikes. Guevara's arms are hanging over the plate when he gets the next pitch from Garia. He swings late but hits a blooper into right field.

By the time the ball is back in the infield, Fe'ao streaks into third base. Guevara moves to second base on a botched cutoff throw. Little League mistakes.

When he gets to third, Fe'ao is excited. He sees Curaçao's third baseman, Denjerick Virginie, staring at him as he slaps his hands together. "What you looking at, *popolo*?" he barks. *Popolo* is Hawaiian literally meaning dark berry, meaning black.

———————— •◆• ————————

Ty Tirpak's turn. Coaching at third base, Layton Aliviado notes that Rudmichaell Brandao is playing back by the bag. Aliviado puts on the bunt sign.

Tirpak is the skinny-guy image in a fun-house mirror. His face is long, his cheeks hollow, eyes high and mouth low, with almost no chin. He's a Hirschfeld cartoon, all long lines. His ears stick out of his short patchy blond hair. At the age of twelve, he's old-school. He says his favorite player is Nolan Ryan.

Ty Tirpak was the most vocal member of the Hawaii team.

As he takes warm-up swings, Tirpak's arms reach behind his body. When he hits, Tirpak loads energy like a stretched rubber band, then snaps his arms and bat forward at the first split-second that he can make any judgment about the pitch. The problem with the elastic swing is that it doesn't leave much opportunity for correction. You snap forward and there's no going back.

Little League does not have a squeeze play, per se, since runners can't leave the base till the pitch reaches the plate. But Aliviado knows Tirpak can bunt, and once the ball is in play anything can happen.

Tirpak gulps a gallon of air as he waves his bat in a tense half arc. Standing a foot off the plate, Tirpak has to reach for the pitch as it veers to the outside part of the plate. Still, he manages to drop the ball down the third base line. In one motion, like Ichiro, he's running to first base.

"When I saw the guy [pitcher Garia] releasing the ball, I thought it was right where I needed it. Sometimes they'll throw a bad pitch, but it was right here [letter high]. It was in the right spot. I didn't want something to come way outside, especially since I was trying to get it toward third. It didn't seem super fast, but I just started to put my bat out and it started to feel faster. After that I just sprinted."

Third baseman Brandao fields the ball, running alongside Fe'ao toward the plate. Rather than taking the ball out of his glove to throw, he shovels the ball underhand with his glove. The throw is late and high, and catcher Willie Rifaela has to lift his foot off the plate to catch it. Fe'ao slides safely under the throw. The score is now Curaçao 6, Hawaii 4.

Vernon Isabella admits he wasn't ready for a bunt.

"I was completely surprised," he says. "I would have hit in that situation. One big hit makes it 6–5. With two guys on board, you are looking for a hitter. He's not one of the best hitters, with the type of swing he had…But that was the most important play of the rally, maybe of the game.

"I told the players that the most important play was at first base, but I didn't know that he was going to bunt. He did what he thought was easier. It was the wrong decision to go to home plate. But he didn't go to first base because he didn't know if the runner would be able to beat it. We weren't going to play the infield in. If the hitter smacks a ball past the bag, then you're in even worse shape."

Curaçao packed the stand with families from the Caribbean territory of the Netherlands.

A split second after he touches first base, Tirpak jumps in the air in exultation, punching the sky like he's spiking a volleyball. Volleyball, one of the more popular games on Hawaii's isles, is Tirpak's best sport. He gets to practice his spike in Williamsport.

Hawaii immediately replaces Tirpak at first base with Harrison Kam, a tiny but speedy outfielder.

———•◆•———

The pressure is getting to some of the Curaçao players. Willie Rifaela, the catcher, starts to cry.

"I told him to stop crying and catch the ball," says Isabella. "But he was one of the guys, his eyes got big when we were playing on TV."

———•◆•———

Before the inning, Hawaii's Zachary Rosete approaches Aliviado in the dugout. "Coach, I can hit." Rosete had a hit earlier in the day, but he was not one of the team's best hitters. But Aliviado decides Rosete is focused and steely.

"I look in his eyes, and I was thinking, 'Wow, there must be something.' So I told [coach] Tyron [Kitashima], 'Put Zach in there. This kid *means* it.' Normally he wouldn't say that. He must be on. When I gave the sign for an outside pitch, he was hanging over the plate. He was eager to hit."

Rosete singles, scoring Guevara. Now the score is 6–5. Still nobody out and Curaçao leads by only one run.

———————— • ◆ • ————————

After Kaeo Aliviado walks to load the bases, Hawaii's best hitters come to the plate.

Kini Enos grounds to shortstop Jurickson Profar. Profar fires the ball home from deep in the shortstop position, forcing out Kam at the plate.

And now Alaka'i Aglipay steps up. All season, he has been the best player in the West Oahu Little League. Aglipay can lift any pitch out of the small ballpark for a grand slam.

But Garia quickly gets ahead, 0 and 2.

Choking up, Aglipay hits the ball to the right side of the diamond—too far for the second baseman to throw home for a force. Profar, covering second base, gets the front end of the possible double play. A DP would end the game and give Curaçao the championship.

Profar is off the bag by two feet when he gets the throw, but umpire Robert Stuart calls him out. Profar rushes his throw to first base, and it's wide and late.

"I knew I didn't have enough time to get both outs," Profar says. "But I thought I had to try something and see what happens." Profar dismisses the Hawaii side's claim that he missed second base. "I know I touched the base," Profar says.

Rosete scores. The game is tied, 6–6.

Hawaii was lost, and now is found.

———————— • ◆ • ————————

Darren Seferina was an unlikely power source for Curaçao in the championship game of the Little League World Series, homering off Hawaii's Vonn Fe'ao.

The game goes into extra innings. Only one championship game—the legendary Gary-Taiwan game of 1971—has gone beyond the regulation six innings.

Vonn Fe'ao burns through the Curaçao batters in the top of the seventh inning. He gets Jurickson Profar to ground to shortstop.

Ahead of Sorick Liberia 0–2 on blistering fastballs, Fe'ao gets him to swing through changeup for a strikeout. Then he gets Lourens to swing through two changeups before fanning him on a fastball.

———————— •◆• ————————

So it comes down to the bottom of the seventh inning. Michael Memea stands at home plate, waiting for a three-and-two pitch from Christopher Garia.

Hawaii's lumbering catcher wags his bat behind his head. The bat barrel bounces up and down as Garia moves into his motion.

Memea gulps and twitches. His face shows some of the signs of approaching adolescence. He wears one of those wispy moustaches that prompt parents to debate when to teach the kid to shave.

On the pitch before, with a three-and-one count, Memea swung late on a high outside fastball. He swings hard but his timing is off. If he gets that pitch again, he needs to bring the bat around quicker. Maybe he should use a lighter bat. Or maybe he needs to coil his body. But he also has to be ready for an off-speed pitch or a curveball.

Garia is not throwing as hard as he did back in the third inning. But he still flings the ball upwards of seventy miles an hour. That seventy-mile-an-hour is the equivalent of a ninety-one-m.p.h. pitch in a big-league game.

Layton Aliviado tells Memea to hack at anything he can hit. Aliviado has enough faith to let Memea swing on a three-and-one pitch. Aggressiveness wins games.

———————◆————————

Mike Memea was an instant celebrity after his walk-off home run gave Hawaii the Little League championship in 2005.

Garia stands on the mound completely exhausted. His thin arms hang by his side as he prepares to throw. His mouth is dry. He smacks his lips to get moisture. No matter. He's still dry.

The full-count pitch to Memea is the sixty-ninth of the game for Garia.

He's reached his limit. At most, he has a few pitches left in his matchstick arm.

The pitcher is the loneliest player in all of sports. Even when they're overpowering hitters, pitchers stand solitary. That's why pitchers act out, taunting strikeout victims, stomping around after close calls, glaring from behind their gloves, waving their arms in exasperation.

Garia is all alone now. He's been throwing hard, under the most physically and emotionally exhausting circumstances after ten days of taxing practices and games. And now his manager coach wants him to stay in the game when everyone in Lycoming County knows he's exhausted.

———————•◆•———————

Garia steps forward softly, kicks high, whips his arm forward, and delivers the same ball that Memea could not reach one pitch before.

But this time Memea sees the ball better and gets his barrel out a split-second sooner.

He lifts his front foot about an inch before beginning his long loping swing. He extends his arms forward, as if he is presenting a sword to an emperor at an ancient royal court. He drops his bat on the ball. The ball hits the bat's sweet spot. Memea holds the bat with both hands all the way through his swing. Then he watches the ball arc. He drops the bat, with both hands, to the ground.

He watches. Christopher Garia watches. Centerfielder Rayshelon Carolina turns his back to the infield as he runs back toward the outfield fence and watches.

The ball veers on a line over the outfield wall, about twenty feet above the field. The ball bounces just beyond the dirt track beyond the out-field fence, bouncing to a chain-link fence that holds the hedges beyond the outfield wall. Fans sitting on the hills start to chase the ball, but the hedge and fence—put into place as a security measure after September 11—stops the ball after a skip.

Home run. Hawaii wins.

When Memea sees the ball clear the outfield wall, he leaps and allows a smile. He holds his right arm high, his index finger poking the sky, all the way around the bases.

Memea arrives home to the clamor of all his teammates. Family members press against the fencing separating the stands from the field, digital cameras aloft. A few players line up by the fence, looking for parents and brothers and sisters. ABC/ESPN TV cameras spill out onto the field. Little League officials run onto the field to award the Hawaiians their championship banner.

As TV cameras and reporters move onto the field, Christopher Garia and his teammates walk off. They're crying, hiding their faces in their hands. For some, the tears come in heavy sobs. Curaçao's players cluster near Vernon Isabella and the other coaches. The Hawaiian bunch celebrates.

In what has become a tradition, the Curaçao players line up along the first base line and bow to the Hawaiian fans. Then they line up along the third base line and bow to their own fans.

Curaçao's players react to losing the extra-inning finale in the Little League World Series.

After the Hawaiians get their championship banner, they run around the circumference of the field. Some players from Curaçao join the Hawaiians in their victory lap.

Mike Memea is numb. As he's mobbed by his teammates, he already wants to move on. The game's over. He resists going to the media room for interviews.

"Can we go swimming now?" he asks.

After winning the championship,
Hawaii's players sign a souvenir bat.

Players from both the Hawaii and Curaçao teams joined each other in a victory lap at the conclusion of the 2005 Little League World Series.

CHAPTER 14

The Life of Champions

*O*N A HOT AND BRIGHT DECEMBER DAY, the players, coaches, and family members of the Little League World Series champions from Ewa Beach took their familiar positions around a baseball diamond at Pearl Ridge Elementary School in Hawaii.

Fathers clustered along the right field chain-link fence, with the best view of the action at first base. They stood close together, as if they were in a football huddle, under a jumbo-sized umbrella that protected them from the hard sun. That group of six, seven, eight dads laughed and talked about the game's plays and their kids' progress.

Along the line closer to home plate, mothers and children sat in low beach chairs, balancing drinks and lunch and answering the steady demands for attention from their other children. They talked about how the kids are doing in school and how to keep up with the demands of work and ferrying their kids around Oahu, and paying attention to the players' brothers and sisters.

Younger children ran from station to station—from their moms to picnic tables to playground equipment to a cinderblock shelter where they play board games.

On the field, five of the players from the Little League champions were getting used to the new field dimensions of "real" baseball. Just months ago, they dominated the field with sixty-foot bases. They were so big that the field couldn't contain them. Now they were playing on ninety-foot bases, the standard-sized field in baseball, half again as big as the Little League diamond. Playing on a bigger field takes some adjustment. Running from base to base sometimes seems like a marathon after Little

League. Throwing from deep right field, or from third to first, takes maximum effort. And the runners lead off the bases, creating a new task for the pitcher.

In this case, the pitcher was Quentin Guevara. Guevara is five feet, four inches, and he weighs 126 pounds, but he has a chance to grow into a full-sized athlete. His father, a guard at the Halawa Community Correctional Center, is over six feet tall and well-built. Guevara is concentrating on sports the way his dad never had a chance to do. And his coach, Layton Aliviado, is trying to help him make the adjustment to the full-sized field.

A batter reached base and Guevara had to figure out how to keep him from stealing at will. The beauty of Guevara as a pitcher is the he steps effortlessly into a high leg kick and twists his body around toward the plate. The high leg kick generates power for his motion. As he grows into a bigger and bigger body, Guevara has a chance to become a prototypical power pitcher.

But the runner was going. Guevara barely noticed as the runner took the long journey from first to second base. Guevara was still rocking into his motion when the runner was one third of the way to second base.

After the steal, Aliviado shouted out to Guevara.

"Quint, you've gotta watch the runner!" Aliviado got more and more animated as Guevara stayed with his full fluid motion. "You gotta use the slide step! You can't let him run on you! Quint! *Sliiiiiide* step!"

The men by the chain-link fence chortled and pointed. The women murmured.

The game took place just a few days before Pearl Harbor Day in 2005. Later, John Baniaga, father of Sheyne Baniaga, pointed to the USS *Arizona Memorial*, visible in the harbor less than two miles away.

"That's where the Japanese attacked," he told me. "My grandparents lived just over there." He points in the opposite direction. "They used to tell us about the planes flying overhead, all the time, during that time. Then that day, they looked and saw the smoke coming up from the harbor. It's kind of what you're trying to deal with on the mainland with September 11, right?"

There's a Hawaiian expression for moving forward—"*I mua!*" That's what everyone was trying to do here. Move on from the world championship. Move on to the next level of play, with a more demanding field and a more physically imposing and athletic opposition. Move on to better schools. Move on to the rest of childhood's journey.

No one really understood just what kinds of opportunities—and demands—would come with winning the Little League World Series.

When they arrived at Honolulu Airport, a crowd of 2,000 friends and well-wishers greeted them with leis, banners, and TV cameras.

When the boys returned to school, principals called assemblies. Girls started pressing themselves on even the most awkward boys: "Can I kiss you? I've never kissed a champion before." Politicians and business people arranged parades. The Los Angeles Lakers came to the University of Hawaii for an exhibition game and the Ewa Beach kids were invited to meet Kobe Bryant and Luke Walton and pose for pictures with the glam cheerleaders. The team also shot a commercial for the Fun Factory video arcade.

Vonn Fe'ao signs autographs and meets well-wishers after earning the victory in Hawaii's championship game.

Resorts invited the players to stay with them. One father took four of the kids on a deep-sea diving expedition at the Ko Olina Beach Club and Hotel, gratis. Companies showered them with gifts—clothes, sports equipment, and fast food for a year.

Wherever the players went, strangers recognized them. Kini Enos and his family sat in a McDonald's one morning, having breakfast on his yearlong free pass, when a man looked up with a stunned look. "He pointed at Kini, like, 'Are you one of the guys?'" his mother Girlie recalls. "Kini just nodded. The man put down his fork and walked over and said, 'Can I shake your hand?'"

A championship can transform the desirability of even the quietest kids in a school. By all external appearances, Vonn Fe'ao looks like a cool kid. His black and brown ringlets of hair flow down his shoulders, and his granite build and tough-guy glare can be intimidating on both football and baseball fields. But he's still shy, and some of the tough kids used to haze him in the school halls and playground. But not so much after the Little League World Series.

Hawaii's Kaeo Aliviado looks into the stands for family and friends after a Series game.

"A lot of people notice me, and I never had that before," Fe'ao told me before the game at Pearl City. "Kids are treating me different. The people that used to treat me bad, now they hang around and they're my friends now. They're boys who used to cause trouble. They would start a fight with me. They would say something about what I looked like, who I hung with, stuff like that."

There's another side to the fame. "They have a target on their backs now," says Darryl Stevenson, Fe'ao's fall football coach. "Other teams have a tendency to take some extra shots. Especially in Vonn's case, because everyone knows who he is now. The kids know who you are, and they want to prove that they're good, too. Vonn's challenge is keeping his composure when he knows everyone's going after him."

When he got home, Fe'ao announced that he would not get his hair cut, even to play football. He knows his flowing curly locks are part of his image. He stuffs his hair under a tight synthetic cap when he plays football. But the hair has its costs to a young boy's ego. A newspaper in Sese Fe'ao's homeland of Tonga reports that Vonn Fe'ao is the first girl to play in the Little League World Series. Sese and Heather and the other parents were amused. Vonn was not.

The University of Hawaii football team invited the Little Leaguers to watch a game against USC at Aloha Stadium. The boys were announced during halftime and took off their hats and bowed to all four sides of the field. The crowd roared. At one point, fans held up a sign reading "PUT FE'AO IN."

———————◆·———————

Layton Aliviado, the architect and construction manager of the championship team, graduated to high school baseball when he got back to the islands. The Saint Louis School, the elite academy that produced a major leaguer named Benny Agbayani, hired him to coach the junior varsity team.

Aliviado's new team struggled in its early going, losing four of its first five practice games. Like all of Aliviado's teams, the Saint Louis players quickly learned that Aliviado demands discipline and brutal conditioning. Early in the season, the team arrived at the field without the bucket of balls. As punishment, they did suicide drills.

"Everybody's got to remember to bring all the equipment," he says. "But we got there and we didn't have the balls. So I thought about it for a day and made them run suicide drills. You start at the end zone on a football field and go to the five-yard line, touch the line, run back, run to the ten-yard line and back, the fifteen-yard line and back, all the way to the fifty-yard line, for twenty minutes. They won't forget next time. And now they're stronger, too."

Aliviado experiences a surge of nostalgia when he hears "Centerfield," the John Fogerty song that blared on the PA system in the Little League

World Series. "I get kind of choked up," he says. "It's full of memories for me, looking at the stands, and thinking, 'Man, we're at the World Series.' Hardly anyone makes it. You don't even dream it until you're almost there."

Aliviado wants to return to Williamsport some day to look at his team's picture on the wall in the cafeteria. "When you look at the Hall of Fame wall and see the champions over the years—well, I used to look at the pictures and wonder if Hawaii could make it. That always stays in my mind. One day, hopefully, I can go back and look at our picture."

———————————— •◆• ————————————

The biggest opportunity for the new celebrities—and the biggest problem, too—was school.

Some of the boys missed three weeks of school. Classes started in early August, just three days before the team left for the regional tournament in San Bernardino, California. Quentin Guevara, for one, struggled to catch up. In the first quarter of classes at Waipahu Intermediate School, he got two Fs in English and he didn't do much better in other subjects. He had to go to school as early as 6:30 in the morning for special help. He sometimes spent his lunch hour getting tutoring. He was getting frustrated and sometimes begged his mother to let him give up.

Most parents hoped that their kids could catch up and take advantage of the private-school scholarships that have become part of the new atmosphere around the football fields and baseball diamonds on the western part of Oahu these days. Coaches at elite schools watched the kids perform on TV and they like their physical and mental makeup. But they have to get good enough grades to satisfy the admissions office.

Some players came home more focused and determined. Denise Baniaga says her son Sheyne used to require constant nagging to do homework and help around the house. But no more.

"He's more confident and just striving more," she told me as we watched him play football. "Last year, he didn't push himself at all—he gets a B, whatever; he gets a C, whatever. But this year he's really pushing himself. He knows that he has a chance to get into some good schools. All the moms are trying to get their kids in a place where they can go to college. I never went to college. From our family, none of us did. The men would work right out of high school. For me, I had my first child right out of high school, and I didn't work till later."

She's now a part-time clerk in the front office at Mauka Lani Elementary School. The aspirations of the teachers and staff—and other parents and families—have made a strong impression. "Our school is a distinguished school, we win all kinds of awards," she says. "It makes me want to make sure my kids are doing good."

"I don't want him to be a truck driver like me," John Baniaga said. But the parents don't just appreciate the opportunities that school offers. They also appreciate the way private schools work, free of the bureaucracy of the public schools. "Private schools let you know if your kids are having problems," Layton Aliviado said. "The kids don't get lost. Public school is what you want to make of it, and not everyone's ready for that. Private schools is one team, one dream."

Vonn Fe'ao and Alaka'i Aglipay got the most attention from schools. Fe'ao had a tentative scholarship offer from the Saint Louis School, a Catholic school started in 1846 by missionaries. A Polynesian alum

Kaeo Aliviado and Harrison Kam celebrate Hawaii's victory in the Little League World Series.

volunteered to pay the tuition if he could get admitted. Vonn was also interested in Punahou High School, golf sensation Michelle Wie's school. Earlier in the year, *Sports Illustrated* ranked Punahou fourth in the nation for high school sports. The school offers 115 teams in thirty sports and has won more state championships (318) than any other school in America. *USA Today* ranked Punahou's baseball team tenth in the nation.

Aglipay also wanted to play for Punahou. A couple of years ago, when his parents took him out of school and signed him up to work with a tutor, no one had much hope that he'd score well enough on the entrance tests to get in. But in January of 2006, he shocked everyone by easily meeting Punahou's minimum scores.

When he got his Secondary School Aptitude Test scores, he was so happy that his friends and family could barely recognize him. He never reacted that way to his success as an athlete, which came so naturally.

"You should have seen that smile on his face," Linda Sofa, his tutor, said. "I've never seen anything like it."

Hawaii's Vonn Fe'ao

As travel teams transform the landscape of youth baseball, Little League could reposition itself as the organization dedicated to play for play's sake.

POSTGAME

Finding the Soul of Little League

*W*HEN I STARTED TO EXPLORE THE WORLD of Little League, one of the first people I visited was Tom Galla, who coached the Little League World Series champions of 1989.

That team from Trumbull, Connecticut, became a national story because it defied all the odds in beating the team from Taiwan. Teams from Asia had won the World Series in sixteen of the previous twenty years. The Asian teams were so dominant, in fact, that one year Little League actually banned foreign teams from the tournament in Williamsport.

All these years later, Galla remembers his experience with fondness and pride. He took a bunch of suburban kids and trained them to beat one of the biggest powerhouses in all of sports. It was Little League's version of the *Miracle on Ice*. When we talked, Galla still seemed like he couldn't quite believe that his boys had won the title.

Galla told me how he built the team. He made it clear to the parents that his decisions as coach were final and their job was to support him. He told them to cancel their summer vacations. That summer was going to be all about baseball. Winning the Little League World Series was an extreme long shot. To even have a chance, the team had to focus completely on the goal. It was like a youth sports version of the Manhattan Project. Without total commitment, the enterprise was guaranteed to fail.

"I told them basically that [the coaches] were running the team," Galla told me. "We were working with the kids every day. We said, look, we're going to know your kids better than you, and we're going to know who should be on the field and who's going to play other roles. And it may be for reasons that are hard to explain. We were with those kids every day. In the beginning we had double workouts, in the morning and the afternoon. We took them to the movies, we'd have watermelon after practice, we'd have swimming pool parties. They were *our kids* from July 1 until August 26."

On one matter—the actual selection of the team—Galla gave up almost all of the control that coaches usually exercise.

Typically, the coaches from the Little League organization gather around June 15 to select that year's all-star team. Sometimes the leagues give the team's manager the final say. Sometimes the league's coaches vote. Sometimes they require consensus on every player. But it's the adults who get together and make the decisions.

But the Trumbull Little League let the players in the league decide who would represent them on the all-star team. The league's president went from team to team and distributed ballots. The players picked the first ten players for the twelve-man team. Galla and his assistant selected four other players; two of them would get reserve roles on the team, and two would work out with the team but not play unless someone got hurt or left the team.

"I would have picked the same ten, in the same exact order," Galla says. "The kids got a ballot and they could choose anybody they wanted in the league. And they got it right."

That inspired an idea for reforming youth sports. But more on that in a moment.

————————◆————————

At a dinner party a few months after the 2005 Little League World Series, I met a Little League coach from Connecticut who watched the games on TV. Tad McGwire, a coach in the Branford Little League, commented on the infamous Florida-California game. He was amazed—and disappointed—to see Dante Bichette's pacing and snarling in Florida's dugout. Bichette, the former major league slugger, was unhappy with how the game was going. And his response was to bring the big-league game of intimidation to Williamsport's field of dreams.

As we discussed Bichette's meltdown, we talked about why things get so intense in a tournament like the Little League World Series.

It always comes down to the adults.

The adults are the ones who create an obsessive desire to win.

The adults are the ones to push players when they're hurting.

The adults are the ones making nasty comments from the stands.

The adults are the ones to argue with umpires and play mind games with the other team.

The adults are the ones who have a hard time dealing with losing.

The adults run every aspect of the games in Little League.

Give them credit for how much they care. Coaches devote hundreds of hours to teaching kids how to play baseball—and the best ones also teach them how to get along, mind their manners, and be good teammates. That's an amazing sacrifice. Imagine what would happen if that much help went into tutoring the kids or leading the kids on summerlong projects for Habitat for Humanity or rebuilding the Gulf Coast.

But in the process of giving their lives over to Little League teams, these adults can lose perspective. Because they understand the structure of the competition better—the long train of tournaments, the pool system, and what kind of players you need to win—they care more. As the team advances through the qualifying tournaments, the need to win becomes more and more intense. Winning becomes part of their identity. Coaches feel a swelling need to produce, to show other adults that they're going to make their kids win.

The kids don't even know where Williamsport is, but the adults get fixated on getting there.

The central part of the problem might be that—because they're older and more experienced—the adults assume that only they can run a team. *They* know how to run practices. *They* know how to make a lineup card. *They* know when to bunt and when to swing away, when to use a pinch hitter, and when to make a defensive change. *They* know who should pitch, and how long, and who should come in to relieve.

———————— • ◆ • ————————

Over the course of a long dinner conversation, someone suggested a radical solution.

If Tom Galla could give the selection of his all-star team to the players in the league, why not take things a step further?

Give the game back to the kids.

And you know what? It makes sense.

All relationships involve boundaries. Friends should not press each other to do things they don't want to do. Spouses need to be available for each other, but also have lives of their own. Workmates should not get too intimate with each other on the job. And adults—parents and coaches—should respect their children's growing need for autonomy.

Once upon a time, adults and children in America lived in the same world for part of the day but then left each other alone in their recreational pursuits. Parents set the rules and taught their children, but also gave them plenty of room to be kids. Parents knew that children need to live in their own worlds—exploring the woods, building forts, playing games, making money on paper routes and babysitting, and running in gangs (the non-lethal variety).

But in the last half-century, as Americans moved to suburban pods and life got more fragmented, specialized, and separated, parents started getting more involved in their kids' lives. Parents pressured kids to play sports, take up an instrument, and go to computer camp. Parents started to *manage* their kids. Rather than setting expectations and consequences, parents got deeply involved in the details of their kids' lives.

However youth baseball evolves, kids will always line up for a chance to play the international pastime.

This is a gross generalization, of course. We live not only in the age of the overmanaged kid, but also in the age of the neglected kid. But sometimes, they go together. When parents aren't around after school because of jobs and other obligations, they tend to get more intensely involved in designing what the kids do. It's the old myth of "quality time."

Little League has been part of this process of engineering childhood. Little League was, in fact, one of the first programs in America explicitly designed to involve parents in managing their kids.

Don't get me wrong. There are all kinds of things to like about Little League and the long summer of baseball leading to the World Series.

Playing baseball on a real *team*—regardless of whether the team traveled away from home, or whether the players won international acclaim with their televised heroics—can have a huge impact on children's lives.

If you have a great coach like Hawaii's Layton Aliviado, you learn how to sacrifice and work hard. You learn how to accept a role, support teammates, control your temper, and think ahead. You learn to look beyond your own prejudices and limitations and become part of something bigger. All of these great qualities become a part of you.

Understanding baseball—or anything—can help to understand other things better. The positive habits from one activity can carry over to other parts of life. When you learn to sacrifice, work hard, cooperate, and respect others on the ball field, you can transfer those habits to other realms like school and family life.

Except that it doesn't always work out that way. We all know countless people who excel in one area and are completely sloppy and inadequate in others. It helps to know how to do things right in one area, but it's no guarantee.

The debate over Little League—over its millions of games and the tournaments that lead to the World Series, as well as other programs and tournaments across the world—can be simplistic. It's either the most wholesome place for kids to learn and grow together—or it's an adult-dominated place of excessive competitiveness. In fact, Little League—and all youth sports—can be as good and as bad as supporters and detractors say.

In the final analysis, it's not the league or tournament that matters; it's how people get *immersed* in the game.

When we talk about youth sports—supporters and detractors, stand-patters and reformers—we sometimes assume that the coach provides the key to the whole operation.

Coaching matters because the coach can create an environment where the players and their families govern themselves with intelligence and decency. When the kids embrace values of hard work and play, goals and sacrifice, and achievement and caring for others, the results can be profound. And they can last a lifetime.

In 1998, Judith Rich Harris published a landmark book entitled *The Nurture Assumption* that challenges the standard parent-centric view of childhood.

The standard view is that parents play the critical role in how their kids grow up. All over America, parents scramble to get their kids the best opportunities for advancement. Parents sign their kids up for sports and music, push them to get better grades, finagle to get them into private schools, research summer camps, ride them to do their homework, and make decisions about TV and video games. All of which are perfectly valid.

But what really matters is what kind of environment the kids are going to be in, what kinds of peers they'll be with, and what kind of social system governs this world. It's fine to learn how to play baseball or sing in a choir. But the activity itself matters less than the values and behavior of the other children in the group. Children learn their most important lessons from other children. Children pick up cues of how to behave from other children, and make that behavior their own. Gestures of all kinds—the saunter and the shuffle, the grand gesture and the whispered aside, the raised eyebrow and the intentional inattention, the idolization of a star, and the smirk toward a lesser being—convey the group's values and tell the members how to belong.

When a group of children get together and spend time with each other, they essentially teach each other how to behave. They determine whether the group will be one community or a set of factions with different status. They set expectations, enforce norms, embrace each other, and figure out how to make things work.

Or not.

That's why my favorite scenes from the Little League World Series usually took place outside the spotlight. I was most impressed when the players took responsibility for each other.

The most meaningful moments for me came when two tiny first basemen—Tanner Stanley of Florida's Maitland Little League and Kaeo Aliviado of Hawaii's West Oahu Little League—took charge of the field between batters. After almost every at-bat—and always when some trouble was brewing—they'd bop to the mound, remind their teammates of the situation, and say something positive. "Got your back," Stanley said. "Hey, no problem," Kaeo said.

As I got to know some of the Hawaii players, I loved to see how they contributed to the team's even keel and focus. Wherever he went, Kini Enos loosened up his teammates. Players from other teams constantly talked about how much fun Kini was. When I was in Hawaii, talking to a couple of his teammates, he bounced over to the picnic table where we were sitting and took over. Not in a selfish or egotistical way. He just drew his teammates out. He helped them find their words, reminded them of situations, and jumped up to demonstrate plays.

I was also impressed when I watched Ty Tirpak in the Hawaii dugout, screaming himself hoarse throughout the World Series. A bottom-of-the-lineup hitter, Ty got it in his head that he could help with his high-pitched cheers and frenetic movement. And he might have been right. That kind of attitude can help to create a mindset of optimism.

I was relieved when I saw players from Canada and Guam romp around the Little League complex. I was impressed to see the Japanese team practice together like dancers—and break into laughter in between routines. I smiled when I heard that the players from Westbrook, Maine, tromped down to the field after their games ended to gather samples of dirt from the infield as souvenirs.

These are the things that have a chance of lasting—not just memories, but ways of living—long after the innocent dreams of winning a championship.

———————— • ◆ • ————————

A survey by the National Alliance for Youth Sports found that 15 percent of all children's games involve physical or verbal abuse. Of the thirty million kids playing youth sports, almost half say they have experienced some kind of abuse. The extreme incidents —like the infamous case of a Massachusetts man beating another father to death in a fight over the way their kids' hockey practice was being conducted—get the headlines.

But it's the steady accumulation of smaller incidents that do the most to warp the environment. In fact, 40 percent of all young athletes said they wish their parents would stay away from their games, giving them some room for fun and play.

Little League is just a small part of that larger world of youth sports. And the pressures in Little League pale next to the pressures of some other sports programs—in most places, when some sort of league championship or tournament is not on the line. But Little League is very much a part of the larger culture of competitiveness in America. That culture has been institutionalized in adult-run leagues with volumes of rules and regulations that sometimes seem so far from the simple idea of play.

So I wonder.

Is the top-down, adult-managed approach necessarily the only way to organize youth sports these days? Do adults really know *everything* better than children? Not necessarily. Even if kids need some teaching, they don't need to be directed every moment of their time playing baseball.

Why not give the game back to the kids?

Here's how I'd run things. I'd let the adults do all the organizational stuff—draft the teams, reserve the fields, set up the calling trees, get the umpires, and keep score.

And I'd let the adults teach the kids some skills. Many of the adults, after all, are very good teachers and love to pass along their knowledge and love of the game. As a Little Leaguer, I would have been ecstatic if I ever had someone like Joe Pimentel teaching me how to hit. I would have been thrilled to have someone like Shon Muna showing me how to field a groundball. And I would have benefited from Layton Aliviado's ladder drills. This is all great stuff.

But once the games start, get the adults off the field.

You say it's not practical? Maybe, but think for a minute. Kids have been organizing themselves forever. Only in the past generation have parents and adults become such busybodies that kids feel like they can't organize their own games. But if they're given some broad boundaries, the kids could do the job as well as adults.

The members of the team could vote for a captain to make the lineup. They could pick a game manager to decide field strategy (positioning fielders, changing pitchers, swinging away or bunting, pinch hitting, and so on). Maybe you set strict pitch counts and let the game manager decide when to bring in a new arm. That might take away the pressure for a kid to go one extra inning when his arm is tired.

I asked Tad McGwire, the Branford Little League coach I met at that dinner party, what he thought about the idea. A thoughtful and committed man, McGwire has been coaching for years, but he's watched the Little League World Series pageantry from afar. I thought he would provide a balanced, fair perspective.

He was skeptical. He said the approach might work with all-star teams, but it might not work during the regular season. "I know probably every kid who's going to be on the all-star team this year, and I think they would be fine with something like that," he said. "I'm not so sure about the team in the regular season. There is just such a range of kids."

His greatest fear is that the dominant personalities might exploit the situation. "You could have a *Lord of the Flies* situation. The alpha males take over and put themselves in key spots," he said. "Most kids are very cooperative. I've seen kids ask their coach, 'Hey, why doesn't Bobby have a chance to play?' They have empathy for each other. But a team can be a very delicate thing, and if one thing goes off, the whole thing falls apart."

As we explored the best way to achieve the right balance in youth sports—providing boundaries and instruction, but not micromanaging the games—we talked about how baseball could be given back to the kids.

The older boys on the team would be groomed to take a greater responsibility for running the team. Already, many coaches ask their twelve-year-olds to lead by example. "I pull my twelve-year-olds aside and tell them, 'This is your year. Stay positive, encourage the younger guys, teach them.' They help me set the standards early, and that helps the team for the whole season," McGwire told me. As the year progresses, McGwire gives the older boys more responsibility in running the practices. But when the game starts, he's constantly shouting out instructions. Could he let go a little, cede more control to his bigger kids? "Maybe," he says.

I know these ideas run against the grain, especially for the more competitive Little League programs. Adults usually resist letting go, especially when all the kids have not demonstrated maturity to run the operation. But isn't letting go the ultimate goal of teaching kids?

It seems that every time a new problem arises—in schools, sports, everywhere—the first response is to bring in more experts. But maybe making the league more and more organized is not the answer. Establishing rules, procedures, and hierarchies doesn't always work because it removes the game from the people playing it—the ones who really know how they feel.

Maybe kids would actually learn more if they were allowed to have the game back. Research shows that when you give kids more opportunity to take control, they respond. The best way for kids to learn, the extensive "effective schools" literature shows, is peer tutoring. When you set the stage the right way, kids can do amazing things on their own.

Expanding the kids' control of their own games is worth a try. Why not test different models of running leagues and teams? If Little League can experiment with a pitch-count rule, why not also offer an experiment for giving the game back to the kids?

———————— ◆ ————————

As an organization, Little League faces a major challenge.

All over the country, the best players are opting for travel teams, where they get professional coaching and play upwards of 100 games a year. These players compete against elite competition all spring, summer, and fall. Some of the best travel players take time off their schedule to play on Little League all-star teams to chase the glory of a televised championship. But the best players in Little League's tournaments are really ringers.

Meanwhile, Cal Ripken Baseball, the PONY League, Dixie Baseball, and other leagues have challenged Little League at the community level. Of all the community-based league programs, Cal Ripken is best poised to surpass Little League. Ripken Baseball has a plan for taking over youth baseball—and it has the most compelling figure in the sport to attract followers all over the world. If Ripken gets a national TV contract, watch out.

Maybe Little League, the organization that started the professionalization of childhood, could do something to recover childhood. Maybe, if Little League wanted to provide a true alternative, it could give the game back to the kids.

When Carl Stotz started Little League, you could make the argument that kids needed some help from adults to organize games. It was a nice idea to create a special kid-sized game with some of the trappings of an organized league. It was an especially nice idea to get a few adults involved teaching the kids how to play.

But things have gone too far the other way, toward adult domination of a kids' game. And Little League could set itself apart from the alternatives by taking a stand for the kids again.

Little League would have a new niche. Little League would be the organization that provides instruction and does all the logistical stuff, but then lets the kids play the game without turning it into an adult-dominated, pressure-packed spectacle. So what if the best players continued their migration to travel teams and other leagues? Little League would offer something truly special.

———————— • ◆ • ————————

Something interesting happened when most of the teams got eliminated in the Little League World Series.

Little League offers the also-rans a chance to play each other in "friendship" games—what we used to call pickup games. Little League reserves the fields, arranges for umpires, and even gets someone to announce names over the PA system and keep the scoreboard going.

The all-stars from Maitland, Florida, played the all-stars from Valencia, Venezuela. Even though they lost 13–1, no one from Florida seemed to care. Manager Sid Cash told his players that they could play whatever positions they wanted. The players took the field for the pure fun of it.

"It feels totally different," Dante Bichette Jr. told the *New York Times*. "It feels like a regular Little League game."

"Our guys were laughing on the bench today," Sid Cash said. "That was a little different."

"Maybe for the parents, the game is over now," added Victor Alvarez, the uncle of Richard Alvarez Jr., and the founder of the league. "But it's not over for the kids."

"We had a regular pulse today," said Dan Moroff, the father of Florida's Max Moroff.

With a season of pressure-packed games over—and the boys in charge—the summer had a few hours left for simple play.

Imagine . . .

APPENDIX

———————•◆•———————

2005 Little League World Series teams and results

Pool A (United States)
Northwest: West Oahu, Little League (Ewa Beach, Hawaii)
Mid-Atlantic: Council Rock Little League (Newtown, Pennsylvania)
Midwest: Davenport Northwest Little League (Davenport, Iowa)
Southeast: Maitland Little League (Maitland, Florida)

Pool B (United States)
West: Rancho Buena Vista Little League (Vista, California)
Great Lakes: Owensboro Southern Little League (Owensboro, Kentucky)
Southwest: Lafayette Little League (Lafayette, Louisiana)
New England: Westbrook Little League (Westbrook, Maine)

Pool C (International)
Asia: Chiba City Little League (Chiba City, Japan)
Caribbean: Pabou Little League (Willemstad, Curaçao)
Latin America: Los Leones Little League (Valencia, Venezuela)
Europe, Middle East, and Africa (EMEA): Brateevo Little League (Moscow, Russia)

Pool D (International)
Canada: Whalley Little League (Surrey, British Columbia)
Mexico: Saguro Social Little League (Mexicali, Mexico)
Pacific: Central-East Little League (Mangilao-Barrigada, Guam)
Trans-Atlantic: Arabian American Little League (Dhahrin, Saudi Arabia)

Pool Play
Game 1: Hawaii 7, Pennsylvania 1—In the first inning, Hawaii scored four runs on
    two home runs to win the game early.

Game 2: Guam 6, Russia 2—Trae Santos struck out thirteen batters in his complete-game victory and Calvert Alokoa hit two home runs.

Game 3: Florida 7, Iowa 3—Dante Bichette Jr. allowed a three-run homer in the first inning but only two hits in the rest of his complete-game victory. Bichette and Skip Kovar homered to lead Florida's offense.

Game 4: Louisiana 3, Maine 2—Nick Finocchiaro and Michael Mowatt hit solo home runs to give Maine the early lead, but Louisiana rallied in the bottom of the sixth when a series of misplays undermined starter Sean Murphy.

Game 5: Japan 3, Saudi Arabia 0—Japan's pitcher, Takuya Sakamoto, gave up two hits and struck out eleven batters in getting the shutout.

Game 6: California 7, Kentucky 2—Kalen Pimentel recorded strikeouts for all eighteen outs and Nathan Lewis and Aaron Kim homered to pace California.

Game 7: Curaçao 5, Venezuela 4—Richard Alvarez's grand slam stunned defending champion Curaçao and sent the game into extra innings. Sorick Liberia's sacrifice fly with the bases loaded won the game in the eighth inning.

Game 8: Canada 2, Mexico 0—Chris Fisher allowed only two hits in getting the complete-game shutout. A single by Nathan de la Feraude and a sacrifice fly by Tanner Morache scored Canada's runs.

Game 9: Florida 3, Pennsylvania 1—Skip Kovar and Lee Dunnam batted in runs in the first inning to pace Florida.

Game 10: Louisiana 9, Kentucky 8—In another stunning comeback, Louisiana overcame a seven-run deficit to eliminate Kentucky.

Game 11: Hawaii 7, Iowa 3—Alaka'i Aglipay, Vonn Fe'ao, and Quentin Guevara homered and Aglipay, Kini Enos, and Vonn Fe'ao combined to shut down Iowa.

Game 12: Guam 5, Canada 0—Sean Manley took a perfect game into the fourth inning and gave up only one hit in his complete-game victory.

Game 13: Japan 9, Curaçao 0—Yusuke Taira struck out thirteen batters and gave up three hits in a six-inning complete game. He threw seventy-eight pitches, fifty-one for strikes.

Game 14: California 7, Maine 3—A two-run home run by Michael Mowatt put Maine ahead 3–2 in the fifth inning before California rallied to win. Kalen Pimentel hit a grand slam to lead the attack.

Game 15: Mexico 7, Russia 0—Julio Arciniega threw a complete game four-hitter, striking out seven batters. Mexico collected eleven hits.

Game 16: Japan 7, Venezuela 4—Yuki Mizuma struck out six batters and belted a solo home run to lead Japan. Mizuma relieved Shuhei Iwata after Martin Cornelius, and then hit the biggest home run of the 2005 World Series, a blast that hit the camera tower in center field, about forty feet above the outfield fence.

Game 17: Hawaii 10, Florida 0—Alaka'i Aglipay, who pitched the first inning of Hawaii's first two games, went the distance, striking out seven batters. Sheyne Baniaga and Michael Memea homered and Kaeo Aliviado hit a big double to pace Hawaii.

Game 18: Curaçao 3, Saudi Arabia 0—Curaçao's Sorick Liberia and Saudi Arabia's Andrew Holden both pitched no-hitters into the fifth inning. A walk, two wild pitches, an error, and a passed ball gave Curaçao two runs in the first inning.

Game 19: Pennsylvania 15, Iowa 0—Keith Terry pitched a four-inning no-hitter and he, Greg Guers, Blaise Lezynski, Benn Parker, and Darren Lauer homered.

Game 20: Canada 2, Russia 1—Alex Dunbar struck out ten and tossed a four-hitter; Russia yielded two unearned runs in the first inning.

Game 21: Venezuela 4, Saudi Arabia 0—Victor Sequera and Richard Alvarez combined for a shutout with eight strikeouts and two hits.

Game 22: Maine 3, Kentucky 2—Zach Collett's three-run home run in the third inning overcame a 2–0 Kentucky lead. Sean Murphy pitched the first three innings, giving up two runs (one earned) on three hits. Joey Royer pitched three scoreless innings for the save.

Game 23: Guam 5, Mexico 3—Trae Santos pitched a complete game, fanning the last five batters to win his second complete game of the series. Down 3–1, Guam scored four runs in the fifth inning. With the bases loaded, Manley scored two runs on a single, and another scored on an error on the same play.

Game 24: California 9, Louisiana 3—Austin White and Royce Copeland pitched for California. Reed Reznicek hit a two-run homer and Kalen Pimentel hit his second grand slam in two games.

Records After Pool Play

Pool A

Hawaii	3–0
Florida	2–1
Pennsylvania	1–2
Iowa	0–3

Pool B

California	3–0
Louisiana	2–1
Maine	1–2
Kentucky	0–3

Pool C

Japan	3–0
Curaçao	2–1
Venezuela	1–2
Russia	0–3

Pool D

Guam	3–0
Canada	2–1
Mexico	1–2
Saudi Arabia	0–3

Semifinals

Game 25: Japan 11, Canada 0—Yusuke Taira hit a two-run homer and a run-scoring double scored Japan's first three runs, and then Japan exploded for eight runs in the fifth. Takuya Sakamoto gave up only one hit in four innings and struck out six batters.

Game 26: California 6, Florida 2—Kalen Pimentel beat Dante Bichette Jr. in a battle of the teams' aces, striking out nine batters in six innings. Florida was twice robbed of home runs in the third inning—first when California outfielder Daniel Gibney hauled in a drive over the fence, and then when the umpire called that a ball that went over the fence was a double.

Game 27: Curaçao 16, Guam 1—Christopher Garia allowed two hits and Curaçao scored eleven runs in the fifth inning.

Game 28: Hawaii 2, Louisiana 0—Jace Conrad pitched a one-hitter, but that hit was a two-run homer by Sheyne Baniaga. Kini Enos scattered five hits over five innings for the win, and Quentin Guevara struck out two batters in the sixth inning for the save.

AMERICAN AND INTERNATIONAL FINALS

Game 29: Hawaii 6, California 1—Alaka'i Aglipay dominated California for the first four innings, striking out five batters, getting five groundouts, one pop fly, and one baserunner caught stealing. Aglipay struggled in the fifth and was replaced by fireballer Vonn Fe'ao. In the four-run fourth inning, Hawaii scored two runs on bases-loaded walks and one apiece on a hit and an error. A two-run homer by Fe'ao in the fifth inning scored two more.

Game 30: Curaçao 2, Japan 0—Jurickson Profar outdueled Yusuke Taira, striking out twelve batters. Profar, a star of the 2004 championship team for Curaçao, also knocked in a run and scored a run.

CHAMPIONSHIP GAME

Game 31: Hawaii 7, Curaçao 6—Michael Memea's home run capped one of the greatest rallies in the history of the Little League World Series. Hawaii rallied to overcome a 6–3 deficit in the bottom of the sixth inning to send the title game to extra innings for only the second time in fifty-nine years. The championship was the first ever for Hawaii, and it prevented Curaçao from becoming the third team to repeat as champions.

Acknowledgments

Many people helped make this book possible. The participants in the Little League World Series shared their experiences, honestly and passionately. Others—experts on youth sports, participants in other programs, and people who just care about kids—offered their thoughts as well.

Greatest thanks go to Hillel Black, my incomparable editor who became as enthusiastic about youth sports as I was and guided me through different approaches to getting and telling this story. Michelle Schoob was the copy editor who helped to make some of the book's crooked paths straight. Tony Viardo and Lyron Bennett helped develop a marketing plan. Dawn Pope did the book's design.

My agent, Sorche Fairbank, was always available to offer good advice on this book and all aspects of my writing career. She's not only competent and efficient, but creative as well.

A number of people helped me with my research trips. Deb Bogle got me situated in Williamsport, Pennsylvania. John Kearns, Micheline Soong, and Zeke Kearns offered me their spare bedroom in Honolulu and explained something about Hawaiian culture. The people at the Curaçao Tourist Board, most particularly Vico Rojer, helped to arrange meetings with the right people in Willemstad.

My sister, Susan Casarez, translated newspaper articles detailing the Venezuela age scandal. Kathy Taylor of Earlham College, the only professor of Papiamentu in America, provided useful background on the culture of Curaçao.

Isabel Chenoweth provided the beautiful photography for the book. As usual, she offered constant encouragement. She also suggested a new framework for the book when the first two approaches didn't work.

As I worked on the book, and considered the importance of coaches in the lives of kids playing ball, I thought often about the people who have taught me. Teachers and friends, they helped me find my way at different critical points in my life. To these friends and teachers, I dedicate this book.

INDEX

Abbreviations are explained at the end of the index.

Y

Abbreviations used:
Alabama (AL); Arizona (AZ); California (CA); Canada (CN); Connecticut (CT); Curaçao (CR); Guam (GU); Indiana (IN); Iowa (IA); Japan (JP); Kentucky (KY); Louisiana (LA); Maine (ME); Maryland (MD); Mexico (MX); Michigan (MI); Nevada (NV); New Jersey (NJ); New York (NY); Pennsylvania (PA); Russia (RU); Saudi Arabia (SA); South Carolina (SC); Taiwan (TW); Venezuela (VN)